For Cati,
Thank you for supporting
ELCA World Hunger.
Kathy Hoffman

Snowbirding
from Two Ponds

Snowbirding
from Two Ponds

Volume Three of the Two Ponds Trilogy

Kathy Hoffman

Proceeds benefit ELCA World hunger

XULON PRESS

Xulon Press
555 Winderley Pl, Suite 225
Maitland, FL 32751
407.339.4217
www.xulonpress.com

xulon PRESS

© 2025 by Kathy Hoffman

All rights reserved solely by the author. The author guarantees all contents are original and do not infringe upon the legal rights of any other person or work. No part of this book may be reproduced in any form without the permission of the author.

Due to the changing nature of the Internet, if there are any web addresses, links, or URLs included in this manuscript, these may have been altered and may no longer be accessible. The views and opinions shared in this book belong solely to the author and do not necessarily reflect those of the publisher. The publisher therefore disclaims responsibility for the views or opinions expressed within the work.

Paperback ISBN-13: 979-8-86850-887-5

Other Books by the Author

THE JOYFUL FACES OF MESSIAH

BROOKLYN ART LIBRARY, THE SKETCHBOOK PROJECT, VOLUME 18

An illustrated collection of close-ups (eyes, nose, and mouth) of some of the 2021 members of Messiah Lutheran Church and Preschool in Vancouver, Washington.

LIFE AT TWO PONDS

VOLUME ONE OF THE TWO PONDS TRILOGY

Autobiographical humor: Hoffman is very competitive. She finds challenges in almost every situation. She finds ways to compete with her puppies, her husband, Mother Nature, and even a little mouse! Go for a walk with her through her married life as she overplans every event only to find so many things can go awry. Laugh with her as she carefully manipulates every situation until it explodes in her face!

CHRISTMAS AT TWO PONDS – THE BACKSTORY

VOLUME TWO OF THE TWO PONDS TRILOGY

Reminiscent of Bombeck's style, Hoffman relates true stories of how everyday situations can go so wrong. Cringe with her as she reveals the stories behind her first date ... laugh as her many dogs conspire against her ... sigh as her Sunday school students come up with the darndest answers ... smile as she tries to communicate with her husband of forty years. Life is a learning process ... Hoffman must be a slow learner.

Main Cast of Characters

Husband of forty years – **Harry** – my man of few words

Relatives – **Jon** (Harry's brother) and his wife, **Les**

Neighbors – **Dorothy** and **Rodney**

Pets:

- **Angie** – Corgi
- **Lucy** – Corgi
- **Jack** – Border Collie
- **Cocoa Bean** – Chihuahua/Terrier mix
- **Boris** – African Grey
- **Petey** – Morkie–poo

Vancouver and Havasu Friends – **Larry** and **Wendy**

Tucson Friends and Relatives

- **John** and **Arlene**
- **Phil** and **Judy**

Happy Hour Friends:

- **Dan** and **Linda**
- **Don** and **Sallie**
- **Robert** and **Betty**
- **Emmett** and **Sue**
- **John** from Utah
- **Richard** and **Gail**
- **Mike** and **Karen**

Rincon RV Park Friends – **Irv** and **Kate**, **Kathy** and **Joe**, and so many more … all of them special!

Snowbirding from Two Ponds

Volume Three of the Two Ponds Trilogy

This book is a collection of weird and wonderful anecdotes occurring after we retired and purchased a motor home. We were Snowbirds. We hit the road … sometimes the road hit back!

Dedication

This book is dedicated to my dear friend, Marg Nelson.

A week and a half before we were due to come home from our fifth Snowbirding adventure, I got a text from Marg asking for prayer. She was in ICU ... in Italy ... with a possible heart problem. That did not sound good. She had never had heart problems.

Marg is a tad older than I am. We've laughed together since 1975 when we met at work. She came up through the ranks, going back to school after having a family, and rising to one of the highest positions in the Bonneville Power Administration. She is the strongest woman I know. She meets obstacles head on and what's more, she truly cares about people. Marg is my dearest friend!

I didn't like hearing Marg had something life-threatening. I pulled out all the stops, texted her when I could, prayed for her ... and started planning her eulogy. After all, it's a known fact when someone goes into ICU they don't come out. I got a text back saying even though she was still in considerable pain she seemed to be doing better but would have to stay there a few days. I texted back saying how distressed I was and tried to give her some encouraging words. I failed to mention I was halfway through planning her eulogy. In fact, what I did text was: *Would you get better faster if I dedicated my next book to you?* She fired back a text right away: *Probably would help.* And then came another text with a happy face emoji. I was feeling a little better but suddenly realized I was going to have to come through with the book dedication.

Marg was released a few days later. Keith, her dutiful husband, was glad he no longer had to drive two hours on winding roads to get to the cardiac hospital to see her each day. Marg was glad to be alive and out of the hospital. I was glad I didn't have to finish the eulogy. She got better in leaps and bounds. In fact, before her short visit to Italy ended, she had logged an 18,000-step day ... more than ten miles of walking and climbing stairs. I want to be just like Marg when I grow up.

A week later, Marg and Keith returned from Italy, but Marg was sic ... really sick. A few days later, Keith was sick ... so sick he had to go to the emergency room. They found out they had contracted COVID in Milan. They eventually recovered and were relieved to get back to good health ... I was relieved I didn't have to write two eulogies.

Acknowledgements

I am grateful for my husband who is extremely supportive in his own way. Sometimes the key to a happy marriage is lack of communication. He does his thing; I do my thing; and we often meet in the middle. He reads and plays golf; I do crafts and work on the computer. He tends to keep his own company; I tend to seek community. We cherish our evenings together. Opposites attract ... it's a very good thing! We don't travel a lot, except for snowbirding, which means we relocate to a warmer climate and sit for five or six months, still doing our own things ... in a new location. We finish each day with two kisses and a reminder that we love each other ... immensely!

I am grateful for those who have supported my efforts to raise money for ELCA Disaster Relief and World Hunger, especially the many churches in Vancouver, Portland, and Tucson who have invited me to have book signings. And as always, I'm grateful for you, Dear Reader: Never underestimate the value of your purchase ... It matters!

I'm grateful for Helene Johnsen, my muse. After my mother passed away, I could honestly say Helene was my strongest supporter. Helene died unexpectedly in 2024, leaving a hole in a lot of hearts. The next day, I emailed the family, asking if I could paint a picture for them. Within five hours, they emailed me two beautiful pictures: one of her at seventy-five and another of her as a senior in high school. A week later, covered in acrylics, I mailed four paintings to the family in the Northwest. Painting her eyes, her special smile, and her Italian nose repeatedly was a helpful way for me grieve and stay connected with the family. On the way back from the post office, I began to feel at peace with our loss.

My thanks to Sue Miholer, my editor. The editing process is extremely detailed and labor-intensive. When a writer and an editor click, there is peace and harmony ... but more than that, Sue just

Acknowledgements

makes it fun. She stays up on all the latest changes, including the fact that motor home is no longer one word. I didn't like it but I accepted it so it wouldn't be off-putting to those who care about such things.

Continued thanks to Paul Krueger for making me realize how important pictures and drawings are.

I am grateful for the people at Xulon Publishing who make it easy for me to concentrate on writing and illustrating while they take care of everything else.

I give a nod to all the English teachers who have long given up on correcting my use of ellipses ... those ubiquitous triple dots. When speaking, I have a tendency to mumble and add a few words after I've finished a thought. Ellipses enable me to "mumble and add" in print. When you see ellipses in this book, take little pause ... enjoy life.

ELCA World Hunger: Give thanks for your blessings and be assured the royalties and more from your purchase will benefit the Evangelical Lutheran Church in America (ELCA) World Hunger. ELCA Disaster Relief and World Hunger personnel are often among the first to show up ... both here in the USA and around the world. They show up quickly to help when people are experiencing some of the worst days of their lives. To make additional donations, visit "www.elca.org." Poke the "Give" button and give to your heart's content.

Introduction

My Story

I was the only daughter of two Catholic parents, but I had six brothers. Our names rattled off our tongues in birth order: Larry, Kathleen, Charles, Pat, Kevin, Stephen, and David. We couldn't remember who was who unless we went in birth order. Sixty years later, nothing's changed ... I rattle them off in birth order or risk forgetting someone.

We grew up in a happy stable household in Portland, Oregon. Four of us went to North Catholic High School until it burned to the ground. Kevin, Stephen, and David went to Central Catholic High School. The first four went to the University of Portland, which had a solid engineering school. The boys got degrees in engineering; I got my degree in mathematics. The twins, Kevin and Stephen, got degrees in music. David became a massage therapist.

When I graduated, Larry had been working at the Bonneville Power Administration (BPA) for two years. Graduating college in math, I had only two choices for a career: the telephone company or BPA. (I watch movies now about guidance counselors helping students figure out what they want to do with their lives and wonder where they were in 1970. I never saw one!) I bumbled through an awkward interview with a BPA manager and found myself with a job offer working rotating shift work. I was scared. I knew I didn't know anything, but they didn't seem to care. It never dawned on me they might provide on-the-job training.

I was reclassified as an engineer in the late 70s. On July 14, 1982, I met a tall, dark, and handsome State Farm Insurance agent. We got engaged on August 10 and married on September 10. I had been dilly-dallying around for thirty-four years. Suddenly, within two months, Ka-Blam! ... I was married.

Introduction xiii

Harry's Story

Harry and his brother Jon grew up in Lebanon, Oregon, then lived in Oklahoma on a farm. They moved to Stillwater, and eventually moved back to Oregon, living in Lebanon and Roseburg for four years (and six schools). All this happened before Harry entered high school. He finished growing up in Salem, was drafted into the Army, and served in Vietnam from 1966 to 1968.

He returned to the Northwest and got a business degree. In those days, graduating business majors got a job at one of the big eight accounting firms. His was at Ernst & Ernst. Later, he worked for the State Farm regional office in Salem for eight years. His unit was in charge of processing premiums. He was a good boss. Whenever someone new came to work for him, he'd rummage through their wastebasket after quitting time, find the inevitable check that had accidently been tossed away, and alert the newcomer to the facts of life associated with handling cash or checks. He had weekly staff meetings on Friday afternoons, passing out Dixie cups, taking care of business, and leaving quickly, allowing his team to have some fun boss-free time.

While in the Regional Office, he recognized how much free time agents had ... as much or as little as they wanted. He knew what he wanted to do. He took over an agency in Fruitland, Idaho, while living in nearby Ontario, Oregon. When a longtime Vancouver agent, Lyle Cornelius, retired in 1981, Lyle's policies were up for grabs. Harry jumped at the chance to move to Vancouver and split the policies with Lyle's son, Terry. Tons of customers were loyal to the Cornelius name. Harry immediately lost a third of his book of business as so many customers transferred their business back to Terry ... including me.

Our Story

A year after I transferred my policies, I went into Harry's State Farm office to cancel a policy that had failed to transfer to Terry's office. Within two months we were married, and he had renamed me Kate. (I apologize in advance for any confusion the name change may cause.) We had a small but formal wedding, resulting in a marriage lasting forty-two years and counting. We lived in a nice little ranch style house with a grease pit for four years ... the longest Harry had lived in any one place ... ever! He was starting to get antsy. In June of 1986, we moved to a little house on a hill ... a little house with possibilities ... and two ponds. Years later, in a fit of romance, we decided to name our little house with possibilities. It was a fit of romance, not a fit of imagination. We named it Two Ponds.

We were never without a dog, and frequently had at least three. Vacations usually meant packing a trailer and taking a trip to visit friends in Palm Springs or family in Yuma. Finally, it was time to retire. And so, in October 2017, we bought a motor home. Harry retired at the end of 2017 after forty years with State Farm. I retired at a week later, after twenty-eight years with BPA, followed by ten years of volunteer work, and another ten years selling and servicing policies in Harry's State Farm agency. Once he retired, Harry announced he did not ever want to see snow again. As our new life started unfolding before our lives, we decided it might be fun to experience the sun loving life so many snowbirds had been talking about.

PART ONE

CHANGES ARE A-COMIN'

Chapter 1 ... Owning a Motor Home

Taking the Big Plunge

We fully intended to retire on December 31, 2017, and become snowbirds. The first thing we needed was a vehicle to live in. Harry and I went to an RV show. Ten days later, he went to Milwaukie, Oregon, and looked at some RVs. The next day, he took me to Milwaukie to look at the RVs. A few days later, we put money down on a brown-ish 2014 motor home with only 8,000 miles on the odometer. The floor plan appeared well suited to our needs: king bed in the back; L-shaped couch in the front for curling up with dogs in the evening; three TVs inside, one TV outside, central vacuum; four slides (massive motorized extensions that seem to double the living area); washer/dryer; mirrored wardrobe, and a skinny floor-to-ceiling pantry described by Jim the salesman as "spacious."

I began to realize Harry was taking snowbirding seriously! Before we finalized the purchase, we had Roscoe Brothers Tree Service prune the overhanging trees to allow for at least fourteen feet of clearance. We had never noticed how low the tree branches were hanging. After the trees were limbed up, we felt a sense of Two Ponds becoming light and airy. The sun was coming through the trees again! We were beginning a new chapter.

THAT HORRENDOUS MAILBOX INCIDENT

Jim gave us a detailed spiel as he took us around the coach looking into every compartment. He told us what needed to be done now ... what needed to be done later ... how to maintain everything ... how to get the coach to do what we wanted. I videotaped the whole thing. There was no way I was going to remember everything he was saying. After going around the outside, we went inside and learned even more new stuff. It all seemed pretty important.

When it was time for a test-drive, Harry took the driver's seat. I think it's written somewhere: only men drive motor homes ... but I listened. We drove around a neighborhood to a parking lot where Harry got some good instruction on how to turn, back up, and what not.

The paperwork was all filled out. We were good to go. I jumped into the car and Harry jumped into the coach. We were off and running. Going home was not a problem ... I followed the motor home. It was an easy drive even though it was during rush hour traffic. Harry is a big picture guy; I'm a detail person. It works out well in our marriage. On the easy drive home, I had a lot of time to think of the details of getting the motor home into our driveway. But, when we got close to home, Harry turned before I expected and was approaching from a different direction than I had planned. We didn't have cell phones with us. Too bad we couldn't communicate.

Jim had told us when you make a turn, you drive out into the intersection before you start the turn, because you're sitting above the front wheels. I heard him ... it clicked for me. Consequently, when Harry started making a right turn into our driveway, I began to get alarmed: From my vantage point I could see the mailbox was right in the middle of the turn path, and although the mailbox itself wasn't moving, it was getting closer and closer to the coach. I honked the horn four times. (Four times is the maximum you can honk a horn before the neighbors start looking out their windows.) Gratefully, Harry stopped the motor home. I was pleased, but I still had to figure out how to communicate to him that he was on the wrong trajectory. I stopped the car and was about to get out to have a chat with him when the motor home started moving again. Oh no! I couldn't get to the horn fast enough!

A Horrendous Mailbox Incident was unfolding in front of my eyes. The first thing to go was the yellow plastic newspaper holder ... it was squished in one second. After that, the L-shaped metal bracket holding the yellow newspaper thingy ... it complained with a scree. It fought back against the motor home leaving a perfectly straight scar on the slide. The mailbox was next: As the motor home pressed against the mailbox, the wooden supports, holding up two mailboxes (one for me and one for Dorothy), popped up out of the ground taking both mailboxes for a ten-foot flight. I simply couldn't believe it. The worst part was knowing I would be stuck fixing the problem.

The rest of the trip on the long driveway up to the house went without a hitch. He parked the motor home in front of the house. When I got there, I had to choose my words carefully. There weren't any words to choose. Even though it was almost time for dinner, I was seething. Years earlier we had made a trip to Yellowstone. I felt like one of those hot pools ... bubbling. Without saying anything, I got back in the car and left before I could find a word. Initially, I had no destination, but I ended up driving to Lowe's. I figured looking for replacement mailboxes would help take my mind off things. Lowes didn't have two mailboxes the same size and same color, except for tiny ones ... we needed mondo-sized mailboxes.

As I got closer to home, I realized someday ... probably someday in the far distant future ... I'd laugh about it. The laughter came within a week. Who can stay mad at Harry.

By the time I got home, I had cooled off enough to ask Harry why he didn't wait for me after I had honked the horn. "Oh," he said, "you did? I didn't hear it. I was just trying to make sure I didn't take out the gate." I felt a little better: I'd rather have to replace the mailbox than the gate. Dorothy's son Joel from Tucson and I jerry-rigged a support to last until we could give the entire mailbox assembly our full attention. Nine months later we got to it. We discovered the mailbox supports had been pretty rotten and were close to giving up the ghost even without encouragement from the motor home.

CHAPTER 2 ... INTRODUCTION TO SINGING

NO AUDITIONS REQUIRED

In the fall of 2017, the choir director at Messiah Lutheran, my church in Vancouver, put out an invitation to anyone and everyone who wanted to sing in the Christmas program. We were performing a cantata ... whatever that meant. It sounded like fun and not too much of a commitment. I was in. There were no auditions required. When I showed up, the director asked what voice I'd like to sing. I guessed soprano. After a bit, I noticed some people leaving but I didn't know why. Almost immediately we started practicing the anthems for the next few Sundays. The people who had left were those who had come specifically to sing in the cantata. I missed my opportunity to leave. I stayed on and was hooked.

For the first few weeks, I struggled to hit a high D, which surprised me, but I kept coming to the practices and got to know the other singers. Eventually, when I didn't let the D scare me, I was able to hit it and go even higher. I was still surprised we weren't asked to audition.

I found out our event was called a cantata because all eight of the songs were written by the same composer. During the next few weeks, I practiced day in and day out for the Christmas service with a borrowed CD. The big weekend came. We sang the cantata at three services on the weekend. The cantata was finished, but the exciting songs kept ringing in my head. The earworms were so intense I could hardly sleep for the next two nights. Finally, I put all my thoughts and excitement on paper. That night, I was able to sleep like a baby.

What follows is a one-act play birthed from the excitement of preparing for and performing the cantata. The text is meant to be read with building intensity, until the last few lines, which then taper quickly to a long humble bow. The song incorporated in the script is a glorious hymn. To hear it, google "Pepper Choplin Fall on Your

Knees." After listening to the song several times, I believe you will have a glimmer of the excitement that overwhelmed me.

THE CANTATA – 2017 – "FIND YOUR PLACE TO BE" – A SKIT

It was Christmas Eve. The Singers were ready. With one minute to go, they turned to the Congregation and found their friends and family sitting straight with great anticipation.

The Conductor called for a B Flat … the Pianist responded … the Brass found their note … the Strings brought forth the expected timbre. The Conductor looked at his Singers hopefully, reminding them one last time to sing the vowels and spit the consonants. The Conductor lifted his baton and with the slightest of twitches, the Orchestra and the Choir filled the air with the most amazing strains. Phrases blended together in swells. Each time the Conductor swayed to the left or the right, the Choir united in mushrooms of resonating reverberations. The Conductor beamed!

Song after song … lyrics were synchronized with the Narrator's remarks. Everything was flawless. And then came the Finale: **"Fall on Your Knees."**

The Tall Soprano brightened. The Conductor raised his baton. There was complete silence. Down came the baton … the French Horn tooted its engaging but plaintive cry. The rest of the Orchestra joined in. The Pianist entered last with the sweet dainty introduction so familiar to the Singers. The Conductor signaled to his Sopranos. They took the hint. Immediately, full rich pianissimo tones came from the Choir loft.

Come, See the Child, He is here by the fire. All the Sopranos were singing their vowels, swaying with the swells of the phrases.

Silently come, draw near the manger side.

The eyes of those in the Congregation opened wide in anticipation as the Orchestra and the Choir built to fortissimo: **Look in His face and see the world's salvation.**

Chapter 2 ... Introduction to Singing

The Conductor gently brought them back to the rich, reverent melody: **Feel the holy peace ... Fall on your knees.**

The Conductor repeated the surge: **Open your eyes, now the holy star is rising.** The swaying became more passionate. The Choir Loft creaked in heavenly pleasure.

Rays of the light will shine to touch your soul. The Sopranos felt their souls come alive! The rest of the Singers caught the fever! The Orchestra, eyes widened and eyebrows raised, inhaled as one! The Conductor (who had momentarily been flicking a piece of dust from his tuxedo and wondering where it could possibly have come from) heard the collective gasp and immediately looked up at the Choir. This is it, he realized! Twirling his baton feverishly at the Sopranos, he initiated another crescendo. **Open your heart to the glory and the wonder.** He attempted to bring the Singers back to the reverent melody, but the whole Choir, seeing mezzo-forte on the sheet music, refused to be restrained.

Feel the holy peace ... Fall on your knees. Despite the rebellion, the Conductor was delighted!

The directions on the music glared up from the page stating *With Greater Momentum*. The Sopranos filled their lungs and their souls. They were ready to dance at the top of the treble staff!

Fall on your knees. They nailed the D in unison.

They rose to the E: O hear the angel voices. They had found their place to be! They were soaring and they would not ... could not ... stop! The Tall Soprano thought her heart might burst from ecstasy!

The Conductor took the Sopranos to the uppermost line of the treble staff ... F ... Sharp: **O NIGHT!** It rang out decisively as the Sopranos stretched their necks to hit the top of the note and hung on for dear life ... cool ... crisp ... clear ... for an eternity.

... divine. O night when Christ was born. They settled down on a D as everyone breathed a sigh. But the Conductor took them back to the heights again.

O Night... divine. O night... when Christ was born. The Congregation knew the Singers were in their element.

And then it came: the key change from D to E flat. It should have been a textbook change. They had practiced and practiced for this moment. But something inside the Sopranos snapped. They took on a life of their own. At first, no one realized. The Congregation, the Orchestra, the Singers ... all were focusing on The Conductor. But the electricity in the room was unmistakable. Shock filled every face as the Sopranos, like the key change, took a half step backward and revved up for the onslaught. It was all the Conductor could do to keep up with them!

Come ... now ... and ... fall on your knees as you worship in His presence. The Sopranos owned the treble staff. They went pure and high ... they went rich and low. They went slow and steady ... they swayed as they built up speed.

Thanks be to God ... you have found the holy Child. Up and down the keyboard the Pianist raced, determined to keep up with the Sopranos.

Blessed are all who have seen the Lord's salvation. The Pianist hammered the chords in an effort to regain control of the song. This had never happened in all her years at the keyboard!

The Sopranos sat on their F. They darted down to the safety of an A to escape the Pianist. When the coast was clear they raced back up to their F! They had gone insane! They stretched their necks a full two inches, arched their backs and hurled their words to the rafters in a determined frenzy. **Come and lift your voice ... Let your heart rejoice!** It was a watershed moment. And then they did the unthinkable. They threw caution to the wind and flew from the safety of the treble staff for the heights that only come

Chapter 2 ... Introduction to Singing 11

in dreams ... High G! The Conductor's mouth dropped as they peaked. **And PRA** ...! The Sopranos' heads were flopping wildly and joyously as they hung on to the High G! Earrings glittered in the bright lights. Time stood still. The High G lingered stirringly ... **AAAAAISE!** One Alto and two Sopranos swooned ... **the Prince of Peace.** Three Second Sopranos, dizzy from their maiden flight, took their seats and lowered their heads between their knees. In the end, the French Horn managed to regain a modicum of control. The remaining Sopranos surrendered, happily yielding to The Conductor's baton. **Fall on your knees ... fall on your knee ...** Ever-the-professionals, they held the final long E in a husky pianissimo as the Conductor slowed the tempo ... beat by beat ... **-ees.** The Pianist wiped her brow before concluding the cantata with an E flat from the nether regions of the keyboard.

The Congregation sighed ...
    The Sopranos smiled ...
        The Conductor bowed ...
            The Cantata ... was ... complete.

This one-act play was written with special thanks to David Teeter, our choir director, a demanding yet caring and loving man, aka The Conductor ... who wouldn't be caught dead momentarily flicking a piece of dust from his tuxedo, let alone wondering where it could possibly have come from!

A few weeks after the cantata, Harry and I retired.

Chapter 3 ... Central Oregon

Shakedown Cruise

Our new motor home sat in the driveway for eight months. In June 2018, we had a shakedown cruise but not before I bought a manual can opener. I wasn't sure about this snowbirding thing and needed to bolster my confidence. I stopped by the grocery store one day and happened upon the kitchen appliance section. A can opener was staring me down. I picked it up and, in doing so, I picked up a bushel of confidence. I told myself I was fully committed. It was a cheap little can opener ... kind of hard to use ... but I'll never get rid of it. It symbolizes my commitment to snowbirding and to my husband ... in a way no wedding ring can. Every time I look at it, I'm reminded I am fully committed to snowbirding.

Our shakedown cruise was a trip to Crooked River Ranch in central Oregon for a five-day golf vacation and a visit with Uncle Jerry. I had stopped by Costco and loaded up on all sorts of things ... over-sized things. We had way too much of some things and not enough of others. It was all a grand learning experience.

Peanut Butter

It took five hours to go from Vancouver to Crooked River. We shared the driving. We were both sitting up very high and had an excellent view. I was driving when we turned south on Hwy 97. It was pretty, but slightly boring (drive, drive, drive). I asked Harry if he wanted a snack bar.

He said "No ... do you want one?"

"Yes, please."

"Where are they?"

"Top shelf of the pantry."

Chapter 3 ... Central Oregon

He unbuckled his seatbelt and went to the pantry behind the driver's seat. Crash! (drive, drive, drive) "What was that?"

"The plastic peanut butter jar *[from Costco]* fell out of the pantry. I put it in the sink."

"Will you make sure it's standing upright so it doesn't separate in the sink?"

"I did ... Do you want me to open your snack bar for you?"

"Please ... Thanks." (drive, drive, drive) "Was there a mess on the floor?"

"The plastic lid cracked and some of the peanut butter came out."

(drive, drive, drive) "What did you do with it?"

"I put it back in the jar."

"How much came out?"

"About this much." He held up his palm with fingers pointing upright ... about ¼ of the jar!

I never swerved a bit during the whole exchange, but as soon as we got to our destination, I scooped out about a small fistful of the peanut butter and trashed it (I should have kept it for the dogs). When I looked at the spoon, I saw a dog hair sticking up off the end. (Aack!)

(Note to self: Take the three-jar pack of marinara sauce out of the pantry!)

Frying Pan

We arrived at 6 p.m. I putzed around setting up. An hour later, I was ready to start dinner. At home, I used a ceramic fry pan every day. I fried, seared or steamed almost everything. I had gotten a new ceramic pan for the coach. The directions said to season it in the oven. I seasoned it a week before we left, washed it, and put it in the fry pan drawer ... and there it sat. There were no stores nearby, so I resolved to do all my cooking with what I had on hand ... a big stockpot and an electric slow-cooker. I scrambled our eggs in the stockpot for breakfast each morning.

STOVE

I reached for the stockpot to steam some frozen chicken meatballs. Taking the burner cover off, I turned the dial and lit a match ... nothing. Three matches later, still nothing. I looked around a little and noticed a knob with words and arrows: "Spark (arrow) Spark (arrow) Spark (arrow)." I lit a match and turned the knob once. All I got was a loud snap. Three matches later, still nothing. I wondered how long our matches would hold out, but then I had a brilliant idea: I asked Harry to turn the propane on. He went all around the coach looking for a switch to turn the propane on but couldn't find anything. He couldn't even find a propane tank. (In the eight months since we had had the run-through with Jim the salesman, it appeared we had forgotten some of the instructions.) Finally, Harry opened the control panel above the passenger seat and we both saw the LP switch at the same time. He flipped the switch. I repeated my burner exercise. Light a match, turn the knob ... and still nothing happened. We were getting a little frustrated. I was beginning to think about modifying our menu to have salads and snack bars for fifteen meals. Finally, Harry did what any self-respecting man would do: He spun that knob out of frustration (snap, snap, snap, snap). The burner lit right up ... without a match!

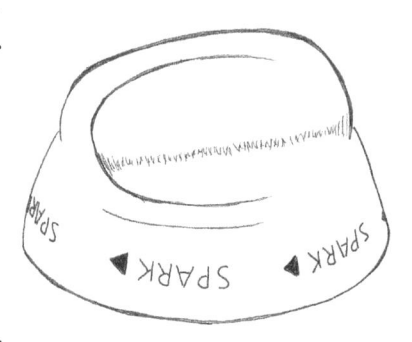

"Oh," was all I could say with a chagrined look on my face.

Chapter 3 ...Central Oregon

FLAVOR

Dinner was uneventful but satisfying. We had our steamed chicken meatballs. There were juices left in the stockpot. The next morning, when it was time to make breakfast, I got the stockpot out of the refrigerator and showed Harry the small amount of liquid in the bottom.

Proudly, I announced, "See, this is what was left from cooking the meatballs last night. I refrigerated it."

"EEW-ICK!" was his response.

"No ... it's flavoring!" I countered.

"So that's what happened to the flavor!"

Sigh.

DOG PROBLEMS

After returning from a golf outing, we checked with one neighbor to make sure the dogs hadn't been a nuisance while we had been gone. She said they were fine.

The next day, however, was a different story. We left the windows open while we were gone. Evidently the dogs fired up every time someone walked by on the gravel. They barked for three and one-half out of four hours. Our other neighbor, a dog-person, had a chat with us rather than complaining to the office. He gave us three reasonable suggestions on how to remedy the situation. We chose the one involving closing the windows and turning on the air conditioning. After our next golf sojourn, he said the dogs had been just fine.

CLOTHES

After taking his shower on the fourth evening, Harry looked over at me. With a sheepish grin, he said, "I have a stack of clothes for the trip ... at home on the chair." There's a lot to learn about traveling in a motor home.

Chapter 4 ... Heading Home to Vancouver

Connecting: Sometimes It's about the Little Things

Harry took the first shift driving home. It drizzled. Immediately, we discovered the wisdom of washing the windshield as soon as we arrive at a location, something we had failed to do a few days earlier. That would have been a good time for Harry to use his EEW-ICK! comment.

As we neared Hood River, I called my good friend Jennifer, the mother of my two little art students. She lived about four blocks from the freeway overpass and had a commanding view of the freeway. I told her exactly where we were. She got her daughter Elena out of bed. They were both standing by the window with their phone listening to me recite the blow-by-blow details of our progress. She described a landmark near her house visible from the freeway. I told her the exact moment we went under the overpass.

She exclaimed, "Oh, it's brown!"

I was delighted, and responded, "I saw a cream-colored Mediterranean home!"

We were both thrilled we saw each other in passing.

Bye-Bye Birdie

We had a successful shakedown cruise: We enjoyed the golf course and learned a lot about the motor home and traveling. We also learned our new lifestyle was not conducive to having a bird. Boris, our twenty-year-old African Grey parrot, had been with us since he was a baby. We had to find a new home for him before we left for the Southwest in the fall. Some would wonder how we could give up a twenty-year-old member of our family. Granted, I think it's a valid concern, but those who would wonder should realize Boris' first word, learned from constant repetition, was "ouch!" ... in my voice. In fact, one of my fantasies, should Harry meet an

Chapter 4 ... Heading Home to Vancouver

early demise, was to slip Boris in the casket with Harry just before cremation. Fortunately, it never came to that. Other than his propensity for biting me, he was a pretty good little bird. A nearby pet shop sold him on consignment six months later.

PART TWO

HEADING INTO THE UNKNOWN

2018–19

CHAPTER 1 ... ON THE ROAD

A New Lifestyle

The memory cells don't work as well as they used to, so I picked November 1, an easy-to-remember date for the beginning of our new lifestyle ... 11/1. It was a pleasant Thursday. All the items on our checklist were checked, all the items on the house sitter's checklist were checked ... we were on our way. We were going to spend a month here and a month there, winding up at home after five months. I had a stack of receipts from RV parks. My head was reeling from the changes going on in my life. It was a lot like traveling overseas and needing to know where passport, keys, wallet, toiletries, snacks, and clothes were at all times. We headed out.

We had a short sleepover at the Corning rest stop off Interstate 5 in northern California. We were back on the road at the ungodly hour of 3:15 a.m. Shortly after the rest of the country woke, I discovered a voicemail from my brother: On November 2, a few weeks after her 98th birthday, my mother died. Those goodbyes had been said four years earlier before her dementia had gotten too bad. There was nothing else to do but soldier on.

Picking Up the Pieces

We alternated driving. After stopping to refuel, it was my turn to drive. With the sun in my eyes, I got confused about the freeway entrance and followed a semi. Too bad. He wasn't getting on the freeway. I had turned a block too soon. There was an abandoned truck stop ahead to the left. It would be easy enough to enter, turn around, exit, and find the freeway. At the entry, there was a wide shallow rain trough instead of a curb ... like something one would find in suburbia. Unfortunately, I assumed speed was the controlling factor. Slowing way down, I entered the parking lot by taking the trough at a 45-degree angle. Even though I was creeping, the motor home pitched violently to the right, then to the left. I heard the sound of major crashing and cupboards springing open behind me.

I announced we were stopping ... in the way a wife of thirty-six years does when she doesn't want any arguments! The massive salt and pepper shakers (pizza parlor shakers) were quaking on the floor of the coach behind the chair. One unbreakable Corelle dish shattered in the kitchen. The rest of the Corelle was still intact. When all was said and done, we only lost thirty minutes and one dish, but it had sounded like all hell was breaking loose! I kept finding little shards of the dish for two days.

TRYING NOT TO PANIC

We had another problem after we left a rest stop at Boron in southern California. The coach was jerking back and forth pretty aggressively. We didn't know why it was happening, but we did know we couldn't drive the speed limit in that condition. Everyone who passed us honking seemed to know what was happening. It turned out to be something to do with the Jeep ... maybe the tow bars locking up. At the same time, we discovered the Jeep battery had run out of juice with our two dogs (the Corgi puppies) locked inside. In a panic, I called the Jeep dealer only to find out there's a physical key hidden in the electronic key fob for just such an occasion. We got the occasion sorted out with no duress for the pooches. They were enjoying their new lazy lifestyle.

Chapter 2 ... Lake Havasu Area

First Stop: Earp

An hour after dark, we arrived at Big Bend RV Resort in Earp, California, forty-five minutes south of Lake Havasu, Arizona. We were cranky, hungry, and a little worse for the wear. The Jeep battery was still dead. Fortunately, our friend Larry, the great mediator, was there to help us recharge the battery, find our site, and set up camp. He had pushed through from Vancouver in one day, towing a rather large boat with his truck. What can I say, he's considerably younger than we are ... by two years.

Our motor home site was underneath two large columnar trees about twenty feet from the Colorado River. It seemed ideal because they provided considerable shade throughout the day ... until I discovered there was no cell service, no internet, and no satellite. My newly purchased Wi-Fi hotspot wouldn't work in our little riverside depression surrounded by mountains. It was a steep learning curve, and I was learning more than I ever wanted to know. Eventually, I found a way to get secure internet by walking about four hundred yards up the bank. Wired again, I got tickets to fly home for the funeral, and after two days with a TV technician, we had a jerry-rigged satellite system allowing us to get some TV reception to see what was going on in the world. It had been a long, dry spell without access to the news ... or to impromptu twitter blasts.

Larry had a mobile home about fifteen sites upriver from us. He and our neighbor in the neighboring motor home had amassed a lot of experience. Both were generous with their advice. We listened fast and hard.

On our first morning, we sat outside with coffee and binoculars. I looked at the road on the other side of the river and announced to Harry the make and color of each approaching car. "There's a little white Mazda convertible!" I had become a car person. A canoe race distracted me from my announcements. There were at least fifty large canoes, each with at least four people paddling, coming down the river. It was a fine race. Lots of hooting and hollering and no motors.

Then the sun peeked out from behind our two trees. Teensy orange heat-activated ants made their presence known. Evidently, it's not advisable to feed the pups in the afternoon sun. I bent down to study them as they were crawling on the dog food in the dishes, then noticed they were coming up my legs at an alarming rate. Thankfully, they brushed right off. We changed our feeding procedure, which took care of the ant problem. But I knew they were there, hiding in the sand, ready to pounce when the heat activated them, again!

Larry had us come to his place to watch the most glorious sunset. Later, the three of us walked back to the coach using our flashlights to illuminate the gravel path. There was something there ... something big. It was so big I could see it was sauntering. It was a good-looking tarantula. We went our way, and he went his. I made a mental note to carry a flashlight whenever I went out after dark!

It's amazing how much energy it takes to do simple things like making the bed when you have to think about every little action. I practiced until I could make the bed in four efficient steps without thinking.

I attended Larry's church, Calvary Baptist, on Sunday. It was a huge church, seating hundreds, with four services on the weekend. The sound system in the auditorium was cranked up so loud I had to wait in the foyer until the sermon began.

FLYING HOME

I was scheduled to fly to Vancouver to speak at the Women's Advent Luncheon. Mom's funeral was to be held earlier on the same weekend. It was an easy matter to move the booking up two days.

Chapter 2 ... Lake Havasu Area

The process to fly to Vancouver was not as easy. We had to get up at 5 a.m. for Harry to run me up to the Chevron Station in Lake Havasu City to catch a shuttle at 6:30 a.m. The shuttle picked up other travelers in town, then drove us north to Las Vegas (a three-hour drive). There was a four-hour wait until my flight. I met a fellow traveler, actually a former classmate, who had worked in the State Farm claims office. She knew Harry. I marveled at how we're all connected.

Chapter 3 ... Vancouver

My neighbor Dorothy and her cousin Sharon picked me up at the airport. I was home and settled in a new time zone by 3:30 p.m. I don't travel much, but when I do, I try to remember I look like an elderly seventy-year-old woman. Sometimes I take advantage: I'm quite adept at looking and acting addled as I've had a good forty years of practice. Other times, I just chuckle ... little do they know ... I'm still in my thirties!

Mom's Services

Mom's vigil was kind of fun. There were so many familiar people and good stories. It was satisfying. When I got home, I watched the end of an episode of The Great American Bakeoff with our charming house and dog sitter, Myrtice.

The funeral was well attended. My brother David gave a eulogy that didn't stray too far from reality. Later in the service, we sang a refrain: *"May the choirs of angels, come to greet you, may they lead you to Paradise; may the Lord enfold you in His mercy, may you find eternal life."* We sang it three times, building momentum with each refrain. It was simple and touching.

The recessional was a hymn set to "Ode to Joy" ... four verses, lungs a-blazing ... no reason to hold back. It was positively thrilling. I marched out of the church with a glorious smile depicting the joy of the moment and the solid conviction that there was no doubt Mom was with the Lord. We had the interment and reception at St. Mary's church and cemetery in Ridgefield. I kept myself low key, enjoying the company of lifelong friends and relatives. Some family members came to my place afterward for an extended visit. It was a pleasant way to wind down.

Choir Practice

I woke with a smile and jumped out of bed to prepare for choir practice with the orchestra. The cantata would be upon us in another month. It was going to be exceptional. All the pieces were by Pepper Choplin. In wonderful Choplin style, the songs built to a frenzy, relaxed, and then flew out of control to the heights of the vocal range. After choir practice, with the help of Jack the Border Collie and Cocoa Bean the Chihuahua mix, I scalped the lawn for the winter and blew the debris off the lawn and the asphalt. Two Ponds, our little piece of heaven on earth, looked pretty smart after a haircut and blow dry.

Myrtice's dad came to visit in the afternoon. He had been duck hunting. The three of us went out for dinner ... good food, good conversation, good company.

Women's Advent Luncheon

The day I'd been looking forward to for more than six months had arrived! It started with the choir anthem at two services. The song we sang had grown steadily on me during the practices, mostly because the conductor showed us how to sing it with panache. Of course, it could be the new risers in the choir loft that let me sit with my feet dangling ... a very rare occurrence. Afterward, I went downstairs for the Women's Advent Luncheon. I was presenting my skit: "The Cantata ... Find Your Place to Be." It went beautifully until I came to the comment about the Bass Section. I pronounced it with a short-a sound making it sound like a fish, instead of a group of singers. I stopped, smiled, and said it right. It all worked out ... thanks to a gracious audience.

Marg always has a jigsaw puzzle going. I puzzled with Marg and Keith for an eternity until I started getting anxious about packing to fly back to Arizona. At home, I finished packing and then tried to pray as usual, but it was almost impossible ... too much excitement. I'm just glad God appreciates the effort (and grades on the curve).

The dogs were very happy I was around again, but Monday morning, Jack got pretty confused as he tried to herd Myrtice and me into the same area. Failing that, he settled down in the dog-hair chair where he could hear her with his left ear and me with his right ear.

I had breakfast with my neighbor, Dorothy. Then my choir buddy, Dorothy Summers (a fellow soprano who tackles the upper end of the vocal range with elegance), whisked me off to the airport.

THE WOMAN IN THE RED JACKET

As I sat at the gate waiting to board for ninety minutes, I noticed a stunning white-haired woman in a bright red jacket. Just for a minute I thought, *Pastor Joel would be proud of me if I went over to visit with her*, but I feared I was still a little too high from the Women's Advent Luncheon presentation, so I resisted the urge.

When we boarded, I found my seat easily. Suddenly, there was a little confusion across the aisle. It was the woman in the red jacket ... she was in the wrong seat. She quickly moved to the seat next to me. We started chatting. We were both glad for the company. Strangely enough, we had a lot of things in common. We talked about many assorted life adventures, including praying. I had gotten the impression she was from Portland as she told me about her life with her husband. When she asked where I was from, our conversation, which had been smooth and natural, became swift and choppy, not even bothering with verbs as we struggled to get as much information as we could in the shortest time possible:

I said, "Vancouver."

She said, "Vancouver."

"Church?"

"St. John's Catholic Church on 87th."

"I used to play the organ there. Messiah Lutheran."

"Oh," she said, "I've been there. MaryAnn."

"I know her!"

"Dorothy Summers."

I squealed with delight: "Dorothy gave me a ride to the airport this morning!"

"I went to the memorial service for her husband."

"I was in the choir singing 'How Great Thou Art'!"

And it just went on from there.

We even exchanged engagement stories. We had great laughs together all the way to Las Vegas ... it felt like God was giving me a big hug!

Chapter 4 ... Lake Havasu Area

Harry Can Cook?

After the shuttle ride from Las Vegas to Lake Havasu, I was exceedingly happy to see Harry. But when we got back to the motor home, I had mixed emotions. He told me how he had reheated things I had left for him, found a Mexican takeout place, and fixed a three-egg omelet for breakfast. These may be fine for a normal husband, but for thirty-six years I'd been laboring under the assumption Harry couldn't cook. He even used the word omelet correctly. I really didn't know what to make of this new disclosure! There were no dishes in the sink, no garbage under the counter, my stash of breakfast bars was still intact, and the blanket he bought had been carefully laid out on the bed with the coverlet tidily tucked on top of it. I was totally impressed! But, in the refrigerator, I saw a freshly purchased 8-oz. packet of shredded Tillamook Cheese. I resisted the urge to stuff it in the freezer on top of the two 40-oz. bags of shredded Tillamook Cheese from Costco. Thanksgiving was coming and I was grateful for everything.

I'll See You Again

I decided to do a little church hopping since I had only two Sundays left in the area. I found three Lutheran churches near the main drag in Lake Havasu City. I went to the one with the most convenient time ... Lamb of God Lutheran Church. It was tucked away in the middle of a residential area. I found out it was a Missouri Synod congregation. There were a lot of Thees, Thous, and a pretty fair amount of ritual. Heavy ritual was not really my style, but I knew I could go elsewhere the following week.

The first thing the pastor did was ask if there were any new people. I shot up my hand and he had me shout out my name. The next thing I knew they were spouting off all the Kathy Hoffmans they had known in the past, including a former pastor's wife. Then an elder came up the aisle to my pew with information about the church tucked in a coffee cup, saying, "We like to mug newcomers!"

"I'm only here for this week," I protested. But they went on with the service possibly lamenting the cost of the mug, which would probably not produce lasting congregational results. The people were amazingly open and welcoming. They made my eyebrows arch.

Once home, I looked at the printed matter and kept thinking how I was looking forward to attending a less-ritualistic Lutheran church the following week. I had coffee in my new mug and reviewed the weekly schedule. There was to be a gathering on Tuesday morning to decorate the sanctuary. I wasn't really a fan of driving forty-five minutes to get to a church, but it sounded like fun and I thought it might help me get into the holiday spirit. So I went.

I met Dell, Linda, Mary (who can't look up without getting dizzy), Karen, Joy, and others. We unpacked ornaments and placed them on the tree systematically. In one hour, everything was in place and looking good, including two trees, some banners, and numerous wreaths throughout the church.

After decorating, I wandered down the hall to where the prayer team was gathering with the prayer requests. I had turned in a request for prayer for eleven people on Sunday and thought I'd like to join them for their prayer session. Pastor Kallio, John, John on oxygen, and Harvey were the prayer team. They asked if I had turned in this prayer request. I said yes as John handed it to me. Pastor Kallio led with a devotional, then each of them prayed for a list of intentions. Thees, Thous, and Almighties abounded. Prayers were spinning out of control. When it was my turn, I took a deep breath and prayed in my own style, which, I have to admit was considerably slower. Twenty minutes after we started, we finished. We all shook hands. Harvey said, "I'll see you again." I didn't want to tell him he wouldn't since I was planning to go to a different church the next Sunday. I smiled and let it slide.

John said, "Oh, Hoffman. My wife's sister-in-law was named Kathy Hoffman. I'd like you to meet my wife. She's up front, decorating." One thing led to another and I trotted back up front and met Karen a second time. Then I looked to my left and discovered an alcove with about eighteen chairs. "Oh, do you have a choir?"

"We sure do," they retorted, "and we practice Thursdays at 4 p.m. Come and join us!"

"But I won't be here to sing," I lamented.

"Oh, no problem, just come and practice with us."

Even though I still wasn't a fan of driving forty-five minutes to get to a church, I went on Thursday. I was disappointed when I reviewed all the songs in the folder and found I didn't know even one of them! And there was no Christmas music. I resigned myself to doing my best, anyway. (And there was Karen a third time!) Clarice, the director, did so many things like my director back home: She told us to sing the vowels and spit the consonants. She drove each phrase until she was happy with the sounds coming from the alto, bass, baritone, and tenor sections. We sopranos just sat there happy we weren't being singled out. She directed us while playing the organ, consequently there was no baton and minimal hand waving. Too bad. But we only practiced one song: "Abide with Me." And then, to my good fortune, Clarice announced that we were going to sing on Saturday night. I was ecstatic. Harry and I were leaving Sunday morning, but I'd be able to sing with the choir on Saturday. After practice, a lady passed by me on her way into the church saying, "Hi, Kathy." Confused, I followed her and asked for a refresher. It was Mary (who couldn't look up).

On Saturday, I was on my way to the choir alcove and passed a man who said, "I told you I'd see you again." It was Harvey from the prayer team. Then John on oxygen came in and waved to me as he took his place across the church in the media booth. I was surprised I knew the names of so many people. While Clarice practiced with the altos, I grabbed a couple of sopranos and went down the hallway to practice cutting loose during the fortissimo sections.

I must say the Missouri Synod people know how to spin a story, too. The deacon got up and made a plea for the Angel Tree the first time I attended and a plea for their sister congregation in Paradise, which had been burned out, the following week. I opened my pocketbook wide. I know the Bible says, "God loves a cheerful giver!" but my husband keeps track of the spending. I didn't have any modest bills in my possession either week. All I had was a couple of big bills. I did what had to be done and made sure I left tracks for tax purposes. I know that God promises to give back a hundredfold, but when the bills get bigger than my comfort zone, it's hard to remember that.

My Lamb of God Lutheran coffee mug is a constant reminder of a warm engaging congregation.

CHAPTER 5 ... PHOENIX AREA

WATER DAMAGE

We were sticking to our travel plan: one month in each spot. Our trip to the Phoenix area was easy. We stayed at Happy Trails RV Resort in Surprise, Arizona, which is essentially the northwest corner of the Phoenix area. The resort sits under the flight path of Luke Air Force Base. Nevertheless, a couple of get-togethers with our friends David and Sheila, who had a place there, made our stay at Happy Trails a memorable one.

The old adage, "Into each life some rain must fall" came to mind when we noticed a spongy floor in the storage bay of the coach. The closer we looked, the worse it got. There was extensive water damage through the storage bay, which had started well before we purchased the coach. We were fortunate our next-door neighbor Mark, an engineer, had decent problem-solving skills. He helped us realize the extent of the damage and find the two leaks (shower faucet and missing seal on one of the basement doors). He introduced us to Bill, the neighbor parked behind us, who knew the right way to fix things and had the tools to do it. We, mostly Harry, were consumed with tearing apart and rebuilding for five days. When he was finished, there was a solid floor throughout the entire storage bay ... destined to outlast the <u>coach</u>!

Chapter 5 ... Phoenix Area 35

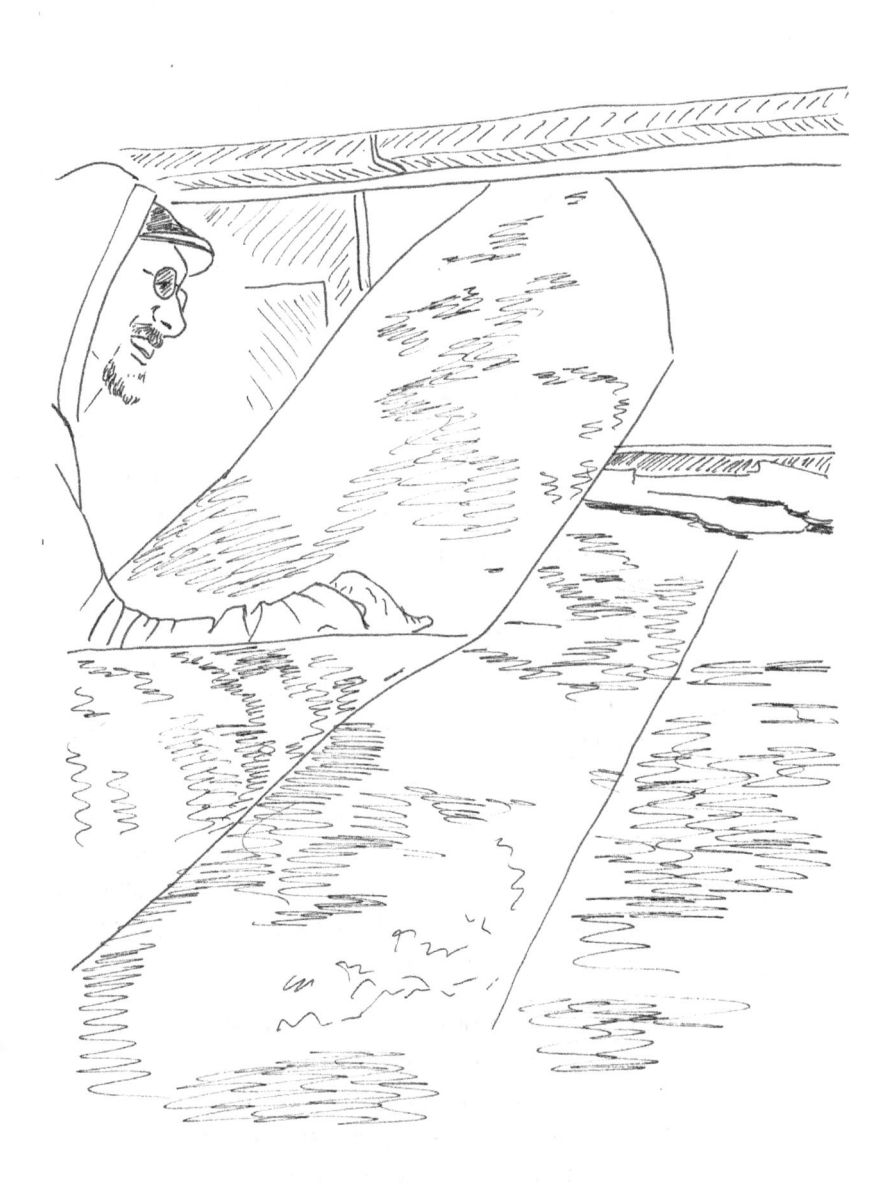

We Got a D-Plus

I had a few days to find a church. A quick search of the internet gave me Spirit of Grace Evangelical Lutheran Church. Their website had an open invitation to join the forty-plus member choir. The choir section was directly behind the altar. It was no place for the squeamish. They put me on the end of the soprano section and gave me a wonderfully familiar booklet "Night of the Father's Love" by Pepper Choplin. We sang from the book each week for three weeks: "The Coming of the Lord," "Angels Are Making Their Rounds" (I knew that one), and "Christ is Born, Nowell." (I could picture Norma from Messiah singing that one!)

There was a high A at the end of "The Coming of the Lord." Ken, our director, waved it off. He said we'd sing the lower notes. I chimed in with "Can we sing it if we know we can do it?" He perked up his eyebrows and said OK, moving me three seats to the left. "You sit with these four ladies. Let's see what you can do." I jumped up because everyone knows you can't hit a high A unless it starts from your toes and move up in a straight line. The other four ladies also thought better of sitting. And then, without the backing of an orchestra, a CD, or the rest of the choir, he made the five of us go through the ending all alone. (I had missed an opportunity to commandeer a high note once back home ... I wasn't about to miss an opportunity again.) We five threw the words to the rafters and nailed the final high A with only the piano to back us up. He asked for a re-do to make sure it wasn't a fluke. We were on top of it! "OK," he said enthusiastically, "Let's do it!" I brought my music home to practice in my spare time. Then I laughed as I realized it's all spare time.

The song for Sunday had a lot of consonants throughout. Ken told us to spit our consonants, as all choir directors are wont to do ... but we didn't do it to his satisfaction. The next week he told the whole choir we got a D-plus. We sang the same consonant-ridden song two weeks in a row. I asked how we did the second time ... all he would commit to was we had improved. Low praise from a choir director!

Chapter 6 ... Singing in Vancouver

Flying Home ... Again

The following week, Messiah Lutheran in Vancouver was having its Christmas program. I flew home to sing in my second cantata, "Christmas Presence" by Pepper Choplin. To hear the cantata, google "Pepper Choplin Christmas Presence."

The conductor had given each of us a CD of the cantata. For three months, I had been listening to the CD as it played on an endless loop. At first, I sang along with the soprano track. Once I had mastered the soprano track, I tried to sing my soprano part along with the alto track. It was humbling, but it helped me understand the nuances of the pieces.

A couple of weeks before the Christmas program, the conductor sent me an email asking me to substitute for one of the handbell players ... Branden. It's hard to sub for Branden because he plays the heavier bells like it's an Olympic sport! But I agreed to do it and vowed to do the best I could. I had the bell music on my phone. As I sat on the airport carpet in the boarding area, leaning against a pillar next to a charging station, I continued to practice. Staring at the music, I raised and cranked my wrists as I played the imaginary bells. I thought maybe I could give my mind and wrists a little muscle memory ... to help boost my confidence. I'm not sure what the passengers waiting to board thought.

The big day finally arrived. The dress code for the evening was red or black. In an effort to stir up a little trouble, I showed up in a hot-pink floral fleece skirt and a bright blue hooded jacket, which would have been a horrible contrast to the dress code. After making my wretched appearance ... and to the relief of my choir and bell mates ... I took off my outerwear, revealing a sophisticated long-sleeved little black dress. Everyone was excited and chatting up a storm. Julia came in with some meringue cookies for the cookie table. Festivity was in the air.

Following the final performance, I went directly home and pounded out my feelings on the computer. A new skit came to life. The words in bold are meant to be sung with reckless abandon ... no holds barred!

The Cantata – 2018 – "All for the Glory of God"

As she rubbed lotion into the pores of her face, her daily ritual, the Tall Soprano heard the thrum of the Bass section in her mind. She had heard it every morning for the past two weeks.

Come and worship, worship the newborn King. Come and worship, worship the newborn King. She was getting more excited by the minute. Today was the day of the cantata. She jumped up and danced from her dressing table to the closet. The calypso beat frolicked in her head: **Come ... and see this tiny miracle. Come ... and see this holy Child.** Her two Corgi dogs were nearby. She leaned forward and invited them, singing: **Oh, come and see.** They came. The dogs thought perhaps there might be some food in it if they complied. **Oh, come and see! Oh, come and see this tiny miracle.** She happily gave each pup a treat. She could hardly wait for the performance to start in a few hours. She dressed meticulously and warmly, knowing there was a major storm on the way. Hair, earrings, necklace, dress, nylons, leather boots ... she was ready. She smiled when she thought of the Orchestral accompaniment, especially the tight, high-pitched tweet from the Flute, which made the song. "How does that first piece start?" She fought to remember ... "Oh, yes. **The World Awaits Your Coming**." What a wonderful way to start the Christmas season.

Then she smiled unassumingly as she thought fondly of relatives and friends who had died in the last year. **Still, they are here ... at Christmastime.**

She was in love with the cantata ... all eight songs. Driving to church, she had her CD player cranked up high, giving her one last opportunity to nail the high note that must be sustained at the very end of the concert. As she entered the back door of the church, she

Chapter 6 ... *Singing in Vancouver*

calmed her excitement with an excerpt from the second song in a minor key: **We are here, God is here, There's a holy presence in this place.** It was a powerful rich addition to the repertoire. **You are full of glory, truth, and grace.**

Goosebumps went up and down her spine as she anticipated the thrill the congregation would feel in the fifth piece when they sang of **Hope to the World, Love to the World, Joy to the World.** She was confident the whole congregation would be smiling at the end of that particular song.

Her thoughts went to the second-to-last song. She had been forced to leave town and had never had the opportunity to sing it with the full Choir and Orchestra. What a fun song. Bouncing from section to section in the Choir, it was sure to be a hit: **Go tell it on the mountain ... Born, Born. I'm gonna send thee two by two.** It was by far her favorite ... playful and strong ... **Jesus Christ is born.**

The cantata was exhilarating. All of the songs blended beautifully with the narrative. The Choir, the Orchestra, and Handbell ensemble worked their hearts out for three full services. The Pastor gave a brief update of the capital campaign for repairs. "We are so close to our goal!" she exclaimed. Those in the pews who were in the know knew this meant the roof, in such great need of repair, would be replaced right after the holidays. The debt on the building would be repaid soon after. Following this good news, she launched into her sermon. A Little Girl, leaning forward with arms folded on the pew in front of her, chin on her hands, listened enraptured, as the Pastor's sermon revealed Mary's feelings when she went to visit Elizabeth ... how she burst into song ... how the song sang her. The Choir wondered at that phrase.

Meanwhile, the Tuba ... who was not used to playing with others and therefore had been admonished by the Conductor after the first service to play louder, and who was determined to be a team player in subsequent services ... had let 'er rip. He had been pumping his lungs for all he was worth. This same Tuba ... exhausted from the effects of three services, and suffering from leg spasms, which were directly connected to the amount of air he was forcing from his lungs ... stretched out his long legs to the left of the Bass Horn. Slouching his 6' 4" frame down in his chair at a forty-five-degree angle, he hoped to be able to control his instrument while affording his quaking legs an opportunity to relax. *After all*, he thought, *there's only one piece left in the cantata*. It was true. There was only one last song to sing and the cantata would be history ... warm and wonderful ... but history nonetheless.

The Pastor returned to her chair. The Conductor raised his baton signaling his disciples: The Choir stood. The Tall Soprano looked out across the congregation in dismay. No one was smiling. It was then she realized the Choir was not singing for the congregation but for the Glory of God. And so it began. The Conductor's baton twitched rhythmically. The lyrics flowed smoothly and confidently:

Angels came to earth one night ... to touch the world with holy light ... and bring a word of hope to the hopeless. Months of practice had familiarized the Tall Soprano with the Conductor's ways ... the retarrrd, the a-tempo, the creSCENdo, the mezzo-piano, the forTISSimo, the tenutoooo, Accelerando, ROBUSTLY, with extra drive. She could see it all in her mind's eye. She could feel it in her soul. Her eyes were on the Conductor. She knew the drill: she was to have her eyes on the Conductor at all times. Whatever his baton told her to do, she must do.

Their word awakened shepherds' ears ... that once were closed by pain and fear. Their eyes would see a glimpse of heaven's glory. She sang for all she was worth.

A glimpse of heaven's glory. Glory to God, Glory to God, Glory be to God in the highest. It was a fitting end to the cantata. **Glory to God, Glory to God, Glory be to God in the highest heaven.** Everyone's voices blended superbly. The Orchestra missed ... not ... one ... note! The Tall Soprano thought it was lovely. She

Chapter 6 ... Singing in Vancouver

smiled as she listened to the familiar words she was singing. Every Christmas, she had heard these words from the Gospel of Luke. **And let there be peace, let there be peace, peace on earth, good will to all.** She felt a momentary twinge of sadness and wondered where it had come from ... perhaps because this was the last song of the cantata. But this was not a sad time. She filled her lungs to announce to the world the happy news and as she did so, she felt her soul come alive again. And the Choir sang on ... building momentum with each phrase. **For unto you is born this day in the city of David. For unto you is born this day a Savior, Christ the Lord.** Dead center in the middle of the final piece of the cantata, it happened. It was not a revolt, as in the previous year ... it was simply a vibrant awakening. After months of preparation, the Choir was no longer singing the words the Angels sang ... no ... they became one with the song! **And this shall be a sign to you, you shall find the Babe in a manger.** The Conductor crouched down and pumped his fist at the Choir and the Orchestra. The excitement was building rapidly.

Suddenly there was a heavenly host. With the realization there was indeed a heavenly host, with the heady, dizzying effects of the music, and with her newly inspired devotion, the Tall Soprano did the unthinkable. No Choir member would ever think to do such a thing. But the Tall Soprano did ... she closed her eyes! She began to sing for the glory of God only ... she *became* an Angel ... she was singing for all her heart was worth ... she was singing to praise God.

At the same time, perhaps because the Conductor had pumped his fist so hard, the most amazing thing happened ... seven-foot wings sprouted from his back. Unused to having his wings on display in public life, he flapped awkwardly to get them under control. In doing so, he took out half of the Alto section to his right. One of the remaining Altos, having a severe feather allergy, commenced sneezing uncontrollably, so much so the new choir risers became unstable. The remaining Altos, all in the top tier, toppled backward from their perch into a vacant spot behind the risers. High heels peared to float upside down in mid-air. The other massive seven-foot plume took out the Flute, the Clarinet, and the First Violin to the Conductor's left. The Second Violin, sitting shorter than most, missed being toppled by a hair. This same Second Violin, left to carry the melody, concentrating on each note, and oblivious to the chaos around him, continued sawing frantically at his instrument. The Trumpets were aghast ... one humongous wing had brushed the tops of their heads. Both darted down into a neighboring pew, fearful if either played an incorrect note, they'd be downsized the next year. The Bass Horn stuttered producing a most unusual sound. The Conductor momentarily halted his attempt to restrain his errant plumage and turned his full attention to the Bass Horn. But all was lost. The Bass Horn's music went flying. He grabbed for it but missed. In doing so, he dropped his instrument ... right on the left toe of the Tuba. The Tuba fell on the floor, tears in his eyes, legs akimbo, nursing his big toe, grateful he had been wearing sandals as he watched his toe swell to the size of a fist. Ever the professional, he bit his lower lip to keep from screaming in agony as the Sopranos were rising to the top of the treble staff. **Praising God and saying ...** They were in the zone. No longer were they singing about the Heavenly Host. The Choir was the Heavenly Host. Everything the Tall Soprano had within her was thrown into the next triplet as she sang ... **Glooory to God.** She continued non-stop ... **Glory to God. Glory be to God in the highest**.

At the exact same moment, the roof, which had been scheduled for repairs right after Christmas, succumbed to the ravages of the winter storm raging outside. Shingles flew from the gables, unbeknownst to those inside. Underlayment was ripped from the plywood. Naked to the storm, the plywood gave up the ghost. A gaping hole, right above the piano, opened to the heavens. The deluge dumped in from above. The Pianist, drenched to the skin, watched as the notes ran down the page like cheap mascara. Prone to feverish emotional outbursts and outraged at the inconvenience, the Pianist hissed at the Conductor, "Don't stop now! Keep twiddling your baton!" The rainwater, trapped in the orchestra pit, was rising. The Facility Engineer,

Chapter 6 ... Singing in Vancouver

sitting in the front pew, as he was not yet a true Lutheran, was starting to question the wisdom of putting the electrical outlets in the floor throughout the Orchestra Pit. The Handbell ensemble, seeing the rising water, quickly jumped up on their platforms ... all but one, who was intently bent on turning up the bottom corner of each page, ensuring the page turns would proceed smoothly should the handbell piece ever be played again in some future year. The Bass, with her never-ending optimism and her joyful smile, concerned about her new sparkling black four-inch heels, which might be damaged from the rising waters and might then look bad with her tight black mini skirt, jumped up backward to the riser in the Alto section. She strained to keep her instrument upright as *it* strained under the stress of her forty-five-degree incline ... yet she played on. And the Choir sang on. Inconceivable as it may have seemed, they had all closed their eyes by this time and were completely unaware of all the bedlam around them.

Glory to God ... Glory to God. Glory be to God in the highest heaven. Having been exposed to a glimpse of the "other side," the Choir now knew what it would be like to live in peace in the presence of the glory of God. And the Choir sang on. **And let there be peace ... let there be peace ... Peace on Earth, Good Wi-i-i-il to all.** "Had the message been heard?" they mused. "Better safe than sorry!" They repeated the message yet again. First the Bass, Baritone and Tenor sections ... **And let there be peace.** In an effort to ensure this crucial message was heard and understood, the Altos (who by this time had righted themselves and were peering up from behind the risers) and the Sopranos repeated the imperative: ... **Let there be peace.** Then the whole Choir in unison: ... **Peace on Earth, Good will, Good will to all** ... Nothing was separating them from the glory of God. **Sing Glory to God.** They threw their hearts open, filled their lungs, and went for the gusto ... **Sing Glory to Gah-** ... The Conductor, having controlled his wayward protuberances, lifted his hands, his head, and his eyebrows ... this was the secret signal between him and the Tall Soprano, which meant *hold it ... hold it until I pinch it off!* She held it ... no matter how her

Part Two – Heading into the Unknown ... 2018–19

s ached, she vowed to hold it until the final measure regardless of how long the Conductor lingered ... *Pinch* ... **-ahd!!** The formerly stoic congregation burst to their feet, erupting in thunderous applause. The fierceness of the storm paled in comparison. Tears were flowing from every eyeball. The Little Girl in the second pew was screaming with delight as she jumped up and down. A woman bundled up in a wheelchair nodded her approval. As the applause faded, a deep confident voice came from somewhere in the rafters. People looked around but couldn't find the source of the voice, but they listened ... "Go in Hope, Peace, Love, and Joy. Be the Presence of Christ to the world." They responded, "Thanks be to God!" The Tall Soprano knew in her heart of hearts, of all her life experiences, there was no greater privilege than singing glory to God.

After the cantata, the Tall Soprano was eagerly chatting with her friends and relatives. She noticed an elderly woman slowly approaching. The old woman was hunched down and mumbling to no one in particular. She was wearing an unusually gaudy hot-pink and white floor-length fleece skirt, short black boots, a black sweater, a well-worn hot-pink scarf across her shoulders, and an incongruous vivid sky-blue hooded jacket. The Tall Soprano felt for her. As the old woman passed on her way to the side exit, the Tall Soprano heard her muttering repeatedly, "I'm no Branden ... I'm no Branden." The Tall Soprano thought it might mean something to someone but not to her. She reached for a bright little meringue cookie topped with cracked peppermint and smiled.

Chapter 7 ... Phoenix Area

Home to Harry

The flight and shuttle ride home were noneventful. After a big welcome-home hug, Harry asked if I'd had anything to eat. When I said I hadn't, he told me there was a helping of stew in the refrigerator. When I hesitated, he said he would fix it for me. My eyebrows hit my hairline. I thanked him and told him I'd get it. He gave me directions on where to find the microwave bowl and how to hit Reheat and Start. I dumped a healthy amount of stew into the bowl. As I got ready to put the lid on, he said I needed to mash it down so it would heat properly.

I was warming up to his unexpected abilities in the kitchen.

"What am I," I asked, "window dressing?"

"Yup," he said.

Dental Floss

We had bought twelve packs of dental floss from Costco. We had also gotten little containers of floss with every dental appointment. Consequently, we had plenty of floss around. We preferred the mint or cinnamon flavors. So did Angie! As soon as we'd leave the room, Angie would jump up on Harry's chair and root around his tray. When I remembered, I watched out for it.

One fine day, I was polishing the driver's window from the outside. Lucy was sitting right next to the window inside the coach. I swiped up down up down. Lucy's nose followed up down up down. I was tickled but suddenly remembered Angie. She was standing on the floor looking at me. But she wasn't watching what I was doing ... she watching to see whether or not I could see her. When I finished, I went to the back of the motor home to run a load of laundry. When I returned, Angie was quietly lying in her pen ... dismantling a dental floss container!

... Lost again!

Oh, that Angie ... we lost her again ... inside the motor home! She had two favorite cool spots in the bedroom. I trekked almost the full length of the forty-foot motor home, looked under both sides of the bed, and came up empty. I returned to the front of the coach and checked behind the two chairs in the living room. I still came up empty. As a last resort, I checked the front. Lucy was draped across the driver's seat. And there on the floor ... tucked way under the dashboard as far from the living area as she could be ... was Angie, in her new favorite spot.

A Magnet

I found a tiny little bar magnet just outside the coach. I thought it was unusual because I hadn't seen it in the three weeks we'd been there. No matter. I snatched it out of the gravel and saved it because you never know when you'll need a tiny little bar magnet.

Aretha Hoffman?

Undaunted by our low grades in the first part of December, the Spirit of Grace choir popped right back and enthusiastically sang during the two services on Christmas Eve. Since there was an hour to kill between services, the church provided a lovely buffet for us. Also, since the choir had sung "Fall on Your Knees" by Pepper Choplin two years earlier, I offered to perform my skit as a surprise. The director accepted. It was a little intimidating to perform it for people I didn't know, but I cut loose on the high notes, nonetheless.

Saving Money

I ordered three unmentionables on the internet on December 16. I was pretty sure I read they guaranteed delivery by Christmas, but they did note I needed to allow up to ten business days. If I had paid twice as much, I could have gotten two-day delivery from Amazon Prime. Nevertheless, I was convinced I had an okay chance of getting them before we left the Phoenix area on January 1. It was kind

Chapter 7 ... Phoenix Area

of important to get the delivery because the mailroom in the park (a contract post office) made it crystal clear they don't forward anything. The next day, UPS arrived in front of our coach. I was impressed ... but it was for the neighbors. I waited and waited ... and waited. I didn't know if my unmentionables were coming by UPS, FedEx, or USPS. After a week, I started getting nervous and contacted the company. They were in China! I started sweating on the last weekend of the year. The people in the mailroom were most helpful. I told them in a hushed voice exactly what I was waiting for (using a three-letter word instead of saying "unmentionable"). They said they'd hold the package and would call me if and when it finally came.

Chapter 8 ... Casa Grande

On the Road Again

We had a tiny sprinkle of snow early on December 31 and rain for the rest of the day. Ice fell off the awning as we retracted the slides the next morning. It was January 1 and we were on our way to Casa Grande, a couple of hours south ... without my package. As we were leaving, I discovered the steps weren't acting right. They wouldn't retract. It was New Years Day: There was no chance of getting a repair person out. We decided to make a run for it. We were going two hours away. How hard could it be? I was pleased the roads were dry as we left. It was too bad the steps didn't retract because the public works people were in the middle of a big road improvement project on Interstate 10. It was a little scary driving in the right lane with concrete barriers threatening to kiss our extended steps. It was easy sailing after we turned south. We arrived without incident at Palm Creek RV Resort in Casa Grande.

Palm Creek

After we got settled, I checked the tracking number. The package still hadn't left China. A week later, it was in Los Angeles. It's a good thing I didn't do the math, because gas, time, and postage, as well as anxiety, would have made Amazon Prime's two-day delivery look pretty cheap, even at double the price!

The next day, a mobile RV service was doing some work for a neighbor. When I asked him about the step, he showed me where a small magnet had broken off. The magnet was needed to complete the circuit in order for the little motor to retract the steps. It was an easy fix. He said as long as I did the work, he wouldn't have to charge me for a service visit. He handed me a replacement, told me what to do, and the rest was history.

Palm Creek RV Resort was huge. It had a lot of activities, including:

Chapter 8 ... *Casa Grande* 49

- Pickleball ... 32 courts ... it was said to be the largest pickleball complex in the western United States. Harry didn't have the knees for it anymore; I didn't have the coordination.
- A pretty little eighteen-hole par-three golf course with water running through the back nine.
- A nondenominational service at 9 a.m. on Sunday, with a forty-member choir. The teaching was solid and provocative ... in a good way.
- Cards, Mexican Train, and Mahjong on weekdays.
- Bible study or dog agility on Tuesday. (Bible study won out.)
- Jigsaw puzzling in the library. (I was one of the half dozen regulars.)
- Computer club and cell phone classes.
- Fitness center.
- Lawn bowling, shuffleboard, stained glass, silversmith, woodworking, quilting, painting, crafts, lapidary, water aerobics, and yoga.

I checked on the card playing. It seemed like a good way to meet people. The card people said there was a big two-hour show that night. I talked Harry into going and got tickets. I gave it a six out of ten; Harry gave it a solid 2. Bottom line: We had a good time watching "The Edwards Twins" (identical males about sixty years old) impersonate some of the greats, including Dolly, Sonny and Cher, Barbara Streisand, Bocelli (the blind tenor), and Frankie Valli. The Frankie impersonation had me rolling in the aisles. Unlike the other impersonations, it was *not* spot on. We were in the back row ... a good place to be. I'm glad I wasn't up close enough to see caked-on makeup.

WHEEL OF FORTUNE?

The main road through the park was three miles long. There were streets jutting off both directions. It was a big park (almost 2,500 sites), but the strangest thing about staying there was that regardless of how many people were staying there, everyone disappeared at dinnertime. I got so engrossed in the jigsaw puzzle, I suddenly realized I was alone in the library. I walked about a quarter mile back to the coach through the neighborhoods at dusk and ran into only one other person!

Staying Connected

Little things helped me stay connected to my home base:
- Pastor Debbie said something about God's mercies being new every morning ... it made me miss Kay, my prayer partner of ten years.
- I read a book to keep up with my Tuesday Breakfast Book group back home.
- I was looking forward to mailing my Christmas cards before Easter!

Choir

I joined the choir at our Palm Creek Community Chapel and was enjoying the differences in choir directors. Some were more actively involved than others, but no one exhibited the full body workout demonstrated by my choir director in Vancouver.

The choir director at Palm Creek asked for one person to sing the high G the next week. Helen and I shot up our hands. The director asked if our voices blended well. "Perfectly!" I hollered. (How does anyone know the answer to that question.) Several people tittered ... the director would have to decide. As it turned out, our voices did blend nicely as we nailed the high G together. A few weeks later we had a little trouble with one of the measures ... I kept missing the note, but I was confident Helen would find it and everything would be just fine. I stood next to her, just in case. The measure in question came and went. Neither of us hit the note. It was hard to stand there and smile when it ended, knowing we had tried to no avail.

Chapter 8 ... Casa Grande

DAILY LIFE

We got three balls for the dogs. They knew enough about fetch to run and get the ball and enough about sharing to take the fetched ball back to their individual crates. Pbfft ... sisters!

I had a little problem with my photos. I accidentally deleted all 417 pictures in my gallery in less than five seconds. Believe me, I was shocked! My phone gave me no prompt like *Do you really want to delete 417 photos?* After two hours on the phone with Sam from Verizon around midnight and two more hours with Oliver from Samsung the next morning, I discovered it was possible to delete something and have it be unrecoverable.

On the news, they suggested going to twinning.popsugar.com to find out what celebrity you look like. I had high hopes until I found I had a solid 83% match with Bruce Dern! Maybe Harry was right about my new haircut being way too short.

As I became a seasoned traveler, I discovered three rules for a happy motor home experience: keep the dishes washed, the counter cleared, and the bed made.

THE UNMENTIONABLES

The mailroom in Surprise called saying I had a package waiting. *All right!* But then they said they had given my package to the new renter in my old space. He had opened it, realized it wasn't something he would normally wear and returned it to the mailroom. I called our friends, David and Sheila, who graciously forwarded it to our new location. The whole process took about a month. But hey, I saved $45 by ordering from China instead of Amazon Prime.

They didn't fit.

I had to email the company. I was concerned whoever was on the end of the email transaction might not understand my English, so I took great lengths to make sure my comments were direct:

> Dear Sirs,
>
> The bras I purchased were not the ones that were sent. The bras I purchased had a picture associated with them showing wide straps with lace overlay. The bras I received had narrow straps that cross in the back and no lace overlay. The packaging showed a picture of bras with wide straps. The bras in the package were not as advertised on the front of the package nor on the internet website where I made my purchase.
>
> These bras are too small. They are extremely uncomfortable. I removed the padding and was very surprised that the bras are still too small. I re-measured and verified my bust is xxx inches. The packaging noted that a medium bra was indicated for an xxx-inch bust. The bras I received came in plastic bags labeled "M" and should have been the right size, but they did NOT fit (see photos).
>
> Sincerely,
> Kathy Hoffman

Suffice it to say, it was not pretty. Sadly, the photos I included were not among the 417 photos I had accidently deleted. *[Please do not look for those photos in this book ... they have been deleted from my life!]* I ended my email by requesting they get the order right. Here is the response I received from the company within twenty-four hours:

> "I'm really sorry. Maybe the warehouse made a mistake. We can give you five dollars as compensation. Or you can send the product to us if you want full refund."

Rather than checking to find out how much it would cost to ship the bras back, I emailed the company requesting they provide a post-paid mailing label. I never heard back. Sunk cost! Two years later, after fussing the entire time, I went to Amazon Prime and placed an order. *(Sigh!)*

Chapter 9 ... Palm Springs Area

Desert Hot Springs

By the time we were halfway through our first snowbirding adventure, I was starting to get into a bloom-where-you're-planted mindset. We were getting much better at packing, traveling, and getting settled. We had a six-hour drive from Palm Creek to Desert Hot Springs. It's only a few hundred miles ... just about right for retired people. Our reservation at Caliente Hot Springs started on February 1. Rain was in the forecast. Within ten minutes of completing our setup, the rain started coming down. We were grateful for the timing.

Golfing

A nice little nine-hole par-three golf course was woven tightly between park models. The fairways were narrow, hilly and lined by patio doors, bay windows, and ponds. There's a warning sign at the first hole for all golfers: if one hits a ball into somebody's yard one should not retrieve it. Between the narrow fairways and the ponds, Harry and I managed to lose three balls each per round of golf. After five rounds and fifteen balls, we moved on to public courses.

We were told the winter was a little harsher than normal. (Since then, I've discovered people say that every year.) We decided to go golfing at a course on the San Andreas Fault. The wind was blowing ferociously. When we hit the ball up into the air, we didn't know if it would go left, right, forward, or come back to us! Same with chipping and putting. We had had enough after seventeen holes and bagged it We returned two days later and enjoyed playing eighteen holes with very little wind. We were getting a good sense of why there were so many wind turbines in the Coachella Valley. We were at the west end of the valley getting the full force of whatever came from Los Angeles.

Chapter 9 ... Palm Springs Area 55

BIBLE STUDY

I found an unscheduled Bible study. I liked it because we reviewed what was said during the Sunday sermon and figured out ways to put it into practice. It was very convicting. The next Sunday, the message was on taming the tongue. We had a lively discussion with nary a lull.

I had been reading a book by Bonhoeffer with the Tuesday Breakfast Book group back home. (It was a hard book to read. My friend Steve complained it made his brain hurt.) I found a recumbent bike in the fitness room and was pleased to find I could knock off one chapter per exercise session.

CATHARSIS

I was getting used to being a monthly nomad. I checked on Lutheran churches. It's hard to know where to go, but I decided not to opt for the tiny church nearby, going instead to Palm Desert on the other side of the valley. Distance continued to baffle me. It turned out the other side of the valley was about forty-five minutes away.

My new church was Hope Lutheran. There was a lot of energy in that church. (It made me homesick again.) It was about twice the size of Messiah and had a full choir with about three dozen members. After the service, the choir stayed in their chairs. I approached apprehensively. (It was as if I would be addressing the whole choir! Would they be ticked because I was asking to join and possibly upset their balance?) I shed my fears, tapped the shoulder of the organist-director, and asked, "Do you have room for a high soprano?"

The response was immediate. The left side of the front row exploded with life. I was warmly welcomed. When they found out I was from Desert Hot Springs, they paired me with Jerry, who was just down the street from me. He had night driving issues and hadn't been able to attend evening practices. A take-charge woman named Juanita marched Jerry and me back into the choir area, gave us folders filled with music, fitted us with robes, and brightly sent us off into the world until the next practice.

I was disappointed to learn the choir was taking a one-week hiatus. In fact, there were several more disappointments to follow but greater joy at the end. During the one-week hiatus, I checked out the Sunday service held at our park. The preaching was solid, and the two Bible studies I attended during the week were uplifting. I flipflopped. I found myself disappointed I had already committed to Hope Lutheran's choir and to Jerry. Nevertheless, I was determined to fulfill the commitment and bloom where I was planted.

On Thursday evening, Valentine's Day, Jerry and I chatted agreeably all the way to the church for our first choir practice. We were given massive amounts of music (about a dozen songs). I wondered why there were so many. I soon learned the choir would be singing a cantata on the first weekend of March. Our one-month self-imposed limit for an RV stay was scheduled to end on March 1, so I didn't worry about the cantata. Obviously, I wouldn't be there.

One of the songs was "Soon Ah Will Be Done A-Wid the Troubles Ob De World." I did not like that. Blackface issues were all over the news and we were an all-white choir singing to an all-white congregation. In addition, the lyrics in the first verse had a resounding blare of "I want to meet my mother." After four years of rugged emotional abuse from my dementia-stricken mother, and no resolution before she died, I had a second reason for not wanting to sing that song. I was pleased when the director told us to set it aside. There were other less-controversial spirituals, but I didn't have a problem with them. I wasn't going to be there anyway. Juanita tried to encourage me to extend our stay a couple of days to sing in the cantata, but as I told her, our RV reservation ended on March 1.

About mid-month, the weather, which had been nasty, turned worse. Harry was getting more and more discouraged with our first winter on the road. February was looking just like the other months: cold and windy. He told me to check on extending our stay. I extended

Chapter 9 ... Palm Springs Area

it for a week. I would be able to sing in the cantata after all! I told Jaunita at the next choir practice. I found out the cantata was a celebration of the struggle the slaves went through to get their freedom. It was a collection of spirituals and stories in song. I was getting more comfortable with the songs by the minute.

There's always a transition that must be navigated before one can bypass the "technical" and really "feel" a song. That transition happened suddenly when the director told the sopranos he couldn't hear us at the end of one of the songs. It required a powerful three-note ending following a fermata (which means "keep your eyes on the director"). It was like being given permission to cut loose.

He told us to try it again. We puffed up and got on top of it. We burst forth for all we were worth! High G. Nailed it. The practice hall wasn't big enough to hold us! Nobody says "I can't hear you" to a group of high sopranos! With my newly found courage, I practiced the songs at home until I could feel each one of them.

"Soon Ah Will Be Done A-Wid the Troubles Ob De World" had been fed back into the mix. But by that time, I could feel the vision. When we came to "I want to meet my mother, goin' home to live wid God," I blared out the words because I felt the song. When we sang the verse "No more weepin' and a-wailin'," I wailed it. By the time the day of the cantata came, I was a-wailin' every verse ... once on Saturday night and twice on Sunday. But something changed between the practices and the three performances. It felt like a catharsis. Not only did I feel the song, I felt the words. I felt the freedom to let go of the hurt of the last four years. As I wailed, I began looking forward to meeting my mother when I go home to live with God. I could feel the resentment, stuffed down inside me for four years, leaving. It was like raising a gray curtain shrouding my mother's memory. The old adage came to mind: "Holding a grudge is like letting someone live in your head rent free." I know there was lot of good in my mother. With the grace of God, I now felt confident I'd be able to focus on her good points and not on the tough dementia-ridden remarks.

I was able to look back at several disappointments during the past month and recognize how God used those feelings, disappointments, and experiences to heal a wound ... a gaping wound I had not been willing to acknowledge. It was only a short time ... such a welcome catharsis.

MAHJONG

Having learned the basics of Mahjong at Palm Creek, I was excited to discover there were people who played two or three times a week at our new location. They welcomed newbies. From time to time, there were training sessions. I gladly volunteered to help train newcomers. As a result, I learned a lot about strategy from Gisele, a lovely French woman who had played for ten years. Just listening to her talk with her thick accent was a pleasure.

HOT-TUBBING

The big calling card for Caliente Hot Springs RV Resort was mineral pools: five hot tubs and two heated swimming pools. We spent a lot of time in the water ... up to two hours each day. I enjoyed meeting people there. As usual most conversations started with name, location, and chit chat about the weather back home. What was the matter with us! With a little persistence, the conversations turned to common interests and experiences. I was fascinated with a lady who wrote for children's magazines and newspapers.

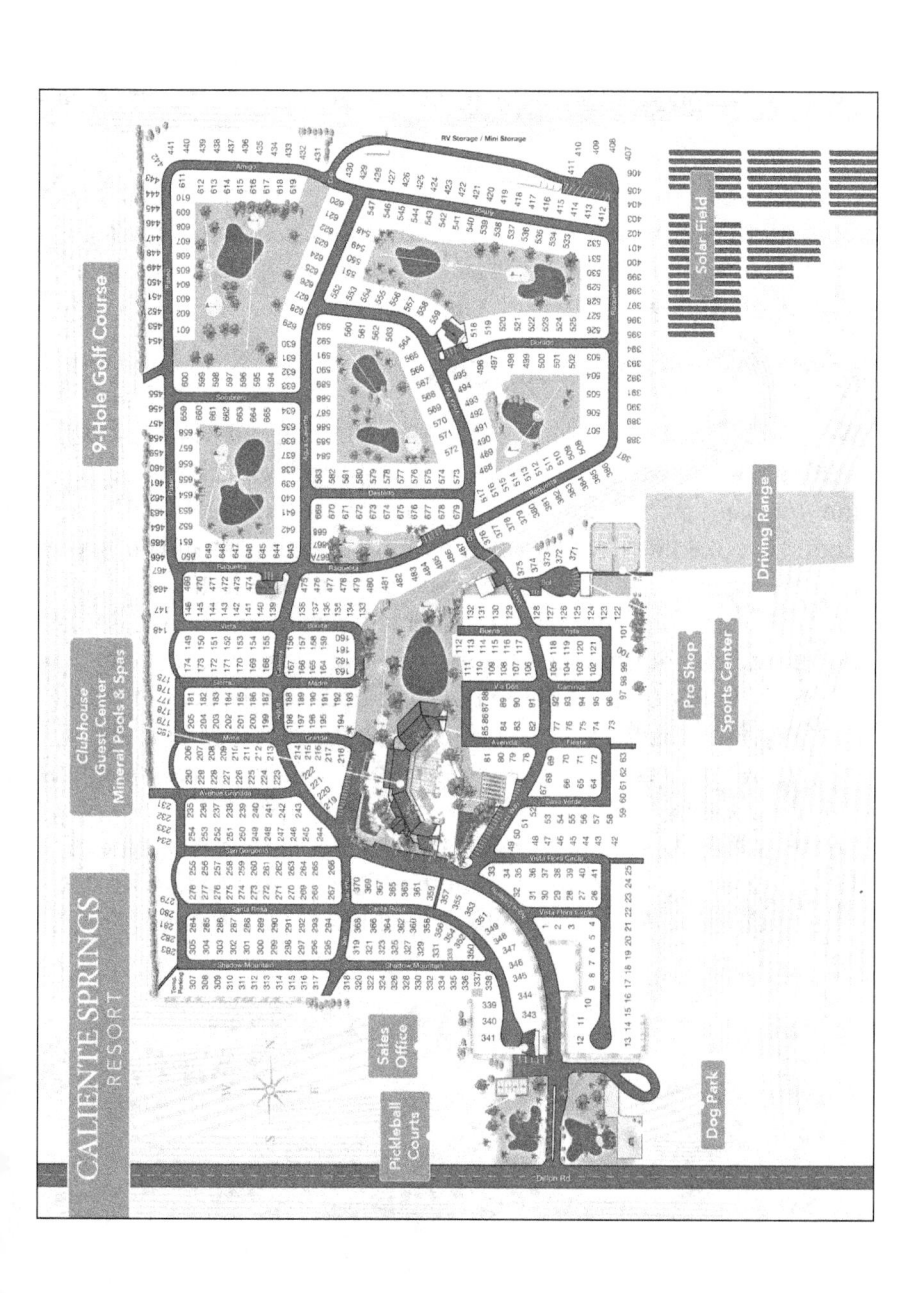

Chapter 9 ... Palm Springs Area 59

Vancouverites

We got together with friends from Vancouver who were staying in Palm Springs: the four men went golfing; the three women went shopping.

I discovered via email my next-door neighbors from Vancouver, Brad and Gwen, had stayed a couple of hundred yards down the road from Caliente Hot Springs Resort for four days! We didn't find out until they had left for Yuma.

More Problems with the Coach?

We came home from late night hot-tubbing on our very last day only to find out we had not turned on the porch light. Harry opened the door and started poking some buttons on the panel inside the door. He poked wildly to no avail. We finally gave up and climbed into the coach. It was then we discovered all the lights were off. (We must have had power because some lights were working. I was just about to tell him when I noticed it was a strand connected to a lithium battery. I held my tongue and dodged a bullet!) It was a mystery. We tried to get the TV to work and pretty soon it got all squirreled up, too. We sat down with our Kindles to read a little. All of a sudden Harry jumped up, went to the panel, and poked a button. All the lights came on. We had inadvertently poked a master switch when we left to go hot-tubbing. That was the switch Jim the salesman had told us we should never turn off! Go figure!

Chapter 10 ... Back to Vancouver

Satellite Dish ... Again

We were a full day into our return trip and decided to stay at a cozy little RV park. The Dish Network didn't work ... again. I wondered where the satellite signal was coming from. I went outside to the front of the coach, positioned myself with the sunset to my right, and closed my eyes. I imagined the scene at the Colorado River spot a few months earlier when we were tucked under the two columnar shade trees. With my eyes still closed, I moved my right arm across my body pointing to the left. *"Sunrise,"* I announced. I swept my extended right arm in a massive arc to the right. *"Sunset,"* I continued. Still thinking about the Colorado River incident, with eyes still closed, I turned my head to the area of the sky where the satellite should be. When I opened my eyes, I was staring into the heart of a densely dressed palm tree ... the only palm tree on our site ... totally blocking the desired path of satellite signal. *(Sigh!)*

The Last Leg

We were looking forward to returning home, but after watching the weather reports, we decided we weren't in a rush. We stayed in some pretty spots and did a little more golfing. There was more wind and flooding even in Northern California. By taking it easy, we were able to get set up before dark each afternoon. As we got more proficient at dismantling in the mornings, we knocked thirty minutes off our prep time.

We had apps on our phones to warn us if chains would be required to get through the pass. When we got to the Siskiyou Summit it was sunny, clear, crisp, and dry, with a smattering of snow on nearby hillsides. It was a gorgeous time of year to go through the mountains.

We were ready to take advantage of the HOV lane for the last fifteen minutes of our excursion. It's something a true Portlander is always concerned about. But we got to Portland an hour before the HOV lane opened. According to our driving app, there had been a traffic jam on that particular stretch of Interstate 5 all day. We shifted to Interstate 205 and rolled into our driveway at about 3:10 p.m. A perfect ending ... almost. We still had a little more to learn about towing the Jeep. When Harry unhooked the Jeep in our driveway, he discovered the battery was dead, dead, dead. We were disappointed but we were grateful it happened close to the house so we weren't stuck somewhere.

After two days of emptying the coach and running everything through the laundry or the dishwasher, we were settled again. The boys (Border Collie and Chihuahua) were happy to see us, the girls (Corgis) showed off their new maturity by running around outside off lead. They no longer seem bent on escaping from the yard.

We slipped back into our Vancouver routines with ease. But we learned some things about ourselves on the trip, especially how we interact in a confined area. We discovered a lot of things can be done to make the area feel larger (make the bed, do the dishes, keep the counter clear, close the cupboards, mop the floors). We were looking forward to our second snowbird outing the following November.

I was proud of myself for emptying the coach, cleaning everything, and putting it back in the coach before I lapsed into my normal lethargy. Then I realized we had to take the coach in for warranty work. I had to empty it again. *(Sigh!)*

PART THREE

WHERE WERE YOU IN 2020?

2019–20

Chapter 1 ... Vancouver

Packing

Packing day was October 31. We were in and out of the coach carrying crates of absolute necessities for the trip. Odd little questions would dart through my mind from time to time ... hovering just above the subconscious level. For example: Why in the world would they put an outlet right above the bathroom sink. The questions didn't need to be answered, they just existed. But electrically speaking, it seemed to be a strange place for an outlet.

Chapter 2 ... Scio, Oregon

On the Farm

We departed as planned on Friday, November 1, stopping seventy miles away in Scio, Oregon, near Salem. We were visiting Jon and Les at their sheep ranch, aka the Farm, for the night. We were close enough to home to run back with the Jeep if we discovered we had forgotten something important.

Jack, the Border Collie, was a lazy sheep dog. Jon and Les had given him to us years earlier because he wouldn't work their sheep the way they wanted. Unfortunately, he had developed a dislike for visitors to Two Ponds and it was getting more pronounced. Jack was going back to the Farm to stay. Jon and Les had recently diversified to cattle. Jack's mother showed a propensity for being a cattle dog. Les was hoping Jack could get the hang of herding cattle, too.

We got to the Farm at feeding time. After we all greeted each other, Les casually turned and walked away. (Whenever Les walks away without a word, I know something special is about to happen.) I followed her to the calf stalls. Five seven-day-old calves ran up to her to get fed. She had a milk bucket complete with six spigots for suckling. When the calves saw Les dump a pail of milk in the bucket, they each jostled for a spigot. They slurped, wagged their tails, and didn't let go until they had demolished two pails of milk.

While Les dumped in a pail of water, they took a breather. Seconds later, they had re-spigotted themselves, draining the water completely. Within ten minutes all five calves were nestled in one stall, under a heat lamp for the evening, right outside the window of our motor home!

Chapter 2 ... Scio, Oregon

I needed to warm up a casserole for dinner. The electric hot plate wouldn't start. It was a little frustrating since I had used the outlet to make coffee in the morning. I plugged the hot plate into the second of the two kitchen outlets with the same result. We activated the propane ... the electrical issue would have to wait. Later at night, I plugged my phone into a different outlet to charge it. But it didn't work either! I was starting to get worried. The three major outlets in the living area of the coach were dead. Harry checked the relays ... nothing had popped. We were grateful the electric mattress pad and the electric heater worked in the back bedroom. There was an outlet in the front of the coach we could use for the coffee maker and for a charging station. We slept on the problem. Breakfast in the morning had to be simple ... no electricity involved ... it was disconcerting.

Goodbye, Jack

Just before we left, we happened to look toward Jon's kennels. Jack was hiding behind the far wall of the kennel with his head peeking out looking at us with the soulful look known well to owners of Border Collies. It was almost like he was saying: *Please don't take me, please don't take me.* It was a good thing ... we could see he wanted to stay on the farm.

Chapter 3 ... Lake Havasu Area

Lake Havasu

We had an easy two-day drive to the Lake Havasu area. We were looking forward to hiring an electrician to fix our outlet problem. We arrived early in the morning at Black Meadow Landing RV Park and spent the rest of the day setting up, reading, and visiting with Larry and his new bride Wendy who were staying at their place about fifteen miles away. Our RV site backed up to a five-hole golf course for park residents and guests. Every night at dusk, about six burros would come down from the hill and enjoy grazing on the golf course and chatting about their day ... "haw-ee." In the morning, before guests woke up, someone from the park would take a bucket and walk the golf course scooping poop. Quaint.

Our first evening we settled down to watch an old episode of Murder She Wrote. Right in the middle of the episode, Harry bolted out of his chair, ran into the bathroom, and poked a red button on the GFI outlet. Instantly, my reading lamp in the living room came on as did the light on the Keurig coffeepot. Joy! It had taken two days to figure out the problem ... but we didn't have to call an electrician.

The next day, I was tidying the bathroom and noticed a healthy splattering of dried shaving cream or toothpaste on the wall ... and on the GFI outlet! (It was way too late to fix blame ... I had to let it go.)

A Patch of Sunlight

Harry called me into the bedroom the next morning. All the shades were pulled. It was very dark. "Say," he asked, "how come there's a patch of sunlight on the floor there?" A little sleuthing later, I discovered cold air and light were streaming in through a damaged seal on the bedroom slide. After a quick patch later and the start of a maintenance list we continued our adventures.

Lovely

We spent a good deal of time reading. I came across an interesting bit from a Louise Penny book: "She was in her early fifties and lovelier than when they'd married. She wore little makeup, comfortable with the face she'd been given." I was delighted. I read it to Harry and asked softly, "Am I lovelier than when we married?" There was a pause. Harry is totally literal ... I got scared. I started to laugh and blurted out, "Don't answer if the response is No!"

His eyes twinkled. After another short pause he said, "I'm hungry." I could live with that!

E-Bike

Harry bought an e-bike for the trip. The first thing he did when we got set up was jump on the bike and ride around the circumference of the little golf course. He looked like something out of a Norman Rockwell painting. Later, he showed me how it worked and off I went. It's a little disconcerting to start pedaling and have the bike propel itself forward electrically. I figured I would get used to it.

Pennies and Pokeno

I decided to give Pokeno a try. The RV park was on two levels. We were parked on the upper level by the golf course. The activity room was at the base of a steep "rustic" grade. I thought it might be a good opportunity to practice riding the e-bike ... Harry agreed. I rode down, greeted everybody, and bought pennies for the game ... six dollars of pennies ... four rolls of fifty pennies and two Ziploc bags of two hundred pennies each. Pokeno is like playing poker and bingo at the same time. There was a twenty-cent ante. And so, with 600 pennies at my disposal, I opened my first bag of 200. The pennies came and went. I finished twenty-two cents ahead. When it was time to go home, I wondered how in the world I was going to carry all that bulk. I had no satchel and no basket. For some odd reason, I chose to carry the four rolls of pennies in my pocket and the remaining Ziplocked pennies ... 422 ... down the front of my shirt. I had no idea how many bumps there would be on the road going up the hill. It was slow going, too. I had to shift into second gear (I hated shifting) in order to get up enough speed to stay upright. I had visions of the two bags of pennies crashing to the ground, Ziploc bags splitting open, and pennies scattering everywhere. I bounced all the way home, arriving safely with 622 pennies intact!

FIGHTING WITH INANIMATE OBJECTS

The next time we played Pokeno, I brought a large cloth bag to carry my bounty. Sadly, I lost ... and lost big. The only consolation was I didn't have as many weighty pennies to carry back the up the hill. Having successfully been in second gear once, I knew it would be a piece of cake to climb the hill in second. There was only one problem: I wasn't going fast enough when I shifted into second. The bike lurched! I wobbled to the side of the road at an excessive speed of one or two miles per hour colliding with a very, very short but sturdy rock wall. I had two seconds to put my eyes back in my head and plan my descent. I had hit the wall with the bike, my shin, and my hands. I found myself lying face down in the natural landscaping ... humiliated. Rolling onto my rump, I immediately looked down the hill to make sure no one had seen what had happened. No one was in sight ... what a relief. I got myself up, clambered on the bike, and peddled gratefully up the hill in first gear. My right hip itched. I scratched it a couple of times without falling off the bike. Once home, I discovered I had shredded my left shin. It wasn't too bad except for one fairly large but shallow scrape. All my wounds were superficial. (Harry took a look at my leg and gasped, "Mercy!") After I cleaned up my shin, I noticed something was still wrong with my right hip. I scratched it again, but it wasn't exactly an itch ... it felt like I was being stuck by a little pin. Every time I sat funny, I could feel the little pin prick. Finally, I took off my rayon culottes and discovered a multitude of shiny miniature cactus needles sticking out of the material. (Note to self: when rolling around in the desert, pay attention to what's there before sitting on it.) With a little judicious plucking, I was able to get all of the cactus pricklies out of my culottes.

Golfing

Golfing was wonderful. Larry and Wendy met us at Emerald Canyon where we golfed eighteen holes on a real golf course. Golf carts were required since the distance between the holes and the changes in elevation were extremely severe. We played on Tuesdays and Thursdays for the whole month. Other times, they came to our park and played at our little five-hole course.

The last time we played Emerald Canyon was Thanksgiving morning. Wendy had put a turkey in the oven before we went golfing. It was finished shortly after we were. The four of us enjoyed a traditional Thanksgiving dinner at their home. Within an hour of returning to our coach, the skies opened and there was a rainstorm so loud we couldn't hear the TV. It was the tail end of the newsworthy storm that brought Thanksgiving traffic on the Interstate 5 Grapevine (the northern entrance to the Los Angeles area) to a halt!

Comfort

Early one morning, I was reading a short story about a kid who ran away from home. About the same time, Harry woke up and was roaming around inside the coach.

"Have you ever run away from home?" I asked.

"Sure."

"Where did you go?"

"I went down to Aunt Mit's house."

"Did your mom know?"

"Oh, I'm sure Aunt Mit called her."

Chapter 3 ... Lake Havasu Area

"How long did you stay away from home?"

"I don't know ... about twenty-four hours."

"Did they know you ran away?"

"Well, sure they did. Everybody knew. I took my suitcase. I had to walk a mile."

"Was Jon in the picture?" (Jon is six years younger than Harry.)

"Oh yeah."

"How old were you?"

"I don't know about ... uh ..."

"About eight?"

"Yeah, about eight."

"What did you take with you?"

"I packed my pillow!" (Harry's all about comfort!)

I was laughing out loud, picturing that cute, gangly little curly-haired boy, with his pillow stuffed in an old suitcase, walking down the street with determination and looking forward to a new chapter in his life. But the seventy-two-year-old man standing in front of me hadn't had his coffee yet, so I figured I'd better not push my luck.

HAVASU PALMS

We had gone past a sign for Havasu Palms about twenty times. It sounded exotic. We decided to go exploring the day before we were scheduled to leave. It was a substandard gravel road dotted with boulders and large rocks, but we figured the Jeep could handle anything for just 4.2 miles. They lied ... it was a full seven miles! We went through water, around washouts, through sand, by gullies, through canyons, and around cliffs until we came to a little community on the shore of Lake Havasu. Most people had dune buggies and/or boats. We saw a sign for an airstrip, which explained why there were dozens of Quonset huts. We turned around and made our way back the seven miles to the main road at about ten miles an hour. I was very happy to be back to the main drag and happier yet when we got to the motor home.

You might wonder if I had visions on this excursion ... indeed I did. I had been watching my phone the whole trip, seeing no bars! I had visions of exploding tires and wondered who would be chosen to scamper up the hillside in case we needed to phone for help. I'm sure glad nothing bad happened ... we were forty-five minutes from civilization even before we started the forty-minute trip to Havasu Palms. Oh those visions! I kept them to myself.

The next day we were on the move again. We planned to stay in Palm Springs for December, Tucson for January and February, and return to Casa Grande in March.

Chapter 4 ... Palm Springs ... Reuniting

December meant reuniting with friends from the previous year. A Centering Prayer group I had attended at the Catholic church in Palm Desert was still going strong. But the big thrill for me was returning to Hope Lutheran and singing in the choir. I had been looking forward to returning for Christmas all year! I was right on time to participate in yet another cantata. All the songs were familiar. We sang our hearts out. I was also one of the readers of commentaries between the songs. One of my lines was from the host of angels: "Glory to God in the highest, and peace to His people on earth!" I did my best to be the embodiment of the host of angels as I projected the words with gusto ... after the delivery no one was dozing.

Chapter 5 ... Los Angeles ... Christmas Dinner

The highlight of our month was Christmas dinner with our Pamplin cousins on Harry's side of the family ... in LA. We were concerned about driving in LA traffic. We'd been watching the morning news all month and had seen horrible tie-ups ... driving in LA is not for lightweights! Even though it appeared to be a straight shot from Palm Springs to Autumn's home we didn't want to leave anything to chance. We packed up the dogs at 10:45 in the morning and hit the freeway for a 2 p.m. dinner. It looked like we would arrive about an hour early (every hostess' worst nightmare). We lucked out: traffic going westbound into LA was light, but it was clogged going in the opposite direction. We arrived ninety minutes early. I got to help with the party preparations. Even better, I got to meet people as they showed up, one or two at a time.

We had a wonderful time getting to know the cousins and their grown children. Jim and Sue's offspring, Autumn and Mike, were hosting. Angie and Lucy had a great time too. They ran around with Dodger, a fully grown boxer. It's the first time they'd had a chance to run and play all month. We left shortly after dinner, still concerned about traffic. There was hardly anyone on the freeway ... it was an easy drive back, thanks to Autumn's foresight in scheduling an early dinner. And because Harry likes to dine and dash, we were back on the road when twelve million people were in the middle of their festivities.

Dodger reminded me of how much I love boxers. He came to the sliding glass door and looked in while we were eating dinner. Autumn turned around in her chair and quietly mouthed the word "sit." He sat. Then she mouthed the words "Good boy," and he just sat there smiling and wagging his rump. What a good dog!

Chapter 6 ... Palm Springs Area

Ramon Road

When I'm driving, I prefer the navigator refrain from telling me things I already know. Therefore, when we came back from Christmas dinner, I told Harry I'd been driving all around the desert for three weeks ... I knew my way around and I didn't need him to tell me how to get home. No matter how nicely one says such a sentence, it undoubtedly raises a red flag. It soon became clear to me I had been doing all my driving to the east and south in the daytime, but we were approaching from the northwest in the dark. Pride dictated I continue as if I really did know where to go. I took the Date Palm exit and started looking for Ramon Road, but it was pretty hard to see in the dark. I pulled into the left turn lane. Oops ... it was not Ramon Road ... as Harry pointed out to me. Pride won out again as I continued on Date Palm. I pulled into the next left turn lane ... but it was not Ramon Road ... as Harry pointed out to me a second time. I pulled into the third left turn lane ... which was also not Ramon Road. By that time Harry was getting a little disgusted. Finally, getting tired of trying to make left turns, I stayed in the through lane, almost missing Ramon Road. Despite my pride, we made it home just fine. And it wasn't too much of a strain on our thirty-seven-year marriage.

Lucy's Fine Folly

The resort had four small 8 x 10 chain-link pens near the laundry. If your dogs needed to do what dogs need to do, that was where they did it. Walk a tenth of a mile to the pen area, dogs do their business, and walk back. It was all pretty controlled. Consequently, the girls did not get a lot of exercise in December. But then ... Oh my goodness! How in the world do these things happen?

It was a morning just like any other. Harry took the girls out at eight o'clock. Uncharacteristically, I heard him call "Lucy!" I thought, this is not right! I ran to the window and looked out just in time to see Lucy's black tailless rump dart past the shrubs separating our lot from the neighbor's. She was running on the golf course! That was a huge no-no! I figured I'd better get out there quickly and take care of Angie so Harry could chase down Lucy. When I got out there, Harry was calmly telling Angie to get into the pen. Once he had corralled her, he turned his attention to the golf course making the kiss-kiss noise that attracts Lucy. She came running from the neighbor's area ... a jet-black dog against a bright green lawn. But she wasn't coming to Harry; she was running toward the center of the golf course! We were parked right by the third tee. I looked around to see if there were any golfers ... there was no one in sight. The tee box (12' x 30') was a couple of feet higher than the surrounding course ... somewhat like a mini-mesa. Lucy came from the left and disappeared behind the mini-mesa. Sweat was pouring off my brow as I looked at Harry, who was looking to the right. I looked to the right only to see Lucy running in a circle. Uh-oh, she took a little pee break. That was another huge no-no! Thank goodness they watered the lawn frequently. Harry kiss-kissed at her again. She came on the run. But again, not toward Harry; she ran on the far side of the mini-mesa. With her stubby Corgi legs being so short, I could only see her ears bobbing up and down as she galloped along ... Boppity, Boppity, Boppity, Bop. She rounded the end of the mini-mesa and came running back to Harry who calmly told her what a good girl she was. I had watched the whole thing from a stationary position, but I was out of breath! It was like little Billy in the Sunday funnies, taking the long way around. I'm glad Harry was in control. If it had happened on my watch, I would have been out there flailing my arms, yelling, and chasing her farther away ... calling attention to the debacle. Dogs! Good grief! Later, I asked Harry why he didn't chase her down and get her off the course. He told me she had done something wrong to get attention, so he gave his attention to Angie. *(Sigh!)*

Chapter 6 ... Palm Springs Area 79

BUGS, BUGS, BUGS

Harry had found some stacking dispensers for the inside of the motor home. One tub holds a full bag of dog food ... a mondo bag ... the other a full bag of dog treats. The bins have a rubber seal. They're very well designed: bugs cannot get into the food. Isn't that nice!

Imagine my shock when I opened the dog treats, dug out a large scoop of treats, filled a small plastic container, and noticed some black spots on the treats like flaxseeds. On closer inspection, I discovered the flaxseeds were moving. Well, that didn't seem right! I looked back at the bin. I was horrified to see there were bugs crawling around the opening and more bugs on the floor. Even though they had wings they didn't seem to be at all interested in flying. Also, with a few sharp taps they fell to the bottom of the plastic container. It was easy to separate them from the treats. We had been concerned about bugs getting into the treat bin, but we had never considered them coming out of the treat bin. Thank goodness for the rubber seal!

Chapter 7 ... Tucson

Rincon Country East RV Resort

It took all day to drive from Palm Desert to Tucson, but when we arrived at Rincon Country East RV Resort, we sat up and took notice. People waved and smiled as we drove into the resort and, as we were soon to find out, the behavior was not an anomaly. We had a reservation for two months because it was a requirement: A reservation for February required an additional reservation for either January or March.

My Brother Scoffed at Me

Whenever we arrived somewhere, my job was to park the motor home, level it, and extend the slides. I always had to coordinate with Harry who was taking care of the outside duties, so I didn't mistakenly conk him in the head with a steel beam. It was all simple enough. My next job was to call Dish Network with our new zip code so Harry could sort through the TV channels. I did my job, Harry did his job, but the dish didn't do its job. It moaned and groaned and complained as it searched and searched for the satellite. There were no line-of-sight obstacles. I called Dish Network in hopes of resolving it by phone. No luck. They said it was going to take a week to get someone out to check our equipment. We decided to throw more technology at the problem: I called Cox to arrange for internet service, but it was going to take them a week to get someone to our place. We decided to tough it out … what choice did we have?

The Dish guy came out on day four and discovered we had a broken part. He said a replacement might be available by mail. We asked about upgrading to a new dish, but he said it would take him, personally, two days to make it happen. I complained to my brother Kevin who scoffed at me and told me I had first-world problems. In the meantime, our new neighbor Rich said he had "a guy" who upgraded the dish on his rig. He gave me the name; I called and left a message on Saturday, got a return call early Monday morning, and by 2 p.m. we had a new dish fully installed and all the how-to training we needed. Technology is great when it works.

Church Search

I had a little trouble finding a church, initially. The first weekend I went to two churches but their services were a little too ritualistic for me. The second week I planned to go to two other churches. I liked the first one, Tanque Verde Lutheran Church (TVLC), so much I stayed for a second service. The choir sang at the second service. The choir director was a real pistol. I knew I had found my church. Right after the service I joined the choir, the handbell group, and the Bible study.

The choir director, Jen, turned out to be a ton of fun! She had a deep throaty voice, taught at the middle school, and had the energy level required for such an endeavor. During practices, she flitted and danced back and forth as she was energetically explaining what was expected of us. Whenever we did something right, she sprang up and exclaimed, "Yah, yah, yah, yah, yah" and we went on to the next issue. Her enthusiasm was contagious. Everyone was giving it their all.

LAUNDRY DAY

Laundry day in Vancouver was predictable: sort the clothes into four piles, throw 'em in the washer, throw 'em in the drier ... it all gets done. But laundry day in the RV was a well-anticipated event. The spin cycle on the washer was like a kids' ride at Disneyland. We would be sitting around reading serenely when all of a sudden, the coach would start to shake like there was an earthquake. It was great! I regretted only getting to do laundry every ten days!

TECHNOLOGY PROBLEMS

Harry and I were trying to use the computer, but the Malwarebytes Update message kept coming up, repeatedly. Finally, I just hit the update button to get rid of it. One problem solved.

A couple of days later, I was unable to access the internet. I was at the end of some detailed spreadsheet work for my brother's estate ... this was serious. A reasonable person would think: Go to Settings, hit Wi-Fi, and you'll be just fine. That's exactly what I did, but I couldn't find Wi-Fi under Settings. I asked Harry what he thought I should do. He said, "Go to Settings, hit Wi-Fi, and you'll be just fine." I wasn't. (I had him show me just in case I was missing something ... I wasn't.) I called HP. They said, "Go to Settings, hit Wi-Fi, and you'll be just fine." I was hopeful. But after about twenty minutes, they told me I had to talk with Tech Support for

$99. I was at my wit's end. I slept on it. In the middle of the night, I woke up wondering how they would be able to connect to my computer if I don't have internet. Not my problem, I concluded, and went back to sleep.

The next day, I got up with determination, took care of my morning duties, and called Tech Support. He said, "Go to Settings, hit Wi-Fi, and you'll be just fine." It didn't work any better than it had the day before. However, he didn't abandon me. He had me plug my phone into the computer, which allowed him to access my computer. Technology is great when it works. He went to Settings and couldn't find Wi-Fi. After two-and-a-half hours on the phone, he restored my Wi-Fi and my computer was working just fine. The culprit was the Malwarebytes Update ... it had erased my Wi-Fi! Everything was back to normal, I had Norton Antivirus installed, and all my questions had been answered. It was well worth the $99 ... plus some for Norton ... plus some for a service contract ... plus some for something else, but I couldn't remember what. I was heading for the poor house, but I was wired!

WE ARE NOT BUYING ANYTHING

The unforeseen consequence of two-and-a-half hours with Tech Support was exceedingly low resistance. Harry came home at lunchtime and told me he had been to La Mesa RV ... and did I want to go see a coach he had been looking at? Foolish me, I said yes, trying to be a supportive wife. Before we left, I gave him the wife stare known to men and women everywhere. I said, "We must agree we are not buying anything ... we're just looking!" (The exclamation point was a byproduct of the wife stare.) He agreed.

We toured the coach ... it seemed huge. I took it for a test drive ... it was impressive. On the way back to the dealership, our salesman got a text. The coach we were driving had just been sold. Well, you know what happened next: We fell prey to the fear-of-loss syndrome. (Will we ever learn?) The salesman took us to the main office and sat us in the waiting room while he ... still holding my

Chapter 7 ... Tucson

driver's license ... went to talk to the big boss ... the "one behind the door." We were being held captive.

After about fifteen minutes, he came out and said they had an exact replica of the coach I had driven. It would arrive at the lot within three weeks. It sounded a little suspect to me. He took us back out to the original coach where I sat with him and went through the list of options comparing the original coach to the soon-to-arrive coach. All the options were the same. The salesman and his supervisor wanted us to sign a piece of paper saying we intended to buy. We did. After more trips to see the "one behind the door," the salesman finally came out and asked Harry how he was feeling. Harry said he felt like he was being held captive. It went downhill from there as they dillydallied around, making us wait another twenty minutes. By the time we got my driver's license back and were on our way home, we were both cranky.

After we got back to the park, we were able to clear our heads and think straight. Harry tried to say he was doing it for me, but I wasn't having any of that! As the evening wore on, we became less and less enchanted about the transaction. Harry suggested I contact Jim, our salesman from Portland who sold us our first RV. The next morning, I started texting Jim. By the end of the day, he had located the same coach with a significant upgrade for only a "passel of money" extra. We stalled. He reminded us it was an all-electric coach ... with no propane to deal with, there would be no opportunity for a fire. It didn't take us long to see the benefit of having an all-electric coach. We were getting closer to buying. A day or two later, he called back saying he had a two-year-old coach with an automatic bed that raised up in the back so one could sit up in bed. I knew Harry was going to start drooling. He did ... and so did I. This coach had the fancy upgrade, but since it wasn't new, it was much more affordable. (And the new floor plan was designed to save a marriage.) Jim was arranging to have it driven down to Tucson by the end of February. He said we could put the two coaches side by side, transfer our belongings, and the driver would take our old coach back to Portland. Goodness, who would have thought?

Cousins, Cousins, Cousins

The month was dotted with cousin visits. Phyllis and Bob were staying at Casa Grande (a little more than an hour to the north) and Beau lived in a suburb north of Tucson. The three of them came down to check out our RV site. We had a great afternoon touring, eating, and visiting. There was supposed to be a big yard sale in the park that day. I told my cousins I wanted to look for a beading set as we walked around. When she came, Beau brought a beading set she had used with her daughters and grandchildren. I was very excited. In fact, I used it within a few days to repair my silver ring. A couple of weeks later, Phyllis, Bob, Beau, and I connected with more cousins: Judy and Phil. Lots of laughter. We got on twinning. popsugar.com and checked out our celebrity twins. Once more, it insisted I looked like Bruce Dern! Please ... there's no way I look like him!

A few days later, Judy, Phil, Harry, and I went to Leo's Mexican Restaurant. Having had three introductory Spanish classes, I felt comfortable ordering from the menu ... slowly. (The menu was in English, but I wanted to try out my Spanish). I looked under Combinations and found "3 Zapata." It was my turn to order. "Trace Zapata," I said, with a large measure of pride and a medium measure of confidence. The server looked at me as though I was speaking Greek. I lost my cool. "Oh, come on!" I said, "I know I pronounced it correctly ... I've had three classes in Spanish." She looked at me as though I was still speaking Greek and finally said, "Número tres, Zapata." On instant reflection, I realized I hadn't said "Número" and I had mispronounced "tres" ... I was wrong and she was gracious. The meal was delicious. When I got to Spanish class a few days later, I told our instructor, Debbie, of my failure. She told me by saying "Tres, Zapata" instead of "Número tres, Zapata," the server could have thought I was asking for three orders of Zapata. Oops, no wonder she looked at me like I was a foreigner. Oh ... I guess I was.

Dog Agility Class

One of the winter residents in the park was an AKC rep qualified to teach agility ... AKC-Carol. She offered her time to others who were interested in working with their dogs. I asked the girls if they wanted to join up. Lucy said sure; Angie said why. Lucy won the toss. She showed considerable aptitude for the ring. Unfortunately, her handler had considerably less aptitude. It took a long time for me to train my brain for agility. Once I understood, Lucy followed right along as if she'd been doing it forever.

There were four teams in my class. One lady had a hip replacement and a powder puff on the end of a leash; another had balance issues and a dog who didn't want to work; the last had a smart little Rat Terrier who liked to perform. We were all in it for a good time.

Carol was adamant about giving the dogs treats immediately after they do something ... anything ... as long as they did it correctly. She was also big on giving lots of praise to the dog: immediate, positive feedback! During one class, we had to walk through the course and perform a counterclockwise turn to change the leash from the left hand to the right hand. It took ten seconds to explain but only two seconds to perform. Each of us was concentrating so hard on our turns we got dizzy! We recovered quickly. Carol had me try it again but with a dog. It took me about ten seconds to awkwardly maneuver through the steps, but I did it correctly. "Yes!" she praised me loudly, "You did it exactly right!" (I was so insulted.)

?Habla Español?

Our weekly Spanish class was offered in the game room. Our instructor, Debbie, taught Spanish classes at the University of Arizona in real life. Our class was challenging, but it didn't take long for us to get a lot of words under our belts. Counting had been difficult for me. I decided if I could say 444 smoothly, I would be able to figure out how to say anything up to 1000. I walked around the motor home saying "cua-tro-ci-en-tos cua-ren-ta ca-tor-ce." It was hard to say ... harder to think ... and even harder to know. By the time I could rattle it off pretty well I decided I'd better check my translation. I discovered I was saying 400 40 14. It didn't make sense. I rebooted myself and started saying "cua-tro-ci-en-tos cua-ren-ta cua-tro" ... 400 40 4. That seemed to work a little better but it was difficult to remember throughout the day. When I woke up the next morning, it was easy. How in the world does that work?

My new friend, Kate from dog agility class, was also taking Spanish classes. She decided she was going to drop out. I couldn't afford to lose a friend, so she and I started studying together. Everything started to make sense to us as we worked through all our numbers, verbs, nouns, and homework. One of our assignments was to write a paragraph about our family. We knew enough simple verbs and nouns to do a fair job with the task. Kate wanted to say her brother had a dog. We hadn't learned the word for dog, so we tried el poocho, el barko, and el mutto. Not having any confidence in those words, we looked it up and found out the dog was actually el perro. Kate's husband Irv was charged with guessing which one of the words meant the dog ... by a quick process of elimination he got it right. She and I must have been rummy from studying because we were laughing so hard we had to hold our sides.

Painting

Once a month, McKenna, an accomplished art student from a nearby college, sets up in the rec hall ... individual tables complete with apron, brushes, and five basic acrylic paints (black, white, red, blue, and yellow). The subject is picked a month in advance. She puts a sample at the front of the room. We, a collection of not-so-accomplished artists, come in and pick a table. She walks us through the process of painting another version of the subject. It is always fun to see how everyone's paintings were the same but different. Linda, my RV neighbor, missed the class. When we had a chance, she pulled out her acrylics while I walked her through the steps. The same but different.

GOLF

While I was running around the park doing creative things, Harry and his longtime college friend, John, now a Tucson resident, enjoyed golfing with John's men's group. They golfed twice each week. On a couple of other days, he golfed with another Vancouver friend north of Tucson or some men from the park.

CHAPTER 8 ... TUCSON

MORE BUGS

The bug situation seemed to be under control. However, on closer inspection, I was horrified when I realized the little holes in the treats were not bug-feeding holes but bug-nesting holes! A couple of days later, in the middle of the night, I awoke as if in the painting "Scream," by Edvard Munch, as I realized there were probably bugs in the treat pouch used for agility training. There were, but they were manageable and hadn't left their home for the comfort of the sofa. Harry surmised there were probably bugs in the huge box of treats in the basement of the coach. The good news was, on checking, we found no bugs in the box in the basement!

ESPAÑOL

Spanish class was progressing. I bought a new Bible called Santa Biblia: Spanish in the left column, English in the right. I started reading through my favorite book, Philippians, in Spanish. It was slow going, but I recognized a lot of the words and frequently got the meaning.

We had amassed a surprisingly large vocabulary in a short time. Debbie gave an assignment to write about ourselves and someone else. Here's what I wrote about Harry and me:

We eat breakfast.

We eat dinner.

I talk.

I sing.

I work.

I shop.

Chapter 8 ... Tucson

I draw.

I prepare.

I study.

I chat.

Harry watches TV.

(Too bad I didn't know the words for "golf" and "read.")

The next week we had to write something about our families. We knew the present tense of our verbs, nothing else. Nevertheless, I was able to exploit all the sins of mi familia for the last twenty years. No holds barred! Poor Debbie had to ask what in the world I was trying to say before she could actually correct my paper.

More Relatives

Uncle Jerry and his new wife, Aunt Bev, were passing through the area at the end of February. They decided to stop for a few days.

We had a super visit. They are avid lovers of jigsaw puzzling ... my kind of people! They tried to stay in our park, but it was full so they opted to stay at a park out by the Air Force base. They were treated to multiple air shows daily as Air Force pilots practiced their formation training.

Everything Dog

Dog Agility: Lucy continued to do well in agility classes. I was working her off lead but at one point we had to start over. I called her ... she came! I pretended it was a normal thing. AKC-Carol nodded her approval. Then there was a commotion about fifty feet away near the dog exercise area. One of the dogs got loose outside the pen. His owner was calling him, but the dog would come to within five feet and then dart off (just like Lucy frequently did). Carol turned to our class and quietly expressed her displeasure at this behavior. I was dying inside, hoping Lucy would never do that to me in the ring. But I knew it was just a matter of time. She had the same naughty streak as the little dog who had gotten loose. Thank goodness for treats, with or without bugs!

Fetch and Be Nice: Harry had been working with the girls on fetching with soft four-inch balls. The girls had each started to come back with the ball, which was quite pleasant. It was much more satisfying than the norm of throwing the ball, having them run to it, look at it, turn around, and come back empty-mouthed. One day, I took them to the exercise pen. We were the only ones there. We played fetch individually for a few minutes. Then I threw the ball and they both raced for it. Both jaws locked onto it at the same time. Step by laborious step they worked their way back in my direction. They stopped, turned ninety degrees, and stood there like statues side by side … both mouths on the ball. I was pretty sure there was a conversation going on, but, if so, it was non-verbal. It took about thirty seconds for them to let go. We were finished playing.

Bad Habits: I came home from Spanish class one day. Harry said I had failed to tuck the chair back underneath the table. Angie had climbed up on the chair and had gotten into the treat bucket on the table, kicking my knitting project to the floor in the process. No matter how many times I clean the floor there's always a little dog hair on it. Dog hair and knitting projects don't mix. *(Sigh!)*

New coach

Having made the decision to change coaches, we spent the rest of February mailing paperwork from Vancouver to Tucson and back … and waiting. We were told it would take three days for the driver to bring the coach from Vancouver to Tucson. (The driver was limited to ten hours per day.) But what we didn't know was the guy who assured us we would have it by the end of February (not Jim) no longer worked for the company! More waiting. Finally, in the first week of March we heard something! The waiting had ended … the coach was on its way!

Chapter 9 ... Tucson

Uncle Jerry and Aunt Bev

I was disappointed Jerry and Bev were staying for only a few days. But they started with three days and extended to six. Being about fifteen minutes away tended to limit our visits. When they were scheduled to leave Tucson, they called me. Bev said, "Can you go outside?" I scratched my head and went outside. She said, "Walk down to A Street." I knew I couldn't trust the dogs inside alone, so I leashed them up and we walked down to A Street with my phone in hand. She said, "Turn left." And there they were ... on A Street ... in our park! They had moved and were staying for "a week or so." We got to have several more visits, but when "or so" came, they surprised me by saying they were going to stay another three weeks! I was thrilled!

Bad Habits

Angie continued to be a little sneak. I went next door to show something to Linda. When I came back, I looked in the coach. Lucy was sitting in the driver's seat politely looking at me. I stealthily peered around the corner. The Tupperware container full of dog treats, which had been on the table, was now on the floor ... open ... with Angie's snout stuffed right inside. Moving only her eyes, she looked up at me with a guilty lilt to her eyebrows. Dogs ... gotta love 'em.

The New coach Was on the Way

The waiting had finally come to an end. Jim the salesman told us it would arrive on Friday, March 6, but since we wanted morning delivery, they would deliver it on Saturday. That was too bad because Saturday was the day of the long-awaited Dog Agility Trial. Assuming the coach would arrive early, I was lamenting having to forego the dog trial.

On Saturday morning, I started packing the old coach. Anything for the bedroom and wardrobe went into white plastic bags; anything for the kitchen, office or living room went into boxes or bins. It looked like the new coach would be delivered at the very same time as the dog trial!

I drove the old coach to the RV storage area, parking it near the agility ring. There was plenty of room to put the old and new coaches next to each other for the transfer. I was a little surprised Harry went golfing, leaving me to navigate the streets and figure out how and where to park the coach. But it had to be done. Drive slowly and use the mirrors to back up … how hard could it be? In no time at all, I was in place and ready for the transfer. I got a phone call letting me know the new coach was still on the way. It was 10 o'clock and time for …

Dog Agility Trial

Lucy and I were primed. All of our hard work for the past two months was coming to fruition. About twelve chairs were set up facing the fenced arena. Another twenty-five people were milling around getting excited about the marvelous show to come. It was a Norman Rockwell moment … a bit of Americana. Expectations were high. Lucy was one of four dogs signed up for novice agility. AKC-Carol was the emcee. Her husband, Charles, was the ring assistant. (About a week earlier, Carol had singled out a couple of teams to run their dogs off lead. Lucy and I were among the chosen, but we hadn't practiced off lead, let alone off lead in front of an audience! There was a mad scramble as we prepped, daily.)

Linda went first. She was running her Border Collie mix, Lady … off lead. "JUMP, JUMP!" she hollered. Lady took the first hurdle head on, went around, and came back through the second hurdle the wrong way. Oops. Undaunted, Linda continued to the Hoop (a three-foot Styrofoam ring suspended about a foot off the ground) … "HOOP!" … Lady flew through, flawlessly. "TABLE, TABLE, TABLE!" Lady ran to Table (a painted shipping pallet five inches

Chapter 9 ...Tucson

high), leapt on, and struck a seated pose. "DOWN!" She went down. The crowd cheered. "TUNNEL, TUNNEL, TUNNEL!" Lady jumped up and ran through the L-shaped Tunnel (a two and one-half foot diameter plastic tube about ten feet long) ... "WALK-IT, WALK-IT, WALK-IT!" ... she went up, over, and down the four-foot-high Bridge hitting the mandatory ramps on each end. Lady was brilliant! Linda was running to keep up with her. As she reached the A-Frame, Linda gave Lady the familiar command: "CLIMB-IT, CLIMB-IT, CLIMB-IT!" Lady liked the audience better and walked around to the other side of Linda ignoring the A-Frame. The crowd was rooting for Linda. Linda gave the command again and Lady turned back proceeding up and over the A-Frame without any trouble. Linda was obviously happy, so was Lady. In fact, Lady was so happy she turned around and went back up the down ramp and perched royally at the top looking back at the crowd. The crowd went wild. She came back down, made an effort to go through the last three hurdles, and was finished.

Two other women ran their dogs on lead. Nothing untoward happened.

And then it was Lucy's turn ... off lead! We walked into the ring where I unleashed her. With a heart filled more with trepidation than hope, I gave the leash to the ring assistant. Lucy, not used to being the center of attention in a big crowd, was so anxious she had Xs in her eyes. She looked around and saw Carol. (Carol had given Lucy a yummy treat once. Lucy had never forgotten.) She immediately ran to Carol. I called her and called her ... nothing. I threw a treat at her. She felt it hit her side. She turned and snagged it. I struggled to get her attention. Finally, for some unknown reason, she came back to me. I put her in position for the first hurdle and said, "Ready?" She wasn't ready. She ran back to Carol thinking she might still get a treat. That didn't happen. (I couldn't look Carol in the eye.) After getting into position again, I took her through the first Jump without a problem. She ran around the second Jump and came back the wrong way just like Lady had done. Oops. We tried it again with success. She went through the Hoop and onto the Table. I was shouting all the same words Linda had shouted! But then I paused: I had to figure out where to stand so Lucy could go through the next hurdle, but Lucy had her own needs. She needed to have me thinking and speaking a little faster than I was capable of doing. She probably figured if I was having trouble with the trial, she'd have to take charge ... so she ran to the Teeter Totter and up she went! (She hadn't finished training on the Teeter Totter, but it was too late to intervene.) Down she ran! I woke up to her needs shouting, "TUNNEL, TUNNEL, TUNNEL!" Through the Tunnel she charged, up and over the Bridge, and around to the A-Frame. But just like Lady, she ran around to my right instead of going up and over the A-Frame. In retrospect, I wondered if she was trying to emulate Lady. I brought her back around with "CLIMB-IT, CLIMB-IT, CLIMB-IT!" and she was up and over the A-Frame like a pro. The crowd roared. By the time she came down I was lost in my head again, trying to think of what to say and where to stand to get her through the last three Jumps. With her eyes filled with Xs, Lucy ran to the gate as fast as she could and stopped on a dime ... like a pointer. She was finished. I turned to the emcee with a shrug, "I think Lucy's finished." We both were!

I saw Harry watching in the wings. Later, I asked him what he had thought. With the slightest of upturns to the edges of his mouth, he said, "Lucy provided comic relief."

After Lucy and I finished, the more experienced handlers were to take their dogs through their paces. There was only one! But Tom's Gizmo, a well-trained Shih Tzu, performed impeccably doing all the novice actions perfectly as well as showing us how to negotiate the Teeter Totter and the Weave. He looked happy to be doing it. Too bad we didn't follow Gizmo. Maybe Lucy would have emulated him instead of Lady.

THE NEW COACH ARRIVED

Patrick, the driver, arrived an hour later at noon. Kate drove me to the front gate in her golf cart. We led him through the park to the storage area where the old coach was waiting. I snapped a picture

Chapter 9 ... Tucson

of the two coaches and sent it to my brothers. Kevin, noticing the height of the new coach, texted, "Will the new coach fit in the carport at home?" Two years earlier, we'd had a builder come and raise the roof on the carport to accommodate the motor home. The new motor home looked a little higher than the old one. When Kevin asked the question, the only answer I could come up with was, "I hope so!"

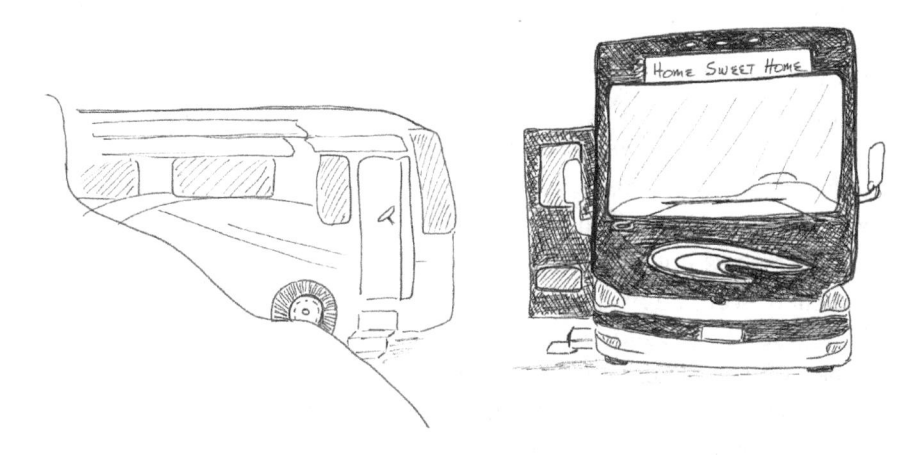

With a little bit of this and a little bit of that, we were in full swing with the transfer. I was in the old coach. Linda and Bev were in the new coach. I had given them free rein to load the cupboards however they wished. Linda's husband, Dave, and Uncle Jerry were schlepping bags and boxes from the old coach to the new. Patrick was taking Harry around the new coach explaining things to him. I started throwing white garbage bags of clothes and towels to the front of the old coach. They would end up on the bed in the new coach. When there was a reprieve, I loaded bins with lots of side holes with kitchen stuff. In the middle of loading the bins, my bag of pearl tapioca exploded. Fortunately, it all stayed in one of the bins. I was glad for a nearby wastebasket. (I didn't know what would have been worse ... tiny pearl tapioca or bugs!)

The temperature got up to eighty-one degrees by noon, seeming very hot for Tucson. The whole transfer took only two hours. After I was sure everything was out, I invited Dave and Bev to go in and check. Dave found something, but it belonged with the old coach. Bev found something and I was sure happy she did ... otherwise, cousins Sue and Jim Pamplin would have been pretty mad at me: The dog plaque they had given us for Christmas was securely taped to the wall with double back foam. I was able to pry it off and give it a place of honor on the wall above the fireplace in the new coach.

I drove the new coach back to our site past Kate and Irv's house (with a little toot on the air horn) and backed it into the RV spot. There were several helpers wanting to guide me. I just watched for Rich and followed his lead. The parking went slowly but smoothly. When it was finally in place, I noticed a little crowd had gathered. The park was not originally designed for forty-foot motor homes, but there were a few spaces large enough to accommodate such a behemoth. I gave another little toot on the air horn and they cheered. When I finished up with Patrick and his paperwork, I started putting things away where they might live permanently. All the helpers had gone home to cool off. Fortunately, Bev and Linda had not noticed a hidden floor-to-ceiling pantry: I had a completely empty pantry in which to stock canned goods ... which freed up another cupboard ... and so on and so on. Within two hours, Harry and I had cleared bags and boxes off the bed and were able to make the bed for the night. With adrenaline still pumping I got almost sixty percent of the rest of the coach secured. We were tired and happy by the end of the day. The adrenaline lasted me well into the next day.

PERSON OF FEW WORDS

Usually it's Harry, my man of few words, who doesn't participate in conversations. This was adequately demonstrated by the peanut butter fiasco on our first trip when I had to pull the information from him bit by bit. As it turned out, being a person of few words can be contagious.

Chapter 9 ... Tucson

Jim the salesman had told me the new coach was equipped with induction burners, not gas burners. I was pretty sure I did not have the right pans for induction burners. It didn't matter that evening because I pulled something cool from the refrigerator for dinner. The next day, I checked to see if I could use my pots and pans with the induction burners. As expected, they didn't work. But it really didn't matter because I had a two-coil electric burner from Walmart purchased during one of our faux electrical crises. All through the transfer, I was comforted knowing I still had a way to cook. I knew I would be able to get by with the two-coil electric burner from Walmart until I could figure out where to get the kind of pots and pans I needed. On Sunday evening, I reached for the two-coil electric burner from Walmart. I knew I hadn't put it away; therefore, I assumed Harry must know where it had gone. Perhaps he had stowed it with some items down below in the storage area. When asked about it, he said, "Oh, that? We didn't need it anymore because we have fancy induction burners! I put it with the free stuff by the park's garbage bins for anyone to take."

(Dear Reader, if you had been in charge of preparing the meals, you would have known why I said what I said next.)

Until then, everything else had gone my way. But at that point, the adrenaline had worn off and I was raw. Oddly, the two-coil electric burner from Walmart was my tipping point! I lost it. My vocabulary was reduced to a single word akin to No ... and there I stood in the middle of the coach, pulling my hair repeating, "No, no, no!" The stress of the last few days descended upon me ... preparing for the dog show, packing the coach, arranging for helpers, switching coaches, signing paperwork, learning about the new coach, unpacking, putting things away ... my mind had been on overdrive for about a week with anticipation, execution, and aftermath. I had given it my all. I had fully committed to the entire process. I had nothing left.

Finally, I grabbed a flashlight and walked to the garbage area to see if my precious two-coil electric burner from Walmart was still there.

Of course, it wasn't. And why would it be ... it was still perfectly good! On the way home, I stopped by Kate's and told her how I had lost it. She and Irv laughed with me. The next day, Harry and I went to the kitchenware department of Bed Bath and Beyond where I made him pay through the nose for his sins!

PARTY TIME

By Monday we were ready for guests. I had brownies, coffee, and cocktail napkins for anyone who wanted to come in and look around. People came in ... one, two, and three at a time ... staying for up to an hour. I had a nice opportunity to visit with each of them. Everybody has an experience. If you listen closely to their stories, you can save yourself a lot of grief in the future! Open house visitations continued for a few days and then started to dwindle. I enjoyed the little spontaneous visits. Most of them occurred while Harry was out golfing. He's not a "sosch" (pronounced like the first syllable of social). Anyone who was involved in the move, or had known about it, was invited. Anyone who had given us advice was invited. Anyone who walked by and just wanted to come in was invited. We had our helpers over for a cozy dinner in the coach on Friday: Jerry, Bev, Linda and Dave. There was plenty of room to entertain. By Friday, March 13, almost all of the visits had taken place.

THE LOWERING OF THE BOOM

And then ...

- By Friday, March 13, 2020, restaurants were closing.
- On Saturday, March 14, bell practice was canceled.
- On Saturday, March 14, the Sunday service was cancelled.
- On Saturday, March 14, life seemed to be cancelled.

The only thing not canceled was the painting class on Sunday in the rec hall. The tables were set up for something called "social distancing." Linda and I attended and enjoyed painting "Lizard on Path." Who knew it would be the last social event of the season.

Chapter 9 ... Tucson

The following Tuesday, all of the activities in the park were cancelled ... including the pool, hot tub, and gym. The only things left open were the restrooms, mailroom, and the office. Nearby golf clubs and grocery stores were still open. We were finally understanding what the people up north in Washington were experiencing.

RISING FROM THE ASHES

And then ... new fun things started happening:

- My church in quarantine back home started a phone tree to check on people in the entire congregation. The assignments were made by age. I had ten young families with two or three children under the age of ten. Although we didn't have a lot of life in common, we did find common ground ... it was all about building relationships.
- The 6 a.m. Tuesday Breakfast Book group went to something called Zoom. The COVID-19 pandemic was forcing us to be tech savvy. One woman on Zoom told her German Shepherd not to fret because the voices of the people were on the computer. Immediately, those who had pets shoved them in front of their cameras. It was a happy moment for dog lovers! (I heard the Humane Societies in New York had been emptied of dogs. It was a good thing.)
- Our Sunday service went online. I started feeling connected again!
- The church needed a volunteer to offer tech support by phone to people who don't know how to connect with others online. I volunteered, assuming no one would call unless they weren't tech savvy at all. It wasn't a big stretch for me.

Harry was still golfing about three days a week. I walked the dogs around the park and chatted with people from a distance. Some friends had left for Sedona and Indiana, giving me a chance to get caught up on my reading ... Dietrich Bonhoeffer and Louise Penny!

Chapter 10 ... Heading Home

Technology

The whole COVID adventure was helped by the existence of great technology. We were all in the same boat ... online. But technology failed me in two ways. Supply and demand no longer worked as expected. Our Keurig pot gave out on April Fool's Day! I was boiling and straining for a few days. Amazon couldn't guarantee two-day delivery. We were scheduled to leave on the fourth ... but it arrived in plenty of time. The second failure was the battery on our handheld vacuum. It's a must if you have dogs who shed as much as our Corgis. We limped home and ordered a new battery, immediately.

Living in a motor home at the beginning of COVID was actually a good thing. We watched the news and kept hunkered down, touching foreign things as little as possible, but when "they" threatened to close state boundaries, we started getting worried and left for home.

Shame on Me

On leaving our final RV site, Harry said "You can just turn there. Right?" I looked at "there." Smack dab in the middle of "there" was a cable stanchion sticking two feet out of the ground. I thought *"Oh?"* but said "Okay." I started my turn. I was inching closer to the stanchion, but I was watching it in the side mirror. Suddenly there was a loud pounding on the coach. Harry had seen the stanchion and was getting very excited. I backed up, pulled way forward, and restarted my turn, with an internal smile.

Chapter 11 ... Vancouver

Coming Home to ...

We got home on Saturday, April 25. Since the coach was almost as wide as the driveway, I was hanging out the driver's window watching to make sure I didn't stray onto the landscaping. I meandered slowly down the long driveway and up to the guest parking. (All the while, Kevin's question kept haunting me.) Once the coach was secured in a temporary spot, I looked at my flower beds: the only thing I really noticed were the pop weeds (hairy bittercress) in the front yard. They were past their prime and had popped, spreading coiled seeds throughout the yard. I thought of all the people who had been working on their lawns and flower beds for six weeks. I was behind ... way behind.

While I was fussing with the coach, Harry was fussing with the cars and the lawn. The grass was about a foot high. He jumped on the lawn mower. He jumped off the lawn mower, went to the gas station, brought back gas, filled the lawn mower, jumped back on the lawn mower, and raced off to mow the lawn. He was moving at an exorbitant rate: well shy of one mile per hour. He was bagging the clippings and had to make frequent stops to empty the bags. We were dealing with the aftermath of a warm, dry April: the lawn had escaped its bounds, covering the low-growing flowers, which by this time were invisible. After four mowings in four days, we finally had the lawn under control.

Meanwhile, back at the coach, it took me two days to clear the coach and put stuff away in the house. Kevin's question was becoming more and more real to me. I looked at the top of the coach and saw a springy antenna sticking up from the roof, about 18 inches in from the side. The time had come. The new coach was four feet longer than the old one, but it had a better turning radius. Harry and I gritted our teeth and went out after breakfast to do the deed. But parking the coach was almost a nonevent. It loved its new home.

It was a little weird listening to the springy antennae greet each of the rafters as I was pulling the coach forward ... *brrring, brrring, brrring!* ... but the coach fit height-wise even though it stuck out a couple of feet in the back ... behemoth!

MASKS

First things first ... I made a bandana mask with rubber bands for Harry and repurposed a gold sheet for myself. Mine tied behind my head. It was interesting to see how many creative options popped up for masks.

After two weeks, I was still all about masks. I went through my closet and pulled out a lightweight pair of pants I knew I was never going to wear. They were gray. I made a cowl thinking it would be easy to button and pull up to cover my nose if need be. It worked okay ... but just okay. When I took the Weed Eater in to get it serviced, the rep at the counter didn't see beyond the mask. He said, "I'll be with you in a minute ... Sir." I said, "Ok, but next time call me ... Ma'am."

Then I went to Costco. I had to dress my gray cowl up a little bit with some dangly pink earrings so the "Sir" comment wouldn't happen again. Unfortunately, I didn't take into account the number of times I had to move my head (left and right; up and down) as I was shopping. Attempting to keep my nose covered was very frustrating and tiring. On the brighter side, a little teenage chickadee passing by with her mother said perkily, "Oh, I love your earrings!" It was simply encouraging to hear someone say something after two months of isolation!

When I got home, I experimented with more gray masks. Finally, I made a little white mask out of lace. Of course it was lined with cotton material. It had ear straps and a filter pocket. I was a fashionista!

House Mouse

We've had mice before. About ten years earlier, Fred came in and discovered our humane traps. I took him out, across the driveway and released him. His cousin came in while we were down south and made herself at home under the sink in the kitchen ... for a while. Evidently, humane traps are a little less than humane if you aren't there to check them from time to time. By the time we got home, any odor accompanying her demise had dissipated.

Vices

I will tell you right now, once you give up a vice you can't go back. I gave up sugar in 2016. On my birthday in 2020, still hunkered down during COVID, I decided I would have a brownie. It tasted great but at bedtime, my ankles popped out like a balloon animal. Once you give up a vice you simply can't go back!

Full Court Press

Finally, by Mother's Day ...

- the pots had been planted,
- the glass fencing on the deck had been washed,
- the deck itself had been washed,
- the cushions had been put out,
- the creek had been cleared,
- the road had been scraped (and blown and blown),
- the greenhouse had been put in order ... full of new life, promise, and hope,
- the Weed Eater had been taken in for repairs,
- the carpets had been vacuumed,
- the floor had been mopped,
- the lawn had been mowed ... six times,
- the furnace filters had been washed, and
- I was happy to be home!

PART FOUR

PRETENDING TO BE AN INTROVERT

2020–21

Chapter 1 ... Vancouver

Late in Leaving

The motor home had been in the shop for servicing since the first part of July. Since everyone was impacted by COVID, including the parts department back East, no one had any idea when the minor repairs might be completed. Three weeks shy of our November 1 planned departure date, we heard we would probably get the coach back by the end of October. It took an additional two weeks. Harry had already scheduled several mid-month golf games in Vancouver. Rather than cancel the golf games, we took our time loading the coach. At the same time, I was able to empty the refrigerator and clear the kitchen counters in anticipation of tile work, which would be done while we were in Tucson. I also defrosted our chest freezer for the first time in ages. We rescheduled our departure date for November 20.

Little Billy

The night before we left, I moved all the last-minute things to the motor home and completed all the items on my trip list. I was so tired after getting the house ready for the tile work, I just sat down like a lump and yawned repeatedly. At 10:20 p.m., Harry said he was taking the dogs to the motor home to put them to bed. I told him I was going to empty the dishwasher, take a shower, and then come over. Anyone who's ever read the Sunday funnies knows Little Billy, the boy who never takes the direct route. I was Little Billy. I started by emptying the dishwasher. Then I went into the computer room where I unplugged the computer and turned off the lights. While I was there, I heard a crash like ice in an ice maker, which was strange since I had recently unplugged the refrigerator. Next, I went out to water the plants in the greenhouse. After refilling the water jugs for use by my neighbor Dorothy, who had promised to water the plants while we were gone, I went outside to check the gutters on the deck one last time. They all needed a little tending. When I came in, I remembered to put dowel rods in all the sliding glass door tracks. Finally, I put my phone in the last-minute bin destined for the motor home and went downstairs to shower. As I stripped off my clothes, I realized the floor was dirty. In my altogether, with my glasses off, I shook out the rug and dry mopped the floors. I threw a couple of towels in the defrosting freezer chest. I thought perhaps the crash had come from the freezer chest. It had. Great chunks of ice dangled precariously from the freezer basket. I started to remove them, but they didn't want to budge. I felt like I was clambering into the freezer as I propped the lid open with my bare shoulder and wrestled with the ice. Into the sink went those great chunks of ice. One of them was too heavy for me to manage. It shattered on the tile floor. Yikes! Still naked, I cleaned up the mess, finished removing the ice, and went back to my showering. Afterward, I took a minute to scrub the shower floor, got dressed, and went upstairs. I was just locking the house as Harry came over, wondering where I was and why I wasn't answering my phone! Oops, busted! We wandered back to the motor home together. Everything else went without a hitch. Little Billy and her husband were in bed in the coach by 11:20 p.m.

ONE LAST VISIT

I woke up the next morning about 6:30 a.m. I was lying in the motor home all comfy and warm thinking about getting up and going to have coffee with Dorothy, when I heard a little ping on my phone. Dorothy was telling me she was up. I got dressed, jumped in the car, and ran up for one last morning visit. She asked me if I had turned the heat down. I had not. I started a new list. At 7:30 a.m. Harry called to tell me he was ready to start our annual snowbirding adventure! I raced home to join him. [And yes, I remembered to turn down the heat.]

LURCH

After tending to the dogs, we hitched the Jeep to the back of the motor home on the upslope of the driveway in full view

Chapter 1 ... Vancouver

of Dorothy's house. We were ready to leave, and Dorothy was watching. I gunned the motor home. It slid backward a couple of inches and, as I stomped on the brake, it lurched! I repeated my futile efforts a couple more times until I realized the transmission was still in neutral. Shifting into drive made a big difference, but by then, Dorothy had run inside with her eyes closed! It was too painful to watch. By 8:40 a.m. we were on the road. My task was to drive to the Love's truck stop in Troutdale where we would fuel up and switch drivers.

Chapter 2 ... A New Route to Tucson

Clonk

It took an hour to get to Love's in the morning traffic. Even after an hour, we were still getting acclimated to traveling. While Harry was inside paying for the fuel, I was sitting in the driver's seat. I was looking at the passenger side mirror expecting to see him return via the rear of the vehicle. All of a sudden, the coach shook. I made a whiplash turn in the driver's seat, looked out the side window where I saw my husband holding his head, leaning against the side of the coach. He really nailed the side mirror! His forehead was quite a little worse for the wear, but it wasn't a concussion, and it wasn't bad enough to keep him from driving, so off we went.

Making a Run for It

Our route was simple. Drive East to Twin Falls, turn right, drive South to Arizona. We stopped at dark at a rest stop near Boise, which had very narrow parking spots. The dogs got right to business and were quite happy afterward to lie around in their crates. We had a quick sandwich and hit the hay at 7:30 p.m. We couldn't put out the slides, so Harry slept crossways on the bed. I slept on the sofa underneath my new heated throw. It was quite cozy. Harry likes to drive in the dark because there aren't as many people on the road. At 1:30 a.m. we jumped out of our beds, had a breakfast bar with our coffee, and started again. We hadn't yet realized we were retired.

Let's Rumble!

Northern Nevada has interesting topology. It looks like Ursa Major took his claw and scratched the landscape several times creating numerous North-South ranges of hills. Highway 93 snakes down the eastern side of Nevada around those hills. It was my turn to drive and Harry's turn to nap. Rumble strips are great. They are normally on the right side of the road and about six inches past the

Chapter 2 ... A New Route to Tucson

edge of the lane. The rumble strips on that stretch of road were not so great. They were on both sides of my lane, encroaching on the stripes and me! If I didn't put my full concentration on the lane, they would get me ... *thrump-thrump-thrump.* Any time I looked at the scenery, the motor home drifted slightly to the right ... thrump-thrump-thrump. Harry had a little ... *thrump-thrump-thrump ...* trouble sleeping ... *thrump-thrump-thrump.*

"DID YOU TURN ..."

At Ely, Highway 93 intersects US Highway 6. The detour, Highway 6/Nevada 318 is a better road and a more direct route South. We took the detour. It was my turn to nap. Harry insisted I go to the back and lie down. Before I did, I told him to turn left on Highway 318 in twenty-two miles. The whole detour at Ely was just a little confusing. In retrospect, I should have stayed up for those twenty-two miles.

(Note to self: Make sure I have Harry's full attention when I tell him about turns.)

After quite a while, I was finally able to go to sleep. A little later, I was aware of *ka-thunk, ka-thunk, ka-thunk.* It was annoying. *What a nasty road*, I thought as I drifted off again. When Harry pulled off at a gravel rest stop, I got up, refreshed. The rest stop consisted of two garbage cans and one picnic table ... but nothing else. "I don't know where we are!" Harry exclaimed urgently. I looked at the GPS display. There were no roads visible in our location. We were somewhere in the middle of Nevada ... lost. (Some words just don't sound helpful when spoken. Among those words are "Did you turn left on Highway 318?" I hope I don't say that ever again!) A quick look at a better map on my phone showed we could recover easily: we could turn left in twenty miles at Warm Springs onto Hwy 375, drive ninety-eight miles to Crystal Springs, turn right on Hwy 93, and we'd be none the worse for the wear.

ET ... Phone Home!

It was my turn to drive. In about twenty miles, still in the middle of nowhere, we found Nevada 375 and turned left. There was nothing there. I found out later, Warm Springs was a "former" town ... only two abandoned buildings remained, neither of which I saw. There was nothing but an intersection! But it was well marked. Nevada 375 is the east-west road at the north end of Nellis Air Force Base. There were several warning signs to watch for low-flying aircraft. I took it to heart, but evidently the pilots weren't training that Saturday. Interestingly, Nevada 375 is labeled the Extraterrestrial Highway. (It made me smile and think about my brother Stephen who was always ... *thrump-thrump-thrump* ... good for a laugh: He told me about a road in Nevada where there was a motel called the Little A'Le'Inn.)

The Extraterrestrial Highway is a remarkably smooth road. We enjoyed the drive. About halfway along the ninety-eight-mile route, on the right side of the road, was the Little A'Le'Inn. I was so excited! "Oh, Harry, look!" I squealed in delight. "There's the Little ..." *thrump-thrump-thrump*. "Kate! You're scaring me!" I shut up in mid-sentence, put on my best hang-dog look and resolved to keep my focus on the center of the road. A little farther down the road, another huge motor home came barreling my way. I was so focused on my position in the road I almost missed noticing the other driver smiling and waving. *Well, what's the matter with me*, I wondered. *Cheerfulness is a choice*. I got with the program and started enjoying the drive. Toward the end of the Extraterrestrial Highway, Harry saw a Quonset hut labeled "Area 51, Alien Research Center." I missed it, and it's a good thing ... otherwise there would have been more thrumping.

Chapter 2 ...A New Route to Tucson

The Last Time Harry Let Me Drive

The Extraterrestrial Highway is a long straight road traversing three mountain ranges. The elevations would make the passes on Interstate 5 look anemic, but fortunately there was no snow, for which we were grateful. After a two-hour stint at the wheel, I was hitting the rumble strips on both side of the lane consistently. It was a little disconcerting. When we reached Highway 93, a road with one lane going each direction, I had to make a sharp left turn across oncoming traffic to get into the next rest stop. I was going fifty-five mph with a semi coming up fast behind me. Turning a motor home can be problematic: Ours had air suspension, which occasionally gave me the impression we were careening down the highway. Sharp turns are not a good idea. (All sorts of things can get thrown around in a motor home if you turn at other than a crawl.) But then, stopping in front of a semi on a two-lane road is not a good idea either. I signaled. To start my sharp left turn, I veered left about thirty degrees crossing the oncoming lane (no oncoming traffic), hit the brake, and almost came to a stop ... heading to a three-foot drop. Since I was sitting above the wheels, it seemed a little more exciting to my passenger than it really was. When I was going slowly enough, I cranked the steering wheel all the way to the left. The motor home handled the turn very well, but Harry declared it was the last time he was going to let me drive until we reached Tucson!

Our destination was Earp, California, a few hours south of Las Vegas. We wanted to visit Larry and Wendy through the end of the month. As we were approaching Las Vegas, I called Big Bend RV Resort in Earp. The lady at the desk said they were all filled up due to Thanksgiving. She even checked with her boss and called back to confirm. Too bad for us. We were fast approaching a decision point. We decided to abandon Earp and make a run for Tucson.

Who's the Goat Now!

Aside: Now, Harry is not stupid, but since I'm the author, I get to be the heroine. Occasionally, Harry has to be the goat. He just has to live with it.

As we were leaving Las Vegas, Harry's phone rang. I put it on speaker and went back to get a cup of coffee. It was Larry and Wendy. Larry was asking where we were. The sound was up pretty high, so I was able to eavesdrop on the conversation. Harry was telling about my driving competence on the Extraterrestrial Highway. It was a little strange to realize I was not the heroine in his story. I was definitely the goat. I shrugged. It had to happen sometime.

Give It a Rest

We were tired and wanted to stop, but the sun was setting, and it looked like there was only one possibility in sight ... a Love's truck stop in Kingman, Arizona. It was farther than we wanted to go, but we certainly didn't want to park on the side of the road either. Harry drove the extra hour. Together, we navigated the highway exit and the Love's entrance. We refueled. While I got a couple of Subway sandwiches, Harry walked around looking for a parking space for the night. There was nothing available! Love's was almost completely full of trucks. Any empty spots were back-in only, which meant we'd have to unhook the Jeep if we parked there. (It's a good thing we didn't unhook the Jeep. We didn't know it at the time, but the Jeep battery was dead ... again!) There was a Petro truck stop about eleven miles down the road. We knew if they were full, we would be out of luck for the night. But we had to chance it. As Harry was walking the path of the three right turns to the exit to make sure we had a clear way out, I quieted myself and prayed for guidance to find a place to stay for the night. I thought of Joseph and Mary in Bethlehem. I soon came to the conclusion there was no comparison but for the words in Luke's Gospel ... "no room." Harry climbed into the coach, and I started driving. We turned right, proceeding slowly. One more right turn, and there, along a concrete

Chapter 2 ... A New Route to Tucson

wall, was what appeared to be a long empty stretch of parallel parking across from some big rigs. It was unmarked. I wondered if it could be quite that simple. I pulled in next to the concrete wall and crept forward looking around and assessing if we'd be in anyone's way when the big rigs pulled out of their spots. I wondered again if it could be quite that simple. It was. We settled in for the night, waiting for someone to tell us we couldn't park there. No one came. We put the bedroom slide out, ate our Subway sandwiches, and hit the hay.

WHAT'S THAT LIGHT DOING ON?

The next morning, we had our breakfast bars and coffee, tended to the dogs, and put the slide in. We were fresh and ready for the last few hours of our trip. Harry was in the driver's seat. He turned the key in the ignition and discovered an icon labeled MIL was still lit. What in the world?!? Searching through the operating manual and on the internet led us to the conclusion we had a Malfunction Indicator Lamp connected with the engine, which probably had something to do with the emissions system. It didn't sound too bad since it was a newish motor home and had just been serviced. Harry turned the key ... nothing happened. The battery in the motor home chassis didn't have enough juice to start the engine. Thank goodness for the Auxiliary Assist switch. He hit that switch, the home batteries gave a jump to the chassis batteries, and we were on our way. Since it was the start of Thanksgiving week, we noted we had plenty for which to be thankful!

TOO LITTLE, TOO LATE

We were treated to a very pretty sunrise north of Phoenix. I was beginning to enjoy the early morning traveling.

We were supposed to stop at Casa Grande, South of Phoenix, to refuel and switch drivers. After we got through Phoenix, I called the park and found out our site was 387. Good to know. I looked it up on the map. My eyebrows went up. It was a beautiful spot, one of the best in the whole park. Very easy to back into.

When we came to Casa Grande, the navigator-heroine was not tending to her duties. We missed the exit ... Harry had to keep driving to our RV park in Tucson. He could have pulled off to the side of the road, I guess ... but he didn't. Then we got a call from Big Bend telling us there were plenty of open spaces after all. The Canadian Prime Minister had extended his ban on the border due to the pandemic and the Canadians were still not allowed to enter the US. Consequently, the *full* campground was only half full for Thanksgiving ... too little, too late.

Chapter 3 ... Arriving in Tucson

The Day the Jeep Died

We pulled into our park at mid-morning on Sunday. I went to register while Harry disconnected the Jeep. As he finished the sixteen-step checklist to transfer the Jeep out of towing mode, he discovered it wouldn't turn on. Evidently, the battery in his key fob had given out. It couldn't have been the Jeep's battery because we had replaced it a week earlier. When I returned, he used my key and discovered the battery in my key fob must have given out also ... at the exact same time! Too much of a coincidence! Thank goodness we had a portable stand-alone jumper. It's such a relief to have the right tools when you need them. He hooked it up and told me when to start the Jeep. *Grrrrrr* ... click. It must have been an anomaly. I tried it again. *Grrr* ... click. And again. Grr ... click. Each attempt was met with wimpier results. It was hopeless. Fortunately, Denny, a guy in the know, was driving by in his golf cart and offered to get his battery charger. He said it would take thirty minutes to charge his charger before his charger could jump the Jeep. Although the Jeep was parked in an unfortunate location, there wasn't anyone else coming to register that day. We were good to go.

Jump, Spot, Jump ... Jump, Jump, Jump

We took the motor home to site 387. It was at the end of Happy Street (aka H Street), a long street lined with palm trees. We had a commanding view of the mountains to the east. It was a spectacular spot. I don't know what we did to deserve it, but I considered it the best spot in the park. What a snap to park the motor home ... make a right turn on Happy Street and back into 387! We fussed with the jacks, tire covers, slides, and hookups. I waved at those who were gawking ... as RVers are wont to do ... and did my best not to justify their gawking. After about twenty minutes, Denny came back in his golf cart and got the key to the Jeep. A couple of minutes later, he returned and said the Jeep was trying to burn up his battery charger! Then Rich, from three doors down (in the second-best spot in the park with the same unimpeded easterly view as ours ... down G Street), offered to jump the Jeep with his massive pickup. Harry took him up on it and it worked. Pretty soon the Jeep was humming away parked next to the motor home. All was well with our world again. The whole process took two and a half hours! I had to reboot the coach to get the jacks to work, but I was getting used to that. The good news was the MIL icon had gone out! We settled in for the winter ... Harry started with a nice long nap.

THREE-EIGHTY-WHAT?

In the evening, I read through the registration packet and saw a map of the RV sites. One site was circled ... 386! I broke into a cold sweat. Moving the motor home wouldn't be difficult, but Harry would have to reverse his setup procedure. I didn't want to get crosswise with Harry, the office, or any of the other residents. I vowed to get the issue resolved, quickly. The next morning, in the office, Joanne said she had driven by our space and noticed it was empty. (My panic was rising!) She really did mean to put us in 386, but 387 was also available. With a few keystrokes, it was ours for the next five months. I was so relieved.

Chapter 3 ... Arriving in Tucson 121

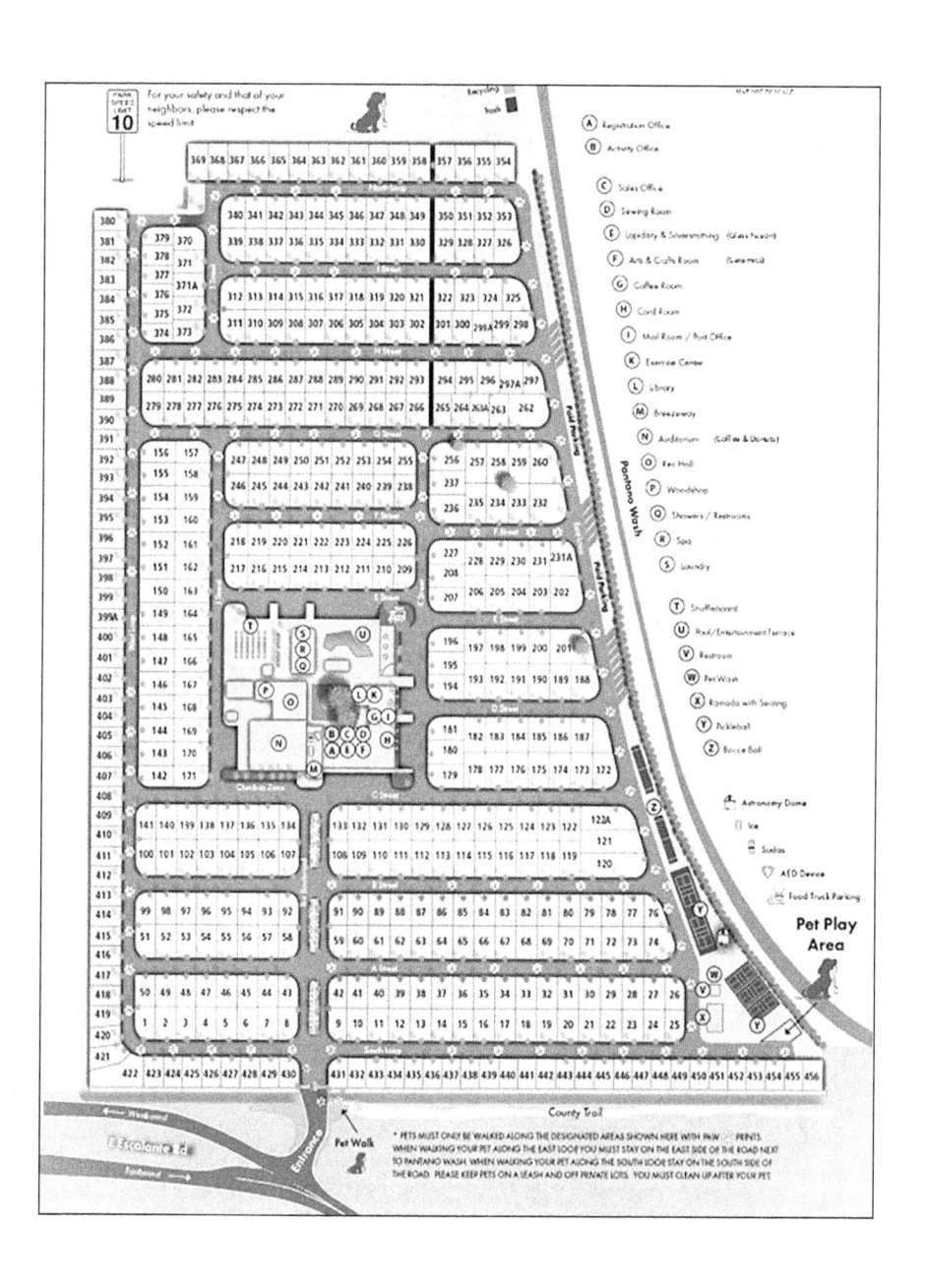

(Park map showing site layout with numbered lots, streets, and amenities)

Speed limit: 10

For your safety and that of your neighbors, please respect the speed limit

Legend:
- A — Registration Office
- B — Activity Office
- C — Sales Office
- D — Sewing Room
- E — Lapidary & Silversmithing (Glass Fusion)
- F — Arts & Crafts Room (Ceramics)
- G — Coffee Room
- H — Card Room
- I — Mail Room / Post Office
- K — Exercise Center
- L — Library
- M — Breezeway
- N — Auditorium (Coffee & Donuts)
- O — Rec Hall
- P — Woodshop
- Q — Showers / Restrooms
- R — Spa
- S — Laundry
- T — Shuffleboard
- U — Pool/Entertainment Terrace
- V — Restroom
- W — Pet Wash
- X — Ramada with Seating
- Y — Pickleball
- Z — Bocce Ball

Astronomy Dome
Ice
Sodas
AED Device
Food Truck Parking
Pet Play Area

Pet Walk

* PETS MUST ONLY BE WALKED ALONG THE DESIGNATED AREAS SHOWN HERE WITH PAW PRINTS. WHEN WALKING YOUR PET ALONG THE EAST LOOP YOU MUST STAY ON THE EAST SIDE OF THE ROAD NEXT TO PANTANO WASH. WHEN WALKING YOUR PET ALONG THE SOUTH LOOP STAY ON THE SOUTH SIDE OF THE ROAD. PLEASE KEEP PETS ON A LEASH AND OFF PRIVATE LOTS. YOU MUST CLEAN UP AFTER YOUR PET.

It Takes Two

We had a narrow escape the next day. Harry and I have often commented it takes two to do the things that one used to do. It usually means two brains. He had mentioned there was no soap in the bathroom. So, when I was setting up house for the long haul, I pulled out the liquid soap. A contractor had once told me how easy it was to fill a plunger soap dispenser. I had assumed it was necessary to unscrew the bottle from below, fill it, and screw it back in. But he showed me how to lift the plunger, pour in the soap, and replace the plunger. I had a full bottle of soap and was ready to do just that. I mentioned to Harry in passing I was going to put some hypoallergenic soap in the soap dispensers. Harry said, "Oh good, you saw I left them out." It was only then I noticed the two plastic bottles on the kitchen counter! If I had filled the dispensers without talking to Harry, I would have poured about sixteen ounces of liquid soap through the hole in the counter, down into a stack of dishcloths, and through to the carpet. I would have been dealing with the sudsy aftermath for years!

Chapter 4 ... Tucson

Silent Night

We stayed hunkered down for most of the winter, wearing masks on the rare times we went to the store and walking the dogs for exercise. The most exciting thing I did was participate in singing "Silent Night," electronically, with the rest of the choir back home. The choir director sent each of us a track of the music. All I had to do was sing along with the music and record myself at the same time ... and make sure my face was framed properly ... and make sure the dogs weren't wandering through the picture ... and make sure the camera was not pointed away from me ... and make sure I was smiling. It soon became obvious to me it would be quite an involved project. I had thought I could do it in one take, maybe two ... but it took thirty-four. Here are some of the takes:

Take 1: Oops, unmentionables were hanging on chair.

Take 2: How did I get so many wrinkles?

Take 3: The camera worked fine but the wrinkles ... (sigh).

Take 4: Needed to sit on floor in front of coach's fireplace.

Take 5: Oh that Angie! She was not supposed to sing.

Take 6: Still hadn't figured how to sit down gracefully.

Take 9: Still hadn't figured how to position the camera.

Take 13: Had trouble starting video and positioning camera correctly; didn't push stop button, video disappeared.

Take 17: Finally started using headphones.

Take 23: Audio was good but camera had slipped into selfie mode: Took video of sofa fibers ... but no bugs!

My brother sent me an encouraging text, which read, "When you record at home you are singer, set designer, dresser, makeup artist, recording engineer, producer, IT person, and lighting designer!" Sadly, the text cancelled the filming.

Take 25: Camera fell over.

Take 28: Passable recording but Angie groaned.

Take 29: Passable recording but Angie groaned ... again.

Take 30: Oops, a text from Dorothy killed the video.

Take 31: The girls cut loose during last verse.

Take 34: Put the girls outside, camera stayed upright, face was slathered with Vaseline (to look younger), lipstick was still okay ... but ... because I was sitting on the floor, I ran out of breath. I couldn't get out the last syllable: "Sleep in heavenly pea ..." was all I could muster! Close enough!

CHAPSTICK

Night was drawing near. It was time for a little chat, a little ChapStick, and a little rest. After we had our ChapStick, I put it back in its precarious place, and wouldn't you know, it tumbled off onto the floor. It's a pretty high bed and I had just gotten settled. I really didn't want to get out of bed and fish around for the ChapStick even though it was right there on the floor ... just out of reach. I decided I would pick it up in the morning. Of course, by the time morning rolled around, there was no thought in my head of ChapStick. Harry and I sat in our chairs watching an episode of "JAG" while we enjoyed our breakfast together. Suddenly I realized something was out of place. I noticed Angie chewing on a dog bone under the computer chair. *That's odd*, I thought, *Angie never chews on a dog bone under the computer chair.* Well, it wasn't a dog bone. She had sniffed out the only edible material within Corgi range in the whole motor home. With Angie it's all about food ... and ChapStick.

COVID Slump

From November through January, I was in a COVID slump. I just couldn't get myself going. I could perform simple mindless tasks like cooking and loading the motor home, but going out for groceries took a little more thought, planning, and energy. *(You, Dear Reader, lived through it ... you know what I mean about trying to second guess all the what-ifs.)* I came out of my slump in mid-January, thanks to two sweet little books: *The Wind in the Willows* and *Watership Down*.

Knitting

I was ready to get back in touch with people. When Kate suggested we teach Kathy, the lady across the street, how to knit, I jumped at the chance. Kathy was up for the challenge and while we were teaching her, Minnesota-Carol went by. She decided she wanted in. We did more laughing than knitting.

We always wore masks when we got together, and we never touched anything belonging to another person. If you've ever tried to learn how to knit, it's a lot like cutting your own hair using a couple of mirrors: Your hands go one way while your mind goes another. Before long I couldn't stand it ... I was touching Kathy's yarn, poking around with her needles, and trying to get my words and my actions coordinated. Eventually, it all came together for her. At least we had masks on and were practicing a modicum of social distancing on Kate's breezy patio.

The third time we got together it was hands-on teaching! We threw caution to the wind by touching everything. What can you do!

At our fourth session, it was a little windy. We decided we could go without masks. I wanted to share some funny littles videos from my phone. Not wanting anyone to touch my phone, I held it out at arm's length and played the videos. They were absolutely hilarious, but because of the direction I was holding my phone, the force of their laughter came shooting in my direction. There was not enough breeze in the world to keep it from being an issue in the early days of COVID. I hoped for the best.

PAINTING

Minnesota-Carol and I usually attended McKenna's monthly painting class. I suggested we do something a little more challenging than the simple cactus planned. Carol wasn't too sure it was a good idea. Neither was I, but hey, I wanted to do a burro, so I tried to talk her into doing one, too. When she was still hesitant, I suggested we have a pre-painting party and do a burro together. She agreed. We found pictures on the internet, selected one, traced it onto the art paper, and proceeded to paint. After we had the basic outline, I told her to paint the burro in seven layers. It totally freed both of us from our inhibitions and off we went. The little burros were very recognizable. It took us two hours from start to finish. Since a painting class was only ninety minutes at most, Carol decided burros would be an acceptable subject for a practice session but not necessarily for the real class. When we got to the class, I painted the cactus, added mountains of Sedona, a clump of rocks, and my little burro. It was a real stretch to get it done in ninety minutes.

I GOT SHOT ... AKA HERD IMMUNITY

The first time I checked the Arizona State eligibility for COVID vaccines, it was limited to people seventy-five and older. I wasn't that old. I stopped checking. When people sixty-five and older were eligible, I started getting serious about finding a vaccine appointment. One night, I accidently found an appointment. I called Kate and Irv, immediately. Thirty minutes later, they had appointments scheduled at same time as mine. We had been ultra conservative about masking, touching, social distancing, and carpooling. But our excitement had peaked and we were getting our first shot. We carpooled! We were so excited we were halfway there before we realized we weren't wearing our masks!

We had to double-mask when we got to the shot site, but the process went very smoothly. When we got inside, one of the Gestapo asked if I was allergic to anything. I rattled off my allergies like a mantra: grasses, weeds, house dust, and epinephrine. "Epinephrine ... what happens when you have epinephrine?" asked the Gestapo. Uh-oh, I could see my appointment fading. I did my best to backpedal to put her at ease. Before long, I got through the line and went right to the injection station where I had to hand another Gestapo my driver's license. (Ick! COVID had done a number on my fear factor. I was still squeamish about having anyone touch my things.) I got my shot and immediately felt a little woozy for about fifteen seconds. I found out the same thing happened to Irv and Kate. As we waited the required fifteen minutes, another Gestapo person helped all of us get appointments for exactly three weeks later. The appointments were all together. Before we left, we each got a three-inch "I got vaccinated" sticker. When we got home, we put our stickers on, and Harry took our picture. It was exciting to be part of the herd!

None of us had much of a reaction, and my reactions were minimal. I thought it was strange I experienced three things at different times during the evening: a headache, an ache in my arm, and a head cold ... each one lasting less than a minute ... just long enough for me to think I might be starting to have a reaction ... and then nothing! But I did get tired. I was wandering around the coach in a three-foot circle unable to do anything later in the evening. I had to take a shower, brush my teeth, and put on my nightgown ... since I was too tired to do anything, I didn't know which to do first ... so I just keep walking around in a circle not getting anything done. *(Sigh!)*

We carpooled again to get our second shots. Kate was too chatty with the Gestapo and didn't answer his allergy question to his satisfaction. Boom! She got stuck with an orange thirty-minute sticker. Phooey!

Each of us had a two-day reaction: Irv had a low-grade fever and stiffness; Kate was lethargic and had a rash at the point of injection; I had sleeplessness. Go figure.

GOLF

Harry was still golfing four days a week with his men's group and park friends, leaving me with tons of time to work on my COVID projects ... writing, painting, cross-stitch, and photo albums.

MAKING LEMONADE ... AN ENTRY FROM ANGIE'S DIARY

Oh my goodness, I had the most special day. Harry went off golfing in the morning, leaving Kate, Lucy, and me in the motor home. We took a walk down the street to the gravel area to do what needed to be done. It was successful, I can sure tell you that! Then we came back to the motor home and had a pleasant time getting treats and just hanging out. The wind started coming up and it looked like it was going to rain but I didn't care because we were in the motor home ... safe, warm, and happy. Life was good!

Well, I probably need to make a correction to the above. When I said our gravel area trip was successful, I was only partially right. Lucy didn't take the opportunity to do what had to be done. And so, a few minutes later Lucy threw-up all over the floor of the motor home. Fortunately, it was a tile floor ... not hard to clean up if you're into that. Well, we all went outside right away.

Lucy was just being a little stinker ... she wouldn't do her business. There's only one thing to do in a case like that when it's so windy outside: One dog goes in the Jeep, the other goes to a new exercise area ... and that's what happened ... and it produced the desired results.

Now ... I always say when you've got lemons, you've got to make lemonade. So I looked around in the car and found some wonderful breakfast bars in Kate's golf bag: Nature Valley crunchy oats and honey. I took them all out and started in on the first one, but I only got halfway through opening it before Kate came along and pulled me out of the Jeep. I don't know why she was laughing and scratching her head, but she took that wonderful treat away from me. Too bad for me. Didn't she know I had called dibs on it?

Chapter 5 ... Tucson

Down the Drain ... So Many Possibilities

I've had a disposal forever. Consequently, my dish scraping practices left a little to be desired when we were on the road. I would say I was pretty good about scraping the dishes. What did go down the drain, I envisioned running smoothly through to the grey water tank. Well, of course, this wasn't the first time I had envisioned something only to have been totally wrong. After three months, I noticed the drain wasn't working properly. Since there were two kitchen sinks with connected plumbing, I noticed it was backing up in the other sink as well. I looked under the sink to see if there was a trap to be cleaned, but there was an extremely heavy drawer in the way, and I just didn't feel like removing it. So I played the wife card and pointed it out to Harry. He got down on his knees and started poking around. He said he couldn't see anything at all. That didn't work out the way I had hoped. I realized I'd have to deal with it myself after all.

I did what came naturally, I put it off for a couple of days. And as one might expect, the situation didn't get better. I started to think about how I might resolve my problem. I could almost imagine two plungers, one in each sink, and me getting a good run at it and plunging down on both of them at the same time. Boy, oh boy, that would sure fix the problem. But then I remembered we always open the grey water valve when we do laundry because we don't want to blow out the seals. I probably wouldn't have had enough power to blow out the seals, but I didn't want to take a chance. Besides I didn't have one plunger, let alone two. I did the next best thing. I commandeered a cheap plastic water bottle. It was pretty flexible. I filled it and inverted it in the gunk coming up from the drain. Then I just let 'er rip. Of course, since I hadn't plugged the drain in the other sink, I had another mess to clean up.

Then, I decided to go at it a little more carefully. I put the metal drain plug in the left sink and stuck the water bottle full of water upside down in the gunk in the right sink and let 'er rip again. Up came the plug from the left sink. I needed to pay more attention to the laws of physics.

Finally, I pressed down on the plug in the left sink, inverted the water bottle full of water, and let 'er rip in the right sink. It actually worked. I was kind of surprised. Then I started to imagine all the stuff going down the drain meeting up with some grease and hardening. So I started working with hot water, such as it was. After about ten squishes from the water bottle, I was getting some pretty decent results, certainly good enough to live through the rest of our trip until I could have someone in the know take a look at it.

DOWN THE DRAIN ... SO LITTLE CREDIBILITY

But wait there's more ... After working on it all day, I told Harry about the problem. Well, Harry had just come home from golf and was tired. In retrospect, it probably wasn't the best time for me to do some show-and-tell on a maintenance problem. Nevertheless, I plowed ahead because it was foremost on my mind. I told him the drain wasn't working right, but I had made a little progress. I showed him the water in the left sink ... it wasn't draining at all. I noticed there was no water in the right sink and thought just for a fleeting instant how strange it was, but I had his attention, so I kept on talking. It wasn't very long before Harry reached into the left sink and pulled out the plug. The water drained immediately taking my credibility with it. He was so tired from golfing there was nothing I could do to resurrect the one-sided conversation ... for the next month and a half! Oh, that Harry! Wouldn't you think I would learn? Not a chance!

SUCCESS

The next day, I told Kate about my dilemma. She suggested a finer strainer and showed me what she had in her sink. I got a couple of those from Amazon and beefed up my scraping practices. Success!

Chapter 6 ... Heading Home

Noisy Trip

There were a lot of sounds on the trip home ... *Dub-dub-dub*, *Thrummm*, and *Nocka-Nocka* ... all in the first day. It was definitely a wild ride.

We left Tucson at 9:15 a.m., heading for Phoenix. I drove for the first hour. While Harry was driving, I tried to rest. I made a makeshift pillow out of my jacket and put my head to the side. And then it started. Rhythmic and insistent: Dub-dub-dub-dub-dub-dub-dub-dub-dub. From time to time, I would open my eyes and look at the pavement. There were so many asphalt worms in the lane it looked like alien handwriting covering the road.

Highway 60 to Wickenburg

Soon we came to a decision point. Harry asked me if he should take the 202 exit. As the navigator, I hadn't fully recognized the immediacy of my duties. I guessed: "No." He stayed on the freeway, and we headed straight into Phoenix. Soon, I realized my mistake. That one was on me.

Aside: Harry and I have a history of navigation concerns. One time, years back, we came to a stop sign at a "T" in the road. Harry asked me whether we should go left or right. I used my gut and said, "Go left." Harry went right. We arrived at our destination. It was so embarrassing! It was pretty typical of my navigational skills for all the years we'd been married. My self-confidence as a navigator is pretty high until he asks me a question.

So there we were, south of Phoenix, and I had made the wrong choice ... again. It only took a quarter of a mile to figure that one out. And so we went barreling toward Phoenix and the unknown.

Phoenix has three bypass routes designed to skirt the heavily populated areas. If you cut diagonally through the Phoenix area, the

Chapter 6 ...Heading Home

route is about twenty-eight miles long ... on a map, it looks like a line bisecting a square. The freeway route we should have taken went twenty miles west and twenty miles north. It saves time and stop-and-go frustration. I was pretty sure the diagonal route had stop lights. (I was right ... it had lots of them ... timed poorly!)

We were still on Interstate 10. I knew I could still salvage the fast route. All we had to do was follow the signs for "Interstate 10 to Los Angeles." And then came a choice "Highway 60 to Wickenburg" or "Interstate 10 to Los Angeles." Harry had had enough of California during the previous two years and more than enough of my navigational prowess. I stumbled for the right way to tell him he should stay on Interstate 10 ... and we'd come to the 303 bypass ... and it would skirt Phoenix ... and it would be a smoother way to get to Wickenburg. But before I could get my long treatise out, he said for the third time, "There's Highway 60 to Wickenburg!" It might have been a statement, but with all the caveats running amok in my brain, it sounded like an imperative. I gave up and spit out the words, "Take it!" I knew it would get us there and I knew I wouldn't have to explain all the intricacies of the route because there weren't any. Suffice it to say, it was a long haul cutting through the heart of Phoenix. But we made it. Meanwhile, I was sitting there choking back an *I told you so* ... because, really, I hadn't actually told him! Harry continued to drive for a while even after getting through Phoenix.

My Stint at the Wheel

The next time I drove, we were heading north on 93 toward Las Vegas. We hadn't traveled the route in the daytime, so when we came around a bend, I was surprised to see a valley of mini-mountains presenting itself in front of our expansive windshield. It looked like giant anthills filling the valley ... like mini-Mt. Hoods. It was quite unusual. I couldn't help but look. You might be able to guess what happened next. There we were, careening down the mountainside into this amazing valley, going through a turn, when all of a sudden, I hit the rumble strip. The *THRUMMM* was deafening.

Harry quietly said, "Slow down." My foot was already on the brake. By the time I got off the rumble strip and could hear again, I realized I was mistaken ... Harry was yelling SLOW DOWN! Soon all was well. And then we passed a scenic turnoff. Of course, we didn't take it, but it just verified there was actually something to see. (My instincts were right for a change.)

My stint at the wheel was going to end as soon as we got through Las Vegas. I was surprised when we had driven through Las Vegas five months earlier. The noise of the tires on concrete made me think we had blown a tire. This time, I was ready for it ... *Nocka Nocka Nocka Nocka Nock ... a Nocka Nocka Nocka Nocka Nocka Nocka Nock* ... miles of it. Other than that, it was uneventful.

AMARGOSA, NEVADA

We stopped about 4:30 p.m. at a rest stop near Amargosa, Nevada, on the southwest side of Nellis Air Force Base. It was a quiet little place just off the road with six or seven corrals, each surrounding a large crystalline boulder. It was neat as a pin, in an arid sort of way. I leashed up the dogs, who had to stop at every post for a little sniff. They were disoriented and anxious about the strange surroundings. They saw Harry about two hundred feet away. They wanted nothing more than to be with him. They acted like they were trying out for the Iditarod Race. Then they saw the motor home. It was all they could do to get me to take them straight back to the motor home, which was surprising since they had already had dinner. All those treats they get whenever they return to the motor home were foremost in their minds.

Once back, I smartly reached for the hamburger bean soup in the refrigerator, well pleased with my preparations for the trip home. We had eaten almost all our food and were down to cereal, a small amount of deli meat for sandwiches, and hamburger bean soup. Breakfast, lunch, and dinner were covered. We could go a couple of days on that fare. With breakfast bars as fillers, we could handle anything. I put the bean soup in the pot, set it on the induction

Chapter 6 ... Heading Home

burner in our all-electric coach, and hit the button ... nothing. There wasn't even a little light on the stovetop to give us hope. We were screwed! We did a little problem-solving for few minutes and then gave up. Sandwiches sounded like an okay alternative. Harry had roast beef while I had an open-faced beet-and-guacamole sandwich. It didn't sound like much, but it was nutritious!

It was really hot. We didn't want to compound our problems by running the generator and the air conditioner. We would be taking a chance on using up too much fuel. (However, had we done so, the light on the induction stove would have come on.) We hit the hay right after dinner, hoping to get an early start the next day. The sun was setting out the window next to my pillow but not fast enough. We needed to keep the windows and shades open for air circulation. I can usually sleep anywhere but not in Amargosa. After lying there with the bright light streaming in on my thin eyelids, our dinners digesting at their own pace, and unable to sleep for a couple of hours, Harry realized he hadn't locked the Jeep. He pointed his key fob at the Jeep and clicked ... no chirp ... nothing! There we were, just off Highway 95, at a junction of two numbered roads, with not a thing in sight, and the Jeep completely out of power! Deader than a doornail! It was good for nothing but being towed by the motor home.

NOT FOR THE SQUEAMISH

Harry thought it would be a good idea to go out and check to make sure the Jeep was locked. *Slam* went the front door ... *crunch, crunch, crunch* on the gravel ... *fuss, fuss* ... *crunch, crunch, crunch* coming back on the gravel ... *CRASH!* Something knocked into the motor home while Harry was outside. It felt like a car rammed us. I asked him about it when he got back.

Aside: We've both had dogs for more than forty years. We know the drill: You have to watch where you're walking!

On the way back from locking the Jeep, Harry came straight back to the motor home, watching where he was walking in a manner of speaking. It turned out he shouldn't have taken the direct route. His eyes were glued to the gravel when his forehead collided with the bedroom slide. I was right when I thought it felt like something had crashed to the motor home. That something was my husband. Troutdale, déjà vu! But at that time, I still didn't know it was Harry who had crashed into the motor home.

The lights were still off in the bedroom. He took off his robe and got back on the bed. Moments later, he said, "I'm gonna need a Band-Aid." I got up, turned on the lights, and saw a sight I never ever wanted to see. There was a rivulet of blood trickling south from a gaping hole in the center of his forehead, running down his nose, and meandering through his mustache to his upper lip. But wait, there's more. There was a second rivulet of blood going north across the broad expanse of his forehead, dawdling in the wispy hairs at the top of his head. I ran the five feet to the kitchen thinking what a stupid time not to bring a bunch of old clean cloths. I wondered for a second if I should get one of my lily-white dish cloths out of the drawer or use the dirty one I'd been using on the dishes, which was in need of a serious bleaching. It was a pretty long second, but begrudgingly, the clean lily-white cloth won out. Between the two of us, his head got cleaned up and I found the gaping hole wasn't a hole after all … it was just a massive dent. There must not be very many blood vessels in the dent area, because after the initial cleanup, it was under control. I got him situated with a couple of Band-Aids and an ice pack and we were back in the bed, trying to find our way to dreamland. We were up and down about two or three more times before the sun set when were finally able to conk out for the night.

Chapter 6 ... Heading Home

LIFE AS A WIDOW IN THREE MINUTES

Seeing my husband with blood running down his face got my mind spinning. Within two minutes I was a widow, driving the motor home back to Vancouver in one hundred-mile spurts, with Harry's poor dead body laid out on the bed in ninety-degree weather. I was anticipating the questions the police would undoubtedly have for me when I made it to the hospital in Portland. I even went so far as to decide that Kaiser's Sunnyside Hospital was too far from home and I'd be better off taking his poor dead body to the Emergency Room at Legacy Hospital in Salmon Creek ... a mile from home.

Having used those two minutes to advantage, I dedicated the next minute to my neighbor's dilemma (a dilemma she didn't know she had). With Harry dead and gone, I'd need to do something with the motor home. I decided to park it on the dike between Dorothy's pond and mine for Dorothy to use when her son and his family came to visit. I still had time to fuss with the complications of draining grey and black water tanks and to figure out how to minimize the number of times they'd have to be emptied per month. I even determined which way the motor home had to face so Dorothy would have a pleasant view before I came to my senses. With that, I drifted off to sleep.

BACK TO BEING HAPPILY MARRIED

We woke at 3 a.m. I asked, "How's your head?"

My man of few words responded, "It's okay."

We were on the road by 3:30 a.m. Harry was driving. Life went on.

An hour later, I asked my man of few words, "How is your coffee?"

"It's okay," he replied.

By 5 a.m. it was time to replenish the coffee mug. I went back to the kitchen to make another cup. Halfway back, the motor home shimmied and I caught myself on the dog crates. Caught up in the moment, my imagination went into overdrive again as I envisioned falling into the crates, breaking my glasses, and having a shard of plastic pierce my eye. By the time I traversed the final five feet to the coffee maker, I was laughing at myself. I had had more than my share of imaginary trips to the emergency room on this excursion and wasn't going to do it again.

With all of the trauma of the head-bash incident, the rest of the trip seemed uneventful. We swapped drivers every so often, holed up in Burns, Oregon, for the night, and got back on a regular sleeping schedule. It took six hours to drive home to Vancouver from Burns. By the end of the day, the motor home was almost completely unloaded. Thank goodness!

CHAPTER 7 ... VANCOUVER

YARD WORK, REMEMBER?

I had a new idea for yard work. I was going to mow the weeds by the bat house and blow off the road. Anything else would have to wait until my yard men came. Two brothers, Sam (20) and Kellen (15), were scheduled to come on Wednesdays for three hours. I surmised this would be enough to keep the whole yard under control and would allow me plenty of time for other things. I was very excited about this new plan. But after thirty-five years of handling my own yard work, it was simply hard to let go.

Aside: Just before we left for the Southwest six months earlier, Kellen and I transplanted daylilies. We must have planted about three dozen of them around the garden area. I had envisioned a profusion of daylilies bordering the garden on our return. But day lilies don't bloom at the end of April.

When the boys came for their first week, I told Kellen to clear out the garden except for the primroses. He said, "What's a primrose?" I pointed it out to him and turned him loose. The next day, I saw something strangely familiar on the grass. As I bent down to pick it up, I realized it was a daylily tuber, one of the many Kellen and I had planted. I cursed myself for not remembering. I thought perhaps there might be a few tubers left in the ground, but it was not likely because Kellen's a perfectionist. It reminded me of the year Harry was banned from doing any gardening: He had mixed up some Roundup on his own initiative and accidentally poisoned all my new crocus starts. He thought they were errant grasses. All one hundred of them had been systematically planted about eight inches apart. The crocus massacre was on Harry ... the daylilies were on me!

Now You See Him …

In a rare talkative occurrence, we had a conversation about the speakers in the living room. They were a little unsightly … five black smudges on the light-yellow soffit in the living room. He was all for taking the speakers down. I asked, "How are we going to hear the TV when we turn it on?"

"We can use the speakers in the TV," he replied.

"But what about the CD player?" I queried.

"Oh, do we still have it?" he retorted.

"If we get rid of it, how would we listen to music?"

"Turn on the cell phone. I run it through the Bluetooth speakers in the barn all the time."

"Well … what if we have a big party and want to play some music?"

"Then I'll go downstairs and turn on the TV."

There was a long pause during which I came to realize we were no longer talking about speakers. Oh that Harry and his disappearing acts!

PART FIVE

REJOINING THE WORLD

2021–22

Chapter 1 ... Vancouver

In mid-October, a day or two after Larry and Wendy left for Lake Havasu, Harry decided he wanted to leave right away. Cathy Basler was going to have a party on the 24th of October and got upset about our change of plans. She and Marg texted me up the yin-yang. What could I do ... the party was ten days after Harry's new arbitrary departure date. For some reason, I read the texts to Harry. About two days later he asked if I wanted to stay for the party. I did ... so we did. ☺

The weekend of October 23–24 was filled with light packing. We still had to take everything; we just took our time packing. Harry did a ton of schlepping from the back door, through the barn, to the motor home. It was the easiest packing weekend yet ... ending with the Halloween party at Basler's home. On the same weekend, we experienced the 2021 Northeast Pacific Bomb Cyclone, an extremely powerful extratropical cyclone. It tapped into a large atmospheric river and underwent explosive intensification, becoming a bomb cyclone on October 24 (according to Wikipedia) striking the Western United States and Western Canada. Thank goodness we had had a lot of trees and dead branches removed. Seconds before it started to pour, I had finished my yard work but I hadn't gotten around to blowing off the road. If I had, I would have had to blow off the road a second time one hour later because the winds were so strong!

On Monday the 25th, we did all the final packing. It still seemed easy. I picked up Alyssa, our house/dog sitter on Monday evening. Harry and I got up early on Tuesday, ate breakfast, finished putting things away in the motor home, hooked up the Jeep, and left for our fourth snowbirding adventure at 9:36 a.m.

It was my brother Larry's seventy-fifth birthday. Even though he's a couple of years older than I am, it was still a wake-up call!

Chapter 2 ... Heading South

We decided to stop in Ontario, Oregon, the first night at 5 p.m. We fueled up and ate Subway sandwiches in the coach. Harry was tired and went right to bed. I stayed up for about half an hour just to give the dogs a chance to get settled and do their business. I think I must have hit the hay at 6:30 p.m. It was impossible to go to sleep so early, but I knew I needed to get my rest because Harry was likely to jump out of bed at any minute and say, "Let's get going."

The parking spot we had selected seemed easy to get out of. We had about a ten-foot clearance in front of us for an easy turn. About midnight, Harry got up to do what needed to be done and looked out the front window. A huge truck had backed into our turn area and had parked perpendicular to us. It was totally blocking our exit. Harry mentioned this to me at 3 a.m. I pondered this problem, as people lying in bed dozing are wont to do. About 4:30 a.m. we decided to get up. We took the dogs out. We also took a closer look at the truck. It was about one and a half feet from our passenger mirror. Our new coach was known for its great turning radius. It was barely possible we could make a tight left turn and be on our way. And that's exactly what we did. I turned the coach to the left while Harry was outside watching the extended mirror and directing me. After we were free, I asked him how much room we had to spare. He said it was only about four inches. By 5 a.m. we were on the move!

Harry drove until daybreak. I drove through the sunrise. Even though we were heading due east, there were a lot of clouds in the sky, making the brightest of the sun's rays a mere intermittent inconvenience.

As soon as we crossed the border into Idaho, we were on Mountain Time. I didn't know what time it was because I didn't know which of our devices adjusted automatically and which didn't. The phone did, the computer didn't, who knows if the radio did or didn't. I wasn't wearing a watch. It was all so confusing! All I knew was

Chapter 2 ... Heading South

it was sunny outside and the shadows were headed a little bit east ... we were together, going in the right direction. Everything else would sort itself out.

The route we took through Nevada was a little forlorn. We went south through Wells. I had been texting with my brothers enroute, but suddenly there was a dearth of texting. I didn't realize it at the time, but we had hit a Wi-Fi dead spot. I was driving when we broke free. Five messages came in, one right after another ... *ping, ping, ping, ping, ping*! Poor Harry didn't know what to make of it; I just smiled and felt loved.

We stopped in Ely intending to stay the night. All of the parking spots at the Love's truck stop were back-in spots. We decided to press on toward the next rest stop ... Sunnyside ... forty miles away.

We pulled into the Sunnyside rest stop at about 5 p.m. It had been a long day, and I was a little concerned about the safety of a roadside rest stop with nothing else around. However, it was a wonderful place to stay. It was a lot warmer than Ely and, because it was out in the middle of nowhere, it was quite pleasant. We were having trouble getting the coach leveled. There were only three cars in the rest stop when we arrived. We moved the coach from spot to spot until we found one we were happy with. We had an early dinner of vegetable beef soup. It was a real step up from the unfortunate Subway sandwiches. Afterward, we did normal things like reading and computer work until hitting the hay about 9 p.m. When we got up in the morning, we found four semis and several large RVs had arrived after we did. In retrospect, it felt like a very safe place to stay. We were up at 4:30 a.m. and on the move in one hour ... again.

Chapter 3 ... Lake Havasu Area

Golfing with Larry and Wendy

Larry and Wendy had been in Earp for two weeks. We rolled in, got set up, and had a nice meal with them ... and another, and another. We golfed with them four times and ate with them six times.

Wendy has always been a good example for me. She has a cheerful attitude and rarely lets anything bother her. When we went golfing with the boys, they insisted we play ready golf: they didn't want any chitchatting when it was our turn to address the ball. And so ... we adapted. We played ready golf and rarely spent time looking for balls that strayed into the bushes. It was rattlesnake country and rattlesnake time ... we were no fools. When we got to the 9th hole at Emerald Canyon, the boys lost their balls in the trees and brush. We waited while they searched. In ready golf fashion, we addressed our balls and continued playing, Wendy said, "It's all about them!" We laughed. It was our private joke. After we both hit, we turned around to see where they were. They still had their noses in the bushes, but they still couldn't find Larry's ball. We decided to continue on. As we addressed our balls and continued playing, Wendy said, "It's all about us!" We laughed even more. It was another of our private jokes.

On the Road Again

We had a great week golfing, hiking, and eating, but the internet connectivity was sporadic. I was glad to be back on the road again. We went south to Gila Bend to bypass Phoenix. When we got there, we turned left on a road labeled *Butterfield 8*. I looked up the movie Butterfield 8, starring Elizabeth Taylor and Laurence Harvey: She had a tragic affair with a rich married man. Things were simpler back in 1960.

Chapter 4 ... Tucson

A Cheery Welcome

We got to Rincon East RV Park and sailed right in like we'd done it before ... which, of course, we had. I masked up and went in to register. They had all our paperwork ready for us. I couldn't believe how efficient they were. I didn't even have to give them my name. The person at the front gate had announced us. Everything went as smooth as silk. The only glitch was the last four digits of the card on file were different than the one I normally use. No problem. I gave them the new card number. I was all paid up and had all the paperwork in hand when I happened to glance at the site number. (Aack!) It wasn't my site, and we weren't Lynn and Fred Rupp. Those lucky Rupps! Their whole five-month stay was paid for with my credit card! Well, everyone in the office jumped into action. Within minutes, the credit card payment was reversed and the paperwork was reissued. The person at the front gate hadn't said the Hoffmans were coming, they had announced "the last check in" had arrived. As far as the office knew, only the Rupps were left to check in that day. Even though they were expecting us soon, I hadn't given them an exact date. The park had changed ownership during the summer. The people in the office were new to me and I to them. There's probably a lesson in there somewhere. I'll probably have to learn it a few more times!

Getting to Know You

After the horrendous mailbox incident, I became the one who parked the motor home in close quarters. We drove right to our spot, turned the corner, and I proceeded to back into the spot. When a big rig comes in, everyone (including me) gawks. Between the Happy Hour group across the street, the sunset in the sideview mirrors, and being married to the navigator, my confidence went out the window. It was a messy job, but no tires were blown, no palm trees were decapitated, and no egos were irreparably damaged.

Once in place, I went out to take a picture of our coach and our view to send to my brothers. Sallie, from the Happy Hour group, bopped up and planted herself right in front of me. Hers was the motor home across the street from us during the COVID year. She invited me to meet the members of the group. I was very happy to meet them and wrote all the names down as soon as I got back to the coach: Sallie and Don, Emmett and Sue, Mike and Karen, Dan and Linda, Richard and Gail, and Betty (with Ozzie the Schnauzer) and Robert. They're light drinkers, so a teetotaler like me didn't feel out of place.

SETTLING IN

After resting for a few days, I started painting and filling the front window of the motor home. (I must not have gotten enough of my art on the refrigerator when I was a kid.) I started with a meercat family, a black-backed jackal, a cougar, a wildcat, and three black panthers. (It's hard to paint black animals.) One of my brothers made a comment about Wonder Woman, so up went a painting of Wonder Me: Lynda Carter's body with my face. Kevin suggested it should be on the cover of my next book. That won't happen!

The cougar looked pretty ferocious. Larry, who was parked ten doors down, wanted me to paint a big cougar on his Cougar trailer when he returned after the holidays. I agreed, estimating I had about four weeks to figure out how to do it.

GOLFING TOGETHER

Harry and I were ready to golf together. We started by carving out Tuesday mornings. Our friend John called and said he would join us. Monday night, I jumped up and said, "I can't go golfing, I have a book signing tomorrow!" Harry and John went, and I postponed until the following Monday, having carved out a new schedule.

The next week, Harry and I arrived at the neighborhood golf course, two miles away. We were about an hour early. The tee times were more of a suggestion, so they let us tee off early, following a

Chapter 4 ... Tucson

threesome. They in turn were following a foursome, which was a subset of a sixteen-some. Boy, oh boy, were they pokey! After we made the turn, the guys in front of us invited us to play with them. Their third had just received a call telling him his daughter had died. He left immediately to get a flight back to Kansas City. Sometimes life gets pretty real!

We were in a golf cart because we were playing eighteen holes in eighty-degree weather. . . and because there was a long distance between some holes. After fifteen holes, Harry remarked it felt like we had a flat. Sure enough, we did. It's pretty nice to have a flat in someone else's cart. The clubhouse sent someone right away with a new cart. We swapped out and rejoined our group at the next hole.

At one point Harry and I decided to get amorous (i.e., kissy-faced). He had a wide-brimmed golf hat, I had a wide-brimmed visor. They were effective at keeping the sun off our faces, but as for amorousness ... it was not a pretty sight. Our headdresses collided and our lips barely connected, but only because we both stuck our lips out as far as we could. There might be easier ways to do things, but we never seem to find them.

PEEK-A-BOO!

Getting a motor home detailed after a long drive from home base was a "thing" in Tucson. I contacted Marco from Desert Detailers as soon as we got settled. He had cleaned our coach the previous year and we were very pleased. It's a family business! Marco came on the appointed morning. The crew began by pressure washing the coach. Harry and I had breakfast while they were setting up, then Harry went off to golf. I, on the other hand, felt the call of nature. It was no problem since all the blinds were closed. As I was resting in the restroom, I felt the whole coach shake. *What in the world*, I wondered. It continued to shake ... I continued to wonder. All of a sudden, I realized one of guys had been climbing up the ladder and was walking on the roof! I could see clearly through the skylight above the shower (next to the throne). Let me tell you, I got out of there as quickly as I could!

A LITTLE DIP

I went to the grocery store to pick up a few things, including dip for Harry. It was 6 p.m. on the day before Thanksgiving. What was I thinking! I had a list in hand, but I didn't know the store, so I had to keep retracing my steps in order to get everything. Finally, I was finished, in more ways than one. Back home, when I was putting things away, I realized I had everything but dip. I apologized to my hubby, telling him, "After I got the cheese spread, I was looking for dip, got distracted, and couldn't hold a thought." We laughed together, hugged, and acknowledged this was our life now. *(Sigh!)*

Chapter 5 ... Tucson

Farmers Market

Every other Tuesday, there was a Farmers Market and Craft Sale in the park. I always had a book-signing table. It took a lot of energy to smile at people for three hours when only about five were interested in buying a book, especially when sitting between two busy craft tables. I began painting a picture at my table hoping it would make me seem less desperate. The other vendors, most of whom got tired at the same rate I did, enjoyed watching the progress.

Painting a Cougar on a Trailer

My Cougar friend, Larry, returned to the park after Christmas with some new information. Nothing would stick to the gel-coat on his rig ... not paint, not decals. The only way for him to have a cougar painted on his rig would be to sand off the gel-coat. Fortunately, he didn't want to go to that extreme. I was off the hook. A month later, I did a double take as I was passing his trailer. He had two half-moon cat eyes, with angry LED eyebrows pasted on the exterior of the front. With just those two decorations and a little imagination, the whole front of his trailer looks like a Cougar!

Golfing

Harry and I golfed together every Monday. We usually used a golf cart, but one day he decided he'd walk the course. Now, I usually sit on the right side of the cart. You wouldn't think it would be a big deal to switch sides, but I had my problems. When I piled into the driver's side, I hit my head on the roof *(Ooh!)* ... kind of hard. The next time I got in, I hit my head again *(Ooh!)* ... and again *(Ooh!)* ... and again *(Ooh!)*. I was bonking my head about 50% of the time. Finally, I tied my sweater to the roof so I couldn't get in without ducking. My bonkage score instantly dropped to below 10% ... but not by much. Harry wasn't very sympathetic ... who would be!

CLUB FINANCING

There was always something going on in the park. There were a lot of clubs, including Lapidary, Woodworking, Astronomy, Bocce Ball, Dog Club, Shuffleboard, Ceramics, Rincon Singers, Arts and Crafts, Design, and more. The park provided staff to organize activities, but they didn't foot the bill unless it was a nightclub show ... even then, they sold tickets to cover the expenses. The individual clubs had their own expenses, usually for equipment. Consequently, they needed to have fundraisers. There were two types of fundraisers. The first type was ticket sales for a dinner or ice cream social. (The Design Club sponsored the Sloppy Joe dinner; the Astronomy Club sponsored the Chili feed. Participants brought their own plates, glasses, napkins, and utensils ... the club provided the food.) The other type of fundraiser was a 50-50 raffle: The club kept half of the proceeds from raffle sales and paid out the remainder as $10 prizes.

DESIGN CLUB

When I explored the park, I found out there was going to be a group activity to decorate the auditorium. I wanted in. I learned the Design Club was in charge of decorating and they were sponsoring the Sloppy Joe dinner the following week. In fact, the Design Club was responsible for decorating the auditorium for every holiday. I joined up right away.

Harry and I went to the Sloppy Joe dinner with the people in our little knitting group: Kate and Irv, Kathy and Joe, and Minnesota-Carol and Scott. Harry golfed with Irv and Joe; I did artsy-crafty things with Kate, Kathy, and Carol; all of us were dog people. We felt right at home with each other. There was a numbered ticket on each table and, wouldn't you know it, our number was called first. We felt like winners from the get-go! We marched through the kitchen, filled up our plates, and returned to the table for a pleasant sociable meal. That's when I realized the dinners were more about relationships and supporting the clubs than about food. But it's nice when the food is good, too.

Chapter 5 ... Tucson

The next morning, I went into the kitchen to see if any help was needed cleaning the previous night's pans. When I walked into the auditorium, the main lights were out. Some of the Christmas displays, including the six-foot nativity scene, were lit up. A Toy Store bedsheet mural, which was hung in front of a window, was backlit by the morning sun. I felt as if I was looking into a toy store from the sidewalk, at night. The whole auditorium was stunning.

COFFEE AND DONUTS

Coffee and Donuts is a weekly event at the park ... every Wednesday morning. It's a venue for keeping guests and residents up to date on the events taking place during the upcoming month. January and February are the peak months. Entertainment, raffles, and guest speakers are also featured. The event is funded by businesses who send reps to give us a ten-minute pitch. We've had businesses like RV sales, healthcare, bike maintenance, and insurance. It's all very interesting. The park has it down to a science. Each week, a business springs for coffee and donuts; One of the clubs sponsors the 50-50 raffle, makes the coffee, serves the donuts, and cleans up afterward. Many hands ...!

RINCON SINGERS

The Rincon Singers is a genial little chorus of about twenty people. Our club's only expense was the top-notch pianist from outside the park hired to accompany us. In December, we sang a medley of Christmas songs at Coffee and Donuts, one of which was *The Chipmunk Song*. We sang it with regular voices the first time and chipmunk voices the second time. Sandy, who was new to the chorus asked me if we could be naughty. Before she clarified what she had in mind, I said, "Sure!" She wanted to have a pushing contest, but she didn't want to surprise me lest one of us would fall and break a hip. (Shoot, we have to think about those things, now!) We planned our mischief. During the presentation, when we sang "Me, I want a hula hoop," it was all or nothing ... we gave it our all. Our "fight" in the soprano section was short-lived ... no one was injured.

The chorus usually sings at the 50th Anniversary Celebration in February. There were twelve couples who had celebrated their 50th anniversary in the last two years. We were making up for time lost during COVID.

Christmas Dinner

For Christmas, there was a big ham dinner at the park at noon. Here's how it worked. Groups of people purchased each table. The money from the sale of tables went to purchasing hams. The people who sponsored the tables brought their own table service and decorated their tables. The Activity Office purchased the hams and delivered one to each table sponsor, who then cooked the ham. The other people at the table provided the side dishes for their table. Since we were visiting John and his wife Arlene in the evening, we didn't go to the Christmas Dinner. It was sure quiet in the park at midday!

More Design Club

After the start of the new year, we tore down the Christmas decorations and stored them in the loft. In less than two hours, the whole auditorium looked like a Parisian café, complete with black-and white checkered tablecloths on every table and a seven-foot Eiffel Tower in the corner next to an outdoor café display.

Happy Hour

Happy Hour, across the street from our RV site, was up and running all through COVID, but I didn't get to know those folks until after I got my vaccination.

Harry kept to himself pretty much, but he was in and out of the coach with the dogs multiple times during the day. He said whenever he went by Happy Hour, he always waved. But they began teasing me about him being reclusive almost to the point of questioning whether or not he existed. Harry's not a joiner, which just increased the mystique. Harry sightings were rare (like Sasquatch or the Loch Ness Monster), unless one was looking out on Happy Street at 8:05 a.m. when Harry walked the dogs every day … like clockwork.

Chapter 5 ... Tucson   155

Robert and Betty

I went across the street to Happy Hour one night. We were having a nice little visit when Robert said something about Betty's feet being cold. Betty agreed, saying she hadn't gotten any of her socks out of storage. She simply wasn't ready for the cold weather. I noticed her feet were smaller than mine and I had some little socklettes that didn't fit me very well. I went back to the motor home and pulled out a pair I knew would match what she was wearing. When I returned, I had my hands on my hips in order to hide the socklettes, and a stern look on my face. Everyone had instant flashbacks to their scolding mothers and started mumbling, "Uh-oh ... uh-oh." I walked over, stopping right in front of Betty. The rest of the group said, "Uh-oh ... it's Betty!" Then I said with a very deliberate voice, "You ... can ... not ... say ... no!" I handed her the socklettes. She accepted them but said she couldn't put them on right away because her feet were dirty. I stood up again and approached her, taking her blanket, saying, with a sigh, "Do I have to do everything?" As I held the blanket up as a screen, she put the socks on and conversations started up again. Suddenly, she announced with a loud slow Kentucky drawl, "Thay's a hole in this one!" I was moderately mortified. A little bit later, Robert asked her how her feet were. She declared "Thay're wa-arm," she exclaimed as she beamed.

Now Robert is just as sweet as can be. When Betty tells him to do something, he immediately responds in an even cadence, "What ... ever ... you ... say ... Dear." Everybody loves him. (He calls me young lady ... what's not to love!)

We all got to talking about the Pajama Dance coming up later in the week and how the organizers said, "Wear pajamas ... but if you sleep in the buff, please go buy pajamas!" For some reason, the next thing we knew, Betty bluntly announced, "Robert isn't wearing any underwear." Everybody got a real big kick out of her comment! Then Betty continued in her thick Kentucky accent, "Maybe Kathy will go back to her motor home and get a pair of Har-ry's shorts for

Robert. Ah'd like to see tha-at!" It just went downhill from there as shock turned into laughter!

... AND OZZIE

Betty has a little Schnauzer named Ozzie. She and Ozzie go everywhere together in her hot pink golf cart. A lot of people have golf carts, but Betty's golf cart has personality! The headlights have gigantic curved foot-long black eyelashes.

Sometimes Robert rides with Betty and Ozzie, but Ozzie gets the front seat ... Robert rides on the back seat ... facing backward! A couple of times per season, the park has a golf cart parade: Robert, still riding backward, waves like Queen Elizabeth. What a sport!

Chapter 6 ... Tucson ... Day at the Races

Robert Stirred the Pot

The horse races in the park were legendary; they occurred at the end of January. For several years, the Astronomy Club hosted a Chili Feed and A Day at the Races at the end of January. Six hobby horses were auctioned off in mid-January. The owners had two weeks to decorate them. As a newcomer, I had not been to the races, but that all changed fast.

Robert wanted a horse, but he didn't want to have any responsibility for decorating the horse. He cornered me one day saying he wanted to have partners go in with him on buying a horse. I liked the idea. I found out horses had sold for up to $180 in the past. It was way too stiff for my pocketbook, but I figured if we were going in as partners it wouldn't be too bad. I hemmed and hawed my way into thinking about it.

The next time we got together for Happy Hour, Robert and I laid out a plan. One by one, the attendees decided they were in: Sallie and Don, Linda and Dan, Karen and Mike, Betty and Robert, John from Utah, Sue and Emmett, and Kathy and Harry. Before long, we had an idea of how we were going to decorate our horse. With potential decorations in mind and a lot of people involved, it looked like our exposure would be about $30 per family. Everyone decided I would be the one to do the bidding since I was the newbie. Robert had stirred the pot ... I was the pot. And that's how it all started.

Getting Ready for a Day at the Races

I was pretty excited about my new responsibility. I checked around to find out how much the horses would sell for and whether or not I should buy one of the first few horses or wait for one of the last ones. Coffee and Donuts was the day of the auction! I was so focused on my bidding responsibility I totally spaced on anything else. But my alarm went off at 8:15 a.m. and I suddenly realized the Rincon Singers were sponsoring the 50-50 raffle. I was supposed to be at the rec hall selling tickets soon. The day was getting bigger by the minute.

I ran to the rec hall to sell tickets and dole out donuts with the rest of the chorus. At 9 a.m., Freedom RV made a short presentation. Then the chorus gave out the 50-50 prizes: We had made $260 from raffle sales and gave away thirteen $10 prizes. After a brief introduction, we went right to the main event: the auctioning of horses for the big horse race.

STEPPING BACK FOR CONTEXT

The Astronomy Club has a magnificent digital telescope housed in a building by the pickleball courts. The building has a sliding roof that is opened after dark on Sunday evenings for special viewing sessions deep into space. They host the annual Chili Dinner and Horse Race. The proceeds from the *sale of tickets* for the Chili Dinner goes to the Astronomy Club. The proceeds from the sale of horses (six hobby horses with plywood heads on five-foot sticks) goes to the Owners' Pool. The Owners' Pool is split among the six winners with a little extra going to the winner of the last race. There's a ton of betting on the day of the races. The proceeds from the betting go back to the bettors, although not on a one-to-one basis.

GOING ... GOING ... GONE!

There were five sturdy-looking horses and one old nag: Horse Number 2 looked like it had seen better days ... much better days. It didn't have a mane. Its long black cardboard eyelashes were falling off. Some wisps of a former mane were hanging off the sides of the horse's head. Five horses had straight sticks, but poor old Number 2's stick was arced forward, making it look like he was an old plug ready to go to the glue factory. He was pitiful.

I wanted him in the worst way!

Chapter 6 ... Tucson ... Day at the Races

I started the bidding on Number 1 ... "$30." It didn't take long before we were at $35 and then $40. The Astronomy Club had imported an auctioneer from The Gaslight Theater in downtown Tucson to run the auction. He was trying to up the bidding increments to $10. I was having none of that ... "$41," I hollered. Pretty soon he got us back on fives and tens. I threw up a couple more ridiculous bids, grateful to be outbid by someone else. Number 1 went right up to $105 and sat there: "Going ... Going ... Gone!" Someone was the proud owner of Number 1, but *I had figured out how the bidding worked.*

Number 2 came up for bid. My strategy was to downplay the horse. "He's lame!" I hollered. Unfortunately, the club leader announced this pathetic horse had won about 30% of the races. I had my work cut out for me. I let the others bid for a little while and then up went my hand. A few phony bids later and I shook my head saying, "It's too much for me." The auctioneer got the bid up to $100.

"Going ... Going ..."

"$105!" I blurted out. Seconds later that lame, bald, pathetic horse was mine (ours). I ran up to the stage and got him.

Number 3 got accolades as being the winning-est horse of all time. The bidding was going up, but I couldn't stand it, I had to get in on it. I was grateful when I was outbid. I mean, who wants to have two horses!

And so on and so on, until we got to Number 6. Now Number 6 had an even sadder story than Number 2 because it was announced to be the losing-est horse of all time. Right off the bat, I bid $20 and then before anyone could say anything, I bid $25. "She's bidding against herself!" exclaimed the auctioneer whipping around on the stage. And then I was finished. I stroked Number 2's maneless neck and muzzle while the bidding for Number 6 went up to $90. Kat from the Astronomy Club had herself a horse. The other three horses had gone for similar prices.

Box Seats

Next up was the auction of three box seats (two people per box). The box seats are coveted because people in the box seats are treated like royalty. Club members bring them their chili dinner, run to place their bets, bring their winnings to them, and hang around to take care of their every whim. I thought it would be fun to get box seats, but Betty said "No, no, no!" in her Kentucky drawl. She and Robert had gotten them one year. The box seats were in front of the tables, right below the stage. Betty said she had felt isolated from her friends. As we sat there through the rest of the auction, Don, one of my silent partners, leaned my way and told me Number 2 was the ugliest horse of all. I beamed. He really understood!

He's a She

The next day at 3 p.m. I sketched out a drawing of our horse, Elizabeth, to be dressed up like the queen. I dropped the sketch off at Happy Hour, but I had to scoot because I was needed elsewhere. Afterward, I connected with Sallie, who had ended up with the drawing. She said the group liked the basic idea. She had some great ideas for how to embellish it. Sallie and I made plans to go to a thrift shop the next day. We'd look for a pastel coat. I was hoping we could find a lab coat in medium blue. Harry and I have golf club covers that look like Corgi heads. One Corgi cover could ride in a handbag attached to Elizabeth's right arm, the other could be in her left pocket. The only thing we didn't know how to do was make her hair. But I was confident we'd get some inspiration at the thrift shop. Sue had only one request … our horse had to sparkle! Our pathetic lame horse was going to be a queen in more ways than one.

Shopping for the Horse Race

We had less than a week to outfit Queenie (new name) so she didn't look like a lame old nag going out for her last run! Sallie and I took off on a shopping spree. Our first stop was Injoy, a gigantic

Chapter 6 ...Tucson ...Day at the Races

thrift store with friendly helpers reminiscent of the 80s. We wandered through the aisles and eventually found a small plaid wool jacket in mint green and white. There were silver chains adorning the pockets. It was perfect. It would fit our Queenie to a tee! As we wandered farther, we found various skirts, but each was a little lighter than the mint green. None of them looked right. Suddenly, we came upon a teal skirt. Holding it up against the mint green jacket, we realized we had hit pay dirt. Off we went to check out purses, hats, and shoes. We found a hat in the exact style the queen wears. Unfortunately, it was almost cherry red making us shudder slightly. Nevertheless, into the cart it went. Style trumped color.

When we got to the purse section, we found a cherry-red purse and sandals to match the hat. We were ecstatic. We found a pair of small white socks, which we could stretch over cardboard to look like lovely delicate hooves. We were thrilled to discover a pearl necklace, pearl earrings, and a sparkly diamond brooch. Finally, we found a dark purple boa interwoven with metallic silver threads, which would be perfect as a royal sash. With Sallie's twenty-five-percent military discount, our grand total came to $31.12. I couldn't believe it!

Our outfit was almost complete. On the way home, Sallie and I stopped by the park's Arts and Crafts room. There was a half skein of champagne yarn just waiting for us in the free bin. It had potential. I crocheted about fifty feet of chain stitches, gathered them together, and stepped back to take a look. When it was stitched to the inside brim of the hat, it would hang down like three inches of curly hair. The earrings would hang from the hat. Queenie would be perfectly coiffed.

Karen had contributed a tiara, which was easily tacked to the front of the hat. We still needed supports for the shoulders, the hat, and the skirt. Robert was enlisted. Soon he had a pattern to take to the woodshop. The woodshop was closed on the weekend, and Robert was a busy man. He was involved in building a shed for Don and Sallie and upgrading the candles at his church nearby. Nevertheless, a couple of days later the supports were mocked up, measured, glued, and ready to be attached to our pretty little mare's body in plenty of time.

Sallie sent me a link to a picture of the Queen as I had been recruited to repaint Queenie's eyes and lips. Karen had suggested our pretty little mare have some teeth. Since only the Queen's uppers showed in her picture, Queenie sported new pink lips and a new set of smudged uppers. A few brushstrokes later and her eyelids sagged slightly ... Oh, those Royals.

DRESSING QUEENIE

At Happy Hour on Tuesday, the impromptu penultimate assembly began. People were concerned when Robert kept looking up Queenie's skirt to measure and adjust the fitting for the hips. Robert was undaunted. Even though he lives a few spaces down from the Happy Hour location, all the tools needed to assemble our pretty little mare were in the back of his truck. He drove to Happy Hour. He did a masterful job of measuring where the hat, shoulders, and hips needed to be supported. Everything was done properly. Even the screwheads: he got to work countersinking them into the wooden supports. A few marks for the tail, and Robert was ready to go to work. We undressed Queenie and took her to his truck for bionic modifications.

At one point during Happy Hour, Robert one of the most mild-mannered gentlemen you could imagine, startled us all by shouting: "Oh ... no!" (With his Kentucky accent, it sounded like "oh now!") It was so uncharacteristic it stopped all side conversations. It seems his beer can had somehow tipped over and was draining into the gravel.

"No problem," said Dan, "I'll get you another beer."

"Oh ... no!" Robert drawled mournfully, slowly shaking his head slowly from side to side, "Betty ... will be so ... upset ... with ... me."

Chapter 6 ...Tucson ...Day at the Races

None of us could quite imagine how Betty could be so upset, especially since she wasn't there. Betty is one of the most social and mild-mannered people you'd ever hope to meet. We were all tickled trying to imagine Betty lowering the boom on Robert.

HAPPY ENDING

I told the group I had a tail for the horse and planned to attach it with a hanger bent to shape. Pretty soon Robert leaned into the back of his truck and fished out several spring steel rods. He said, "Betty made me pack all that stuff in the truck before we left Kentucky. I don't know why ... she made me pack ... it ... but ... she ... did." I was having trouble imagining Betty getting involved with the man stuff needed to fill a truck full of tools. But I went with the flow and gratefully selected one of the rods. I passed it to Robert. While I busied myself pinning up Queenie's skirt, Robert crafted a screw loop at each end of the rod and passed it to me. I bent it in the center and passed it back to him. He twisted it around itself for a little extra strength and passed it back to me. While he was getting some screws to attach the tail to the horse, I wove the rod through the braided champagne yarn. Bingitty, Bangitty, Boom! Our horse's tail was locked on forever. Our pretty little Queenie was looking very smart with her purple sash, her white hooves, her tiara, and her red bag complete with Corgi. She was looking better by the moment.

As usually happens with any group project, there was a major last-minute adjustment needed. Karen was concerned anyone with a hankering could peer into Queenie's cleavage. A modesty panel was required. A quick search of the motor home turned up a hot pink cowl, which was an ideal backdrop for the pearl necklace. Queenie was dressed to the nines. There couldn't be another horse to match her for poise and confidence ... and, with any luck, for speed.

Sue and Emmett planned to run to the auditorium early on the day of the races to secure two tables so our entire entourage could sit together. Harry was going to make one of his rare appearances.

NOSEDIVE

As Happy Hour continued, Queenie, fully dressed, was resting behind me against the front of Dan's truck. The wind kicked up a little bit while we were visiting. Dan and Don could see there was a problem a-brewing. Dan said (in the normal street voice), "Kathy, the horse might blow over." Well, who can hear a normal street voice when we're all laughing? He said it again just as Queenie took a nosedive, literally. We got her upright, none the worse for the wear. I took her back to the motor home to rest up for her big day.

LOST

Somehow, in all the excitement of dressing Queenie, I misplaced my lone needle. It was nowhere to be found, and I needed to do some final basting. I had to go across the street and borrow one from Linda. She looked all through her trailer and barely found one. I got to work. With the basting completed and the skirt tacked to the jacket, Queenie was ready for anything.

SMACK TALK ... TAKE A LITTLE, GIVE A LITTLE

The next day was Coffee and Donuts ... one more time before the Big Race. The Astronomy Club was working on the 50-50 raffle. One member, Katherine, from the chorus, knew I had purchased a horse and, as luck would have it, she had purchased one, too. She started baiting me. She kept verbally jabbing me about how much faster her horse was until I finally declared her horse could kiss our pretty little (oops). Shortly thereafter, I realized that I had used the correct genus but the wrong species. I went back to her and corrected myself ... her horse could kiss my pretty little mare. All was well in our world.

During Coffee and Donuts, Katherine's horse made his debut on the stage. He was actually quite gorgeous. He had a stunningly painted face and a bridle. Afterward, I complimented her on his good looks. But soon she started baiting me again saying her beautiful stallion would beat all of the horses. I couldn't let her comments go. I told

Chapter 6 ... Tucson ... Day at the Races

her she could kiss the championship goodbye ... and I told her why! The revelation marked the end of our conversation!

THE BIG REVEAL

There was a heavy wind blowing on the evening of the races. Queenie was protected by a large plastic sack as Harry and I headed to the auditorium. "Robert," Katherine's male horse, was dressed for the race and ready to go, meaning he was already propped up against the curtain on the stage with a couple of other horses. Seconds later, Queenie occupied the space next to Katherine's Robert.

There was one table reserved for each of the owners. Harry and I sat with Linda and Dan, Mike and Karen, and Sue and Emmett. Sue was wearing a broad-brimmed black sun hat fit for the races. Earlier, Sue had grabbed a nearby table to accommodate the rest of our entourage John from Utah, Betty and Robert, Don and Sallie, and their guests, Michelle and her son Noah. (Noah was 15 ... it must have been a torturous evening for him.)

DINNERTIME

One by one the remaining horses arrived. Wally, not shy around a microphone, was the emcee. He said we would have the chili dinner first and then proceed with the races. After he led a blessing, the owners' tables were called first. Wally called numbers one and two at the same time. Eighteen hungry people jumped up, grabbed their bowls, and ran for the chow line. Nobody missed a beat. Great vats of chili we're waiting for us in the rec hall. We all filed by army style, holding out our bowls as ladle after ladle of chili was dispensed by members of the Astronomy Club. (The chili reminded Harry of his mom's bean soup. She always fixed it on the first evening of every visit. It was a warm memory.) Tiny containers of sour cream, cheese, and diced onions were piled onto our plates or balanced precariously in a spare hand as we proceeded back to our tables.

Robert came by our table and asked if anyone wanted a mint julep. Well, you can't say no to Robert's mint juleps. He had the makings at the other table and said he'd come by shortly with one. I asked him to make mine a tiny one (fingertips spread to one-half inch). But Robert, Kentucky through and through, said they came in one size only. I went to one inch and he rolled his eyes out of pity. Two inches produced a similar response. Not until I hit three inches did he agree to make me the drink.

Betty put some special dip on each of our two tables, saying Robert had been making it all day. Goodness, I was starting to feel a little guilty for reading all day. And so we ate and laughed through the entire meal. I noticed Karen was a little hesitant sitting next to Harry. Perhaps she's not used to someone who doesn't drink, join, or gamble.

When the meal was winding down, I took a large plastic bag from under the table and trotted off to the restroom where I changed into a long black-and-white sundress. On top of everything, I planted a magnificent large-brimmed black poofy see-through bonnet ... reminiscent of the large hats worn at the Kentucky Derby ... right on top of my head. With all the decorations on the hat, it spanned a full eighteen inches. I, too, was ready for the races.

Chapter 6 … Tucson … Day at the Races 167

Harry & Kathy

Linda & Dan

Part Five –Rejoining the World …… 2021-22

Mike & Karen

Sue & Emmett

Chapter 6 … Tucson … Day at the Races 169

John from Utah

Betty & Robert

Part Five –Rejoining the World …… 2021-22

Don & Sallie

Noah & Michelle

THE PARADE OF HORSES

Wally had the owners come up on the stage to introduce their horses. Katherine came up and trotted Robert around the stage. She had him bow a few times.

Next up was our pretty little mare. I walked Queenie out to the edge of the stage to announce her: "This is Queenie! She comes to you from a padded paddock in Hampstead Heath just north of London." (Evidently, the audience was pleased with the introduction ... they applauded.) I continued, "She trained for the races in the canals of Teddington." (They applauded again, but we had a solid backstory yet to come!) "She is accompanied by her trusted Corgi companion, Eva, Duchess of Bristol." (They applauded the Corgi.) After a few seconds, the applause died out. I leaned forward as if telling a secret, "I wasn't going to tell you this, but Horse Number 1 besmirched Queenie. He said he was going to leave her in the dust. But that won't happen." I twisted her back and forth, her tail shimmering in the spotlight, saying, "She's in heat!" And with that, amid hooting and hollering, the introduction was finished.

Number 3 was introduced as Miss Patience. The owner said she was inspired by a recent sermon. Uh-oh, I thought, *this might be a difficult one to beat*. She was dressed in a plumed hat, sparkly mask, and had a feather-light boa wrapped around her neck. Simple but stunning.

Number 4 was called The Snake Charmer. She looked a little sad with a dull gray turban on her head and a multicolored knitted snake wrapped around her neck. When the owner announced the snake had been knitted with love and would soon be given to a favorite grandchild, it all made sense.

Number 5 was called Stargazer. The owner was quick to tell us this horse had no gender. There was a two-foot rocket ship attached to both sides of the stick and a large starry beach ball taped to the top of the head. Even though the horse had no gender, during one of the races it had a wardrobe malfunction and everything had to stop until it was corrected. We're nothing, if not proper.

Number 6, originally booked as the losing-est horse of all time, had a piece of spring steel attached to her head. At the end of the spring steel was a long orange carrot dangling precariously in front of her nose. It looked like this horse might really do something this year!

Chapter 6 ... Tucson ... Day at the Races

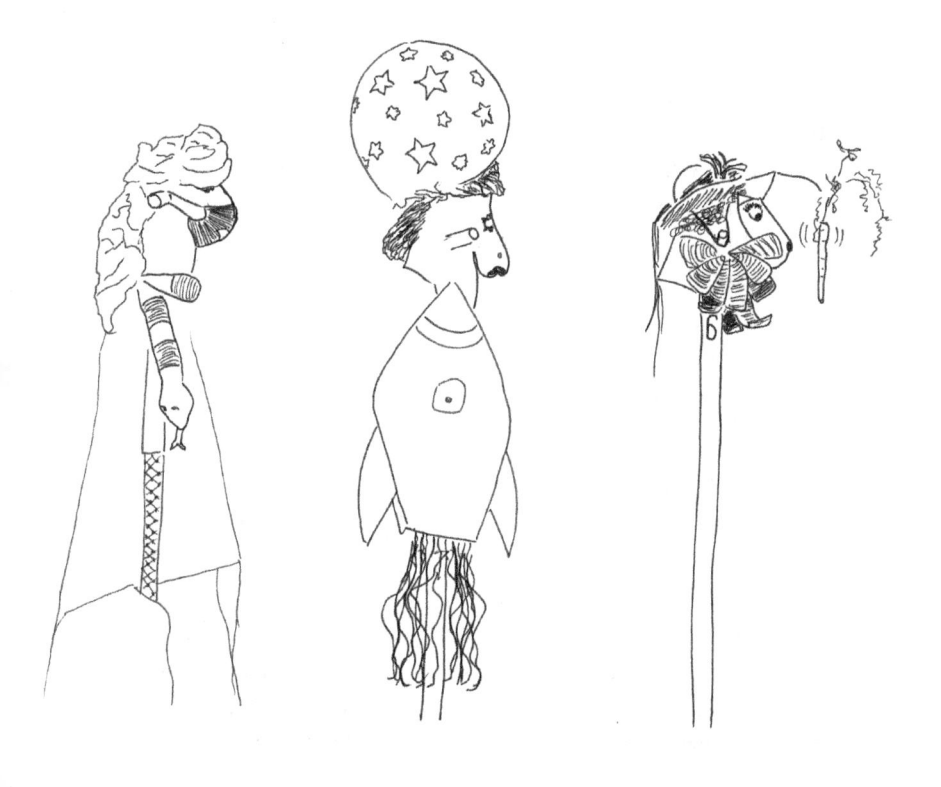

Best Dressed

Before the races started in earnest, Wally announced there would be a contest to see which was the best-dressed horse. One at a time, he had each of the owners bring the horses to center stage. The audience's applause would determine the winner. I was hoping Queenie would be a shoo-in. Robert got a healthy amount of applause. Queenie got noise like you wouldn't believe! Miss Patience got an equal amount of noise … most of it came from Table 3. The owners of Miss Patience were former vineyard owners who had brought some of their bounty … the table occupants were feeling no pain! The other three horses got a moderate amount of applause. Wally declared a tie and said we would have to vote again between Queenie and Miss Patience. From where I stood it was a dead heat. Wally asked if the organizers had two prizes. They didn't. He hemmed and hawed, finally declaring Queenie the Best-Dressed. I gladly accepted a bottle of red wine "on behalf of all thirteen owners of our stable."

The Goal

Here's how a race worked: A six by seven grid of two-foot squares was taped on the stage. All the bingo balls from 1 through 6 and 10 through 69 were put in the bingo machine. When a bingo ball was drawn, the leading number on the ball determined who would get to move: For example, if 26 came up, Number 2 would move one square; if 63 came up, Number 6 would move one square, and so on. The six horses and riders stood behind the starting line. They had to traverse seven squares to get to the finish line. Pretty simple.

Exact Change Only

Before the first race started, the betting lines opened. Wally said the betting had to be done with exact change. No one would be providing any change at any time! Oops, I was a little concerned because I had planned to bet $2 on Queenie in every race, but I had five singles and several twenties. Without the ability to get

Chapter 6 ... Tucson ... Day at the Races

change, I was afraid it might be an expensive evening. The audience approached the betting tables. Staying in character, I bid $2 on Queenie ... and only Queenie. I was pleased when Wally announced there was leftover chili in large tubs and anyone interested could buy some to take home. I got excited at the thought of breaking some of my twenties. I went back to the kitchen and confessed why I was buying the chili. I returned with a bucket of chili, a five, and five ones. Emmett, who had bid $2 on Stargazer in the first race and won $13, was kind enough to break my five. I was ready for a modest bet on every race.

JOCKEYS, WINNINGS, AND MINT JULEPS

Different jockeys were called up for each race. For the first race, Wally asked for volunteers who were new to the park. Janet, a friend from the chorus, jumped up and raced to the stage. She grabbed Queenie. Emmett, right behind her, grabbed Robert. Stargazer won with odds of six and a half to one. Lucky Emmett! Meanwhile, Harry had had his fill of fun for the evening. Waving goodbye to everyone, he took an early departure ... with the bucket of chili and the dirty dishes.

In the second race veterans were the volunteer jockeys. Don was up there riding Robert. It was a dead heat until Number 6 popped across the finish line chasing her carrot.

Since I had been appreciating the smell of the mint julep for about an hour, I took it up a notch. I had a sip ... just a tiny sip, mind you. Each time I sipped, I had to wait for about ten minutes until the buzz wore off.

Jockeys for the third race were chosen from those 65 and under. Stargazer won ... again.

In the fourth race, the jockeys were chosen from people seventy and over. This time the winner was Robert, jockeyed by Don while Linda rode Queenie.

When the fifth race was called, the jockeys were seventy-five and up. One of them had to be helped on and off the stage. Mike was, by far, the best jockey of the night. He raced up to the stage and clambered aboard Queenie straddling her tail. When the time came, he used an imaginary crop like there was no tomorrow. Every time Queenie's number was called, Mike jumped around like a crazed grasshopper and rode her for all he was worth ... advancing twenty-four inches at a time. But still ... she failed to finish. Stargazer won for a third time!

I was beginning to be embarrassed about going to the betting table to bet on Queenie, but I did it one final time. Perhaps this would be her race. According to tradition, the owners rode their horses in the last race. Sue went up to represent our team. This time, Snake Charmer, who had been quite slow in coming out of the gate in the previous race (so much so they had to ask if the gate was open), was the winner. It was all very satisfying.

What can I say. Perhaps our motto should have been "Set the Bar Low." Nevertheless, I was pleased Queenie ran in each race ... never getting stuck behind an imaginary starting gate ... never finishing dead last. We didn't have to worry about getting any money back from the Owners' Pool. The owners of Stargazer got half of it! With our low-bar showing, all we did was feed our horse. *Oh well*, I thought, *maybe next year*. The only horses who weren't "in the money" were the two best-dressed mares. *(Sigh!)*

John was sitting a little too close to the mint juleps at the other table. Every time I came by to say hello, he would see me in my big poofy hat and begin singing the theme from Moulin Rouge: "Whenever we kiss ... I worry and wonder ... Your lips may be near ... but where is your heart?" Oh, those mint juleps!

UNDRESSING QUEENIE

At the next Happy Hour, it was time to uncloak our little Queenie. I got there late just as Robert was leaving. He wanted to know if he should come back with his tool kit. "No," I said, "we can wait another day." And off he went. As I was sitting there, trying to take off the two dozen safety pins, Dan appeared with his electric screwdriver: he couldn't get those screws out fast enough. Oh, those men and their tools! Then Karen started helping with the safety pins. Straight pins, safety pins, basted curls, and earrings ... everything came off. Pretty soon we had a naked mare with a pretty smile, a modest pile of clothing to donate back to the Thrift Store, and a lot of memories.

FOUND

As I was removing the earrings from Queenie's hat, I discovered my missing needle still stuck in the brim of the hat where I had last used it. It had survived traveling to and fro and a full six races, including Mike's jockeying! How in the world did the needle make it through all the commotion for two full days? Linda and I were both shocked.

GENTEEL

When I returned the handful of screws to Robert, he and Betty were fixing dinner, but they said to come in and visit for a few minutes. We laughed when Betty said, "Har-ry shook mah hay-and," as she held out her hand to an imaginary Harry. "He's a re-al gentleman!" Then, in one fluid motion, she raised her wrist, palm down, tilted her head demurely to the side, casting her eyes downward. Did her eyelids flutter slightly? In an instant we were all fifty years younger.

Chapter 7 ... Tucson

Drenched

Sally, from the church office back home, emailed me to ask if I would record a video of the prayer for Sunday's service. I'd done it before with my smart phone. It's not terribly difficult once you get yourself framed just right. I said I would. I planned to do it after Coffee and Donuts on Wednesday.

When I got back to the motor home, it was time to record. It's always a smart idea to check hair, wrinkles, and lighting before recording. My hair was flat: the poofy waves normally gracing the top of my head were lifeless. I tried to renew it by spritzing water on it and using a little gel but nothing would work. Finally, I gave up completely and combed it forward covering my eyes: flat and wet. We'd had a bad rain storm earlier in the week. I looked like I'd been sitting out in it ... a drowned rat! I looked even worse because the morning sun shining through the window played up all my wrinkles. I figured this was probably as bad as it could get! (Set the bar low!) I started the video by saying, "Greetings from Arizona! Contrary to popular opinion it's not always warm and dry here." I finished the recording and sent it in. And they used it! The only person to comment was my dear friend, Marg. Even so, she pussyfooted around it by asking if I was wearing my hair in a different style. We had a good laugh. She was glad to hear it was a one-time hairstyle!

Out to Dinner

At the end of the season, the Happy Hour group decided to go out to dinner. Thirty minutes later we were sitting at a long table on the covered patio at Hacienda Del Sol. Shortly after we arrived, the manager retracted the massive cover resulting in an open-air setting ... ten tables and a piano on a pleasant March evening in Tucson. It was glorious. After we ordered, we continued to visit. In the blink of an eye, four servers decked out in maroon outfits, swept down

Chapter 7 ...Tucson

on our table. Immediately there were hors d'oeuvres all around the table. After a little more conversation, some of the platters were removed and suddenly, there they were again, swooping in from all sides. The serving process took seconds, not minutes. It was impressive.

RUNNING FROM THE LAW

Every Monday, Harry and I went golfing at the course two miles down the road. Usually, we were paired with another couple on the spur of the moment. One time we golfed with John and Tim. We all did the little location dance to get acquainted. You know the drill: Where did you come from? John went first. He was from California, but he had moved up to Port Angeles, Washington. We had an immediate connection because I'd been to Port Angeles. A few seconds later we were commiserating about the closure of the ferry route to Victoria because of COVID. Then it was Tim's turn. He said he lived in Arizona but was born in California. He had lived a lot of other places in between, including Pennsylvania, Kansas, and a couple of states beginning with "I." He ended the diatribe with " ... running from the law." With a chuckle I raised my eyebrows. We completed the dance by finishing with our location ... Vancouver ... not Canada but Washington.

Tim, John, and Harry were all very attentive to their golf game. I had to step up my game to keep pace. As we approached the eighth hole by taking one of two winding paths, John was ready to tee off, but Tim was nowhere to be found. Sometimes it's best not to search too hard. Soon enough, Tim came out of the bushes. He wasn't lost, after all. We whacked our way to the green. When Tim was ready to putt, he reached for his putter but it was nowhere to be found. He looked through his bag twice. I provided a second set of eyes. Nothing. Where in the world was his putter? John walked off carrying his bag to ask the group following us if they had seen Tim's putter. Since Tim and John were both walking, Tim was in a bit of a pickle. We offered him the use of our golf cart to check the bushes on the approach to the eighth hole. He set his golf bag precariously in the passenger seat of the cart. I suggested he leave it with us so he wouldn't have any trouble driving. "No, that's okay," he said, and off he went.

No sooner was he gone than I remembered his comment about running from the law. My imagination took off. I settled on several scenarios, none of which were good. He had managed to commandeer everything we'd brought ... all of our belongings ... bags, clubs, phones, wallet ... the whole shooting match! The only exception was the keys to our car! Was he going to pull a runner? Was this a weekly ploy to rip off golfers? Seconds stretched into minutes. I had already developed a scenario where I would take a run at the six-foot chain-link fence, leap over it deftly, and tackle Tim as he was trying to drive away from the golf course in his truck with our stuff. (I didn't take any time to consider how I could scale a six-foot fence skillfully, when it's hard for me to clamber over a two-foot dog fence, gracefully.)

Fortunately, the fence scenario didn't have to play out, because after what seemed like five minutes, but was probably only two, he came driving back in the cart with our belongings, brandishing his putter. He had left it in the bushes at the previous tee. What a relief! Three holes later I told him I was a writer and he was going to be in my next book. We all laughed. Five more holes later, they each bought a copy of my first book!

Chapter 8 ... Tucson ... All About Dogs

Trick Dog

Most years, the Dog Club sponsors a Dog Exhibition at the agility ring. Those who had been working on agility, obedience, and tricks would have their pets perform for the whole park. I had high hopes for Angie being a trick dog. Those hopes were scaled down to a small set of tricks after three months. This was her repertoire:

Push-Ups: A combination of sits and downs. (The dog follows a treat two inches from her nose as the handler says the magic words ... up, down, up, down, etc.) Naturally, with Angie's short little Corgi legs, I had to bend at the waist to reach her nose level.

Whisper: I wanted her to communicate to me she was tired. Whisper means using her indoor voice to make a little guttural noise rather than a shrill yap. AKC-Carol axed the trick because no one would be able to hear it.

Pillow, Sit, Down, Nap: I wanted her to go to her pillow, lay down with her head on the pillow, and take a nap.

There were several minor difficulties associated with training a dog to do these tricks ... including the one where they learn the trick but then don't feel like doing it. To avoid the difficulties, I had to have treats readily available. As Carol continually reminds us: Give the treat immediately for even a partial effort on the dog's part. Even with the knowledge that she would get a treat, the repertoire was way too complicated. I did some combining. Push-ups and nap were the only two tricks we would perform. They were easy to practice because Harry and I were working with both dogs to learn the nap trick for general use around the motor home (on a rainy day the nap command made it easy to dry the dogs' feet).

EXPLOSION

Now Corgis are famous for their short legs ... and I'm a tall person. Consequently, in order for me to give a treat immediately, I had to bend at the waist into an L-shape. And so I did. It didn't take Harry long to get disgusted with my training techniques. I was working the girls in the living room of the coach while Harry was reading, three feet away. He jumped up and said, a little louder than necessary, "You're doing it all wrong!"

Where in the world did all that testosterone come from, I wondered silently.

He continued to explain to me I shouldn't be doubled over into an "S." Evidently, I was bending at the knees as well as the waist. I was all curled up with my nose next to Angie's. (I had been meaning to take her in to have her hearing checked.) Harry insisted I should be able to train her from a standing position. I asked him if he was upset. And then it came ... an epiphany after thirty-nine years of marriage! He said he wasn't upset and explained he had only two settings: regular and explosive. It was as simple as that. I listened to what he was saying, then took Angie into the bedroom, closed the door, and continued the trick work.

PRACTICE ON THE LOOP

It's important to be able to do the tricks in any situation; consequently, Harry and I both worked with the dogs while we were sitting, standing, or even kneeling. Eventually, I decided we were ready to go out into the world to practice in advance of the Dog Exhibition. While walking the dogs around the Loop, a one-mile dog-friendly circle in the park, I accosted several unsuspecting strangers and asked if we could do dog tricks for them. Most of the people said "Sure." (Silly them ... they were ready to applaud a simple "Sit!") I proceeded to practice the "Nap" command.

Tricks at Anita's Happy Hour

Finally, we were ready for the big time. Angie and I went to Anita's Happy Hour two blocks away to try to nap in front of people I barely knew. When she sat, everyone applauded, killing the mood. I had to tell them there were four or five parts to the trick and ask if they could please hold their applause. The food smells must have been pretty strong because after nattering at Angie, I was soon doubled over ready to poke her on the rear end to get her to comply. What did she care ... I didn't have treats, so she didn't have to do it ... dogs know simple logic. Realizing Angie was not listening, we retreated to the motor home, got the treat pouch, and skipped back to Anita's Happy Hour. With the prospect of a treat, Angie sat ... reluctantly, because of the potluck smells. Unfortunately, she kept looking at all the new people instead of me. My hand signals were rendered useless. It was not pleasant. It was a laborious process, but she eventually came to rest on the cement with her head down. The audience was getting restless. We left quickly, knowing there was more work to be done.

Demonstrating the Proper Way to Train Dogs

Back at the coach, Harry, the one who feeds the dogs, stood erect and gave Angie the commands. "Sit" (she sat), "Down" (she went down), "Nap" (she rolled onto her side after two tries), "Head down" (she went into a perfect sleep mode). The only problem was he didn't tell her to stay, so she stood up, prematurely.

Next, Harry said, "Lucy, sit!" Whereupon Lucy sat, laid down, rolled onto her side, and put her head down. Lucy always knows what's expected of her regardless of what we say. All I could do was sigh. Later I asked Harry if he was going to attend the Dog Exhibition. He said he would probably be there. I instantly thought, *Oh my goodness, the girls would be totally focused on him and not on me.* I banished the thought immediately, knowing anything having to do with dogs was bound to be fun!

Demonstrating the Proper Way to Train Dogs ... Again

Three days later, Harry conducted an impromptu training session. He stood erect and barked out commands:

- "Come!" (Both dogs came running out of their pens.) Angie jumped up on the ottoman. It was not exactly what Harry wanted. He turned to face her.
- "Come!" (He was trying to get her to come to him ... on the floor. She ran into her pen.)
- "Come!" (She jumped back up on the ottoman, laid down, and started barking.)
- "Indoor voice!" (The barking was coming faster and louder.) Harry was fighting a losing battle.

Before I knew it, Harry was completely bent over grabbing Angie by the nose. Lucy came without a command. Then Lucy started to leave. Letting go of Angie's nose, Harry grabbed Lucy by the collar. Angie milled around nearby. Harry grabbed Angie by the collar. He continued to bark out orders while holding their collars. I grabbed my phone and snapped a picture. Within seconds, the training session was over. I held my phone for Harry to see the picture. I was shaking with laughter as I thanked him for showing me the "proper" way to train dogs. He couldn't help but smile.

Chapter 8 ... Tucson ... All About Dogs

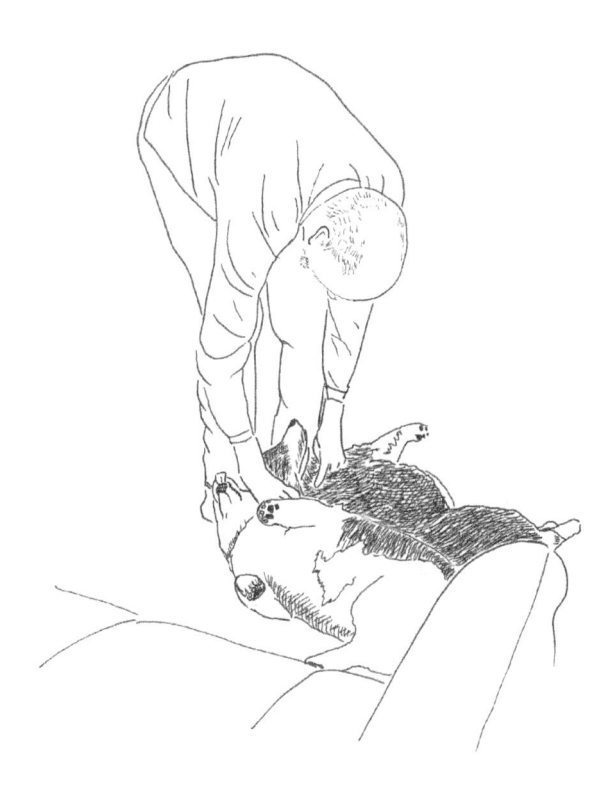

The next day, I went to the agility ring to do a dry run for Carol. She saw I had achieved a modicum of success by working the dogs separately. Carol, always one to push the envelope, said she wanted me to have both the girls do the push-ups and naps, simultaneously. *Oh well, I thought, they'd still be on a lead, and there was still time to practice.*

GOOD GIRL

When the girls got up one morning, I had just finished dictating some thoughts. Angie charged at me and started muttering. I was so pleased she was using her indoor voice I didn't realize I still had the voice-to-text function activated on my phone. When I looked at my phone, later, this is what I saw: "That's a girl ... whisper! ... whisper! ... whisper! ... good girl ... good girl ... good girl ... good girl ... good girl ... can you, can you give me a yawn?"

I guess I'm one of "those" people!

Chapter 9 ... Tucson

Paintings

As February turned into March, people were starting to think about leaving. Some people were looking at the paintings in the front window of the motor home and thinking perhaps they'd like a painting of their dog. As a result, I was hard at work painting during our last couple of weeks at the park:

- Harvey, a spotted Great Dane,
- Bun, a little brown rabbit,
- Gus, an Australian Shepherd, painted from a picture taken on a very windy day
- Ozzie, Robert and Betty's Schnauzer,
- Mia, a little Yorkie who had passed away a month earlier,
- A collie and two African Grey parrots for Sonny and Canadian-Carol's house sitter back home. I had painted a portrait of their grandchildren earlier in the season,
- Roscoe, David and Laura's Miniature Shepherd,
- Boone, a curly black dog with a massive pink tongue,
- Clea and Miss Piggy, two cats for Barbara, and
- Rusty, a Cocker Spaniel, for a visitor across the street.

In between times, I had gotten the ceramics bug. I designed and built some 3D ceramic pockets for air ferns.

Writers' Forum

Jerry, a park resident and author, organized brown bag lunch sessions every two weeks. The sessions were quite well done. For one week, he invited six people to participate in an authors' panel along with him. I was pleased to be invited. We talked about who we were, how we started writing, what types of things we wrote, and the publishing process. We finished with each person doing a four- minute reading from a current or recent work. It was all so interesting. I took several books along hoping to make some sales,

Chapter 9 ... Tucson

but as I looked around the room, I saw many familiar faces ... they had already purchased my book. It made me smile.

Bob, a professional fiction writer, told us in advance the woman in his reading was going to die. He then read a two-minute paragraph detailing her horrifying last minutes stuck in a car on the railroad tracks ... her hands physically glued to the steering wheel ... as a train was approaching. Thank goodness it was fiction. It was a little too startling. The audience seemed a little stunned. After a brief lull, I leaned forward, picked up the microphone, looked at Bob, and countered, "I write funny stuff!"

Mouse

I was chatting with Wayne, a neighbor, at sunset, when Rich came over. Chat, chat, chat. We were talking about life, and got around to the subject of mice. I had a mouse in the coach. Rich said he'd had a packrat chew up his wiring to the tune of $6,800. He had my attention. I begged off saying I had to run to the store and get a mousetrap. Wayne said he had a couple I could borrow. I gratefully borrowed them. The next morning, when I opened the cupboard under the sink in the bathroom, I closed it immediately. The sweet smell of success isn't all it's cracked up to be. After coffee, breakfast, and a little more procrastination, I dealt with our visitor. For the next six mornings, I checked my reloaded trap ... nothing! What a relief!

I'm OK!

The park has a special program for people who are a little less than fully independent. It's called "I'm OK!" People in this situation can still stay at the park, but they must check in with the office by phone every morning. It is a very caring park.

One Hundred

Ruthe Fox, longtime resident of the park turned 100 in mid-February. Her family put on a special celebration. They brought tons of decorations and food for a massive luncheon. Everyone at the park was invited. It was a big deal since it was the peak of the season and there were about 425 living sites, almost all of them filled. If everyone had come, there might have been 650 guests! (But, of course, they didn't all come.) Several of us participated in flower arranging, setup and cleanup.

Ruthe is an inspirational woman full of grace and charm. Even at age 100, she still drove her car, although it was only to go the three blocks to the clubhouse to play cards and Mahjong several times per week.

I visited her when I arrived in November, thinking she might be isolated from everything and everybody. I was wrong! I think she got out more than some people three-fourths her age! Since the park had been a fairly safe haven from COVID, Ruthe greeted her guests without a mask and without a cane … and without dire consequences.

CHAPTER 10 ... TUCSON ... DOG EXHIBITION

The Dog Club's Dog Exhibition was one of the last events of the season. In theory, it was an opportunity to show off how well one's dog has progressed. There were four categories: Rally, Tricks, Agility, and Canine Good Citizen.

AKC-Carol organized the event. She was also the moderator ... and the only one with the megaphone. She had worked with the dogs and handlers weekly and had decided if the dog would be shown on or off lead. If a dog was doing pretty well on lead ... Boom ... she might declare the dog off lead and it would be a whole new ball game!

RALLY

The first category was Rally. Handlers and their dogs performed in the ring, individually. They went to each of ten stations to accomplish the assigned tasks, including left turn, right turn, about face, 360 degrees, come in front and sit-stay, sit-stay allowing the handler to walk around the dog, and more. I know Lucy could have aced it, but you can't win if you don't compete.

TRICKS

After Rally came Tricks. Angie and Lucy were up doing push-ups and nap. They were fashionistas. Paula, one of the residents, had a fancy sewing machine. She outfitted the girls in red bandanas with their names embroidered in white. Carol used her electronic megaphone to make the announcement: "Angie and Lucy, six-year-old Pembroke Corgis, would like to do push-ups for you." I had started them in a sitting position so it would be convenient for the audience to see them. Grabbing a big treat for each of them, I inhaled loud enough for the girls to know this was their big moment. "Down!" I hollered in a loud whisper as I bent down with a flourish, my hands almost touching the ground. They dropped immediately ... a full six inches because they have pitifully short legs. I held my hands palms up and raised myself suddenly to my full height (5' 9"), arms extended in front shoulder high (still holding the treats) ... "Up!" I hollered. They raised the front of their sausage forms and were sitting purposefully in front of me. We repeated the process, exuberantly: "Down! ... Up! ... Down! ... Up!" (The whole thing was way more exercise for me than for the girls!) I could tell Lucy was getting a little bored with the repetition. Fortunately, I didn't get too dizzy and they both made it back to the sitting position without any problems. It was pretty obvious they were doing push-ups. Carol came back to the script announcing, "Sometimes they get exhausted from all their exercise and need to take a nap." With that, I took another deep breath and hollered, "N-n-nap!" This was where it got a little dicey. Angie went down and was rocking slightly but not really committing herself to roll onto her side. Lucy was still sitting... not at all interested in napping. I finished Angie with a hand swipe to the right above her head ... she rolled a full ninety degrees to the left. (I don't know why she always does it backward!) With Angie on her side, I turned my attention to Lucy, "Lucy, down ... N-n-nap!" *Phomp* ... she was down. She knew what to do next, and fortunately, she did it. With both of them lying on their sides, I gave the final command, "Head down ... head down." (If one's good, two's better.) The second attempt worked. Both of them were lying there, flat as pudgy pancakes, on their sides, their forelegs dangling precariously in the air, as if pointing at each other. I had them stay still for a good three seconds so the audience would realize they had done it properly. With an excited, "Okay!" I released them. They popped up and gobbled up their treats and off we went ... three months of work accomplished in less than two minutes. Good grief!

Tucker was the only other dog entered in the Trick category. He was a big, gorgeous, long-haired Golden Retriever. Tucker was entered in all four categories. He accomplished all his tasks like a pro. He liked to perform. Iowa-Carol brought him into the agility ring to perform his tricks. She set out a wooden box. It was the size of an apple crate. (It was really more appropriate for a medium-sized dog.

Chapter 10 ...Tucson ...Dog Exhibition

Maybe that was the trick part!) She told him to get in the box and sit down. At our practice a week earlier, she had had to mash his tail in by hand to get him situated. We were all hoping for the best, but Tucker had already gotten it figured out ... he was sitting pretty as a picture with just the end of his tail hanging out. There was no room to spare. Well done, Tucker! Next, Iowa-Carol turned the box upside down and told him to get up on the box and sit. There was precious little room for a big dog on that little box, but up he jumped and down he sat, smartly. Two tricks down, two to go. He obeyed some hand signals without any trouble. They really were fine tricks! Those in the audience who were having trouble training dogs turned green with envy. His final trick was to push down on a big four-inch button. We heard a *Boy-yoy-yoing*. It wasn't very loud, but the audience quieted down so they could hear it. Iowa-Carol was ready with treats every time he pushed the button. He laid on the ground, paws extended, the button between his forepaws ... *Boy-yoy-yoing* ... treat ... *Boy-yoy-yoing* ... treat ... *Boy-yoy-yoing* ... treat ... Boy-yoy-yoing ... treat. It's a good thing she stopped when she did: The people were starting to question if it was such a fine trick, after all.

AGILITY

After Tricks came Agility. Owners worked their dogs on lead for control purposes and for dog safety. But for the day of the Dog Exhibition, Justice was the first dog to brave the agility ring off lead. Kevin removed her harness, positioned her in front of the first obstacle, and they were off. Under Kevin's direction, she went through the Jump, through the Hoop, and to the Table. The contestant is supposed to stay on the Table for at least five seconds. All the dogs like this spot because it is the one place where they all get a treat, which entices them to stay. Justice planted herself on the Table with a smile. Kevin gave her the next signal saying "Climb-it!" Justice was up and over the A-Frame. With a command of "Walk-It!" she trotted up a ramp, across the full length of a twelve-foot plank Bridge about four feet above the ground, and down the other side to the Tunnel. "Tunnel" sent her through the dark blue plastic tube with a ninety-degree bend at the midpoint. It was a flawless showing ... until the finale: a repeat of Jump, Hoop, Table. When Justice came out of the Tunnel, she was ready for a treat and Kevin wasn't quite where he needed to be, so Justice made a beeline for the Table. Kevin scratched his head, gave her a treat, and they went for a re-do: Climb-It, Walk-It, Tunnel. This time, when Justice went into the Tunnel, Kevin sprinted to his new location: "Jump!" he said. Justice jumped ... and, skipping the Hoop, she ran right back to the Table, again. Fearing similar results from a third pass, Kevin pulled the plug: He and Justice left the ring with heads held high ... to the thundering applause and appreciation of the audience.

Tucker was the next agility dog. It was a thing of beauty to behold him running the course. The audience had recovered from the button incident and was eagerly watching Tucker run through his agility paces.

The final dog to perform in agility was Gizmo, the smart little Shih Tzu who aced the agility ring two years earlier. He's a fixture in the park. Everyone knows and loves him. Gizmo had been working agility for years. He knew what was expected of him. Carol introduced Tom and Gizmo as "a team who is competition ready." Expectations were high ... the pressure was on. It was an easy thing to run him through the agility course ... except if Tom's granddaughter might be standing by the fence with a phone in her hand taking a video ... and to our good fortune such was the case that fine day. Tom called Gizmo. Gizmo walked toward Tom's granddaughter. Tom called Gizmo, again ... same result. Tom approached Gizmo and waved a treat in front of his nose, just barely succeeding in getting him to come to the starting point. Tom began their routine: little Gizmo ambled up to the Jump and hopped right over. Still poking along, he went through the Hoop, sped up a tiny bit, and sat on the Table. He received his treat, then trotted up the A-Frame. He climbed up and over the top and meandered down the other side. He climbed the ramp to the Bridge and politely walked along the plank to the end. (After watching energetic performances by Justice, Teddy, and Tucker, this one seemed laboriously slow.) When Gizmo came to the Tunnel, he balked. Something caught his attention. It didn't take too much effort to get him to go into the Tunnel, but when he came to the other end, he stopped and peeked out at the audience. Too cute! Pretty soon, he was back on track and going through the Weave, which consisted of a dozen plastic three-foot posts standing in a straight line about two feet apart and about twenty-two feet long. Little Gizmo had plenty of room to weave his body through the line of posts back and forth. He was the only dog to attempt the Weave. Even though he strolled somewhat lazily, it was pretty impressive.

CANINE GOOD CITIZEN

After Agility came Canine Good Citizen. It was a test for dogs who had been working on obedience. The teams demonstrated how they could walk around in a circle without having the dogs interact in a negative way. Carol announced two of the teams would do a Meet and Greet. The dogs were supposed to sit patiently while the handlers discussed issues du jour. There were four teams in the ring. Carol picked the two calm ones. Kevin with Justice, and Gary with Teddy. It was a perfect encounter. However, when Justice calmly returned to her spot, Topaz ... a young Boxer mix with way more energy than all the other dogs combined ... lurched. Minnesota-Carol was ready and kept him under control. We all politely looked the other way momentarily, and with that, the annual Dog Exhibition was over. Everybody walked away happy. It was our little bit of Americana for the day.

It's a Small World

While we were still milling around the agility ring, a lady came up and asked if she could take a picture of Angie. I said, "Sure." After she snapped a shot, we visited a bit. She found out I was from Vancouver, Washington, and said her son lived in nearby Portland, Oregon. We dug a little deeper and I found out he was a dean at my alma mater, the University of Portland.

Another time, when I first came to the park, I met Lynn Rupp who made earrings. She recognized my "Live Generously" Lutheran tee shirt. (We had church in common.) She was from the Seattle area. (We had Washington in common.) She knew someone in Vancouver. He was an amazing music director who worked at a church in Vancouver. There was no need to go any further. We both proclaimed in unison, "David Teeter!" It is a small world, after all.

Chapter 11 ... Tucson

Golfing

Out on the golf course, things were looking up. It seemed I had gotten better at putting ... almost overnight. In fact, for three weeks running, people pared with us told me I was a good putter. Well, of course, praise was the kiss of death for my putting. I totally lost my confidence. A golfer named Mark had joined us. I putted and immediately regretted it. The ball was on track to speed past the hole, missing it by six inches to the right. I reached out my putter to grab the ball before I made an absolute fool of myself. Just then, the ball broke to the left and went directly into the hole. There was no way to disguise the fact I thought I had botched it. I got the old hee-haw from Mark ... well deserved.

Happy Birthday, Harry!

Harry turned seventy-five. I wanted to celebrate and was open to doing whatever would please him. I asked him what he wanted to do for his special day. "Nothing" was his answer. It was just as I had expected, but I was glad I checked. He's not a going-out-to-dinner kind of person, so we planned a pleasant meal in the coach to kind of person, so we planned a pleasant meal in the coach to celebrate his big day in exactly the same manner as any of the preceding days. *(Sigh!)*

But hey, I made a batch of brownies ... exactly according to the recipe ... which was something I almost never do. I cut them, keeping them in the baking pan, and started across the street to Happy Hour. "Where are you going?" Harry must have thought I was deserting him. "I'm off to Happy Hour," I said as I departed the motor home. Once there, I stood in the middle of the group and started singing "Happy birthday to you, happy birthday to you, happy birthday dear ... (pause) ... Harry! Happy birthday to you." (One of our pastors had given a sermon urging us to celebrate the special moments in our lives. I thought turning seventy-five was a pretty good reason to celebrate, even if Harry wasn't there.) Around the circle I went, doling out a brownie to each person. People were hesitant to have yet another sugar load, but eyebrows went up when they took the first bite and discovered the brownies were still warm! Success! We had a very agreeable birthday celebration in Harry's honor. You do what you have to do.

Ceramics

I graduated from making geckos to slab rolling. Someone had said they were going to make ceramic pockets to hold various things. Immediately, I envisioned 3" x 5" ceramic pockets to hold air ferns in my sunporch. On the appointed day, I jimmied up a pattern and made five pockets. A week later, when other people saw how cute they turned out, they wanted to make small pockets, too. I arranged to go back for another slab rolling session to show them how to do it. Since I already had enough pockets, I started thinking about what else I could do. I designed a 4" x 4" pattern of lovebirds in the shape of a heart. I glazed them to look like sun conures: bright yellow, with tangerine and bright green accents.

Change, Change, Change!

Three of the beloved people who worked at the park were leaving, as well as Paul and Joyce, two active residents for forty-one years. I knew when I returned home there would be two more changes: our pastors and office administrator were leaving. Change is inevitable ... We do better if we run with it!

Worm Moon

The Rincon Mountains are about ten miles east of our park. Although I have a beautiful view of the mountains, I have no view of the horizon. Nevertheless, when the Snow Moon came up in February, it looked bigger and whiter and brighter than normal. I wondered about the following month's moon. I looked it up online and found there would be a Worm Moon in March. I put it in my calendar. I was looking forward to seeing it on March 18th, but life happened.

St. Patrick's Day

March 17th was the Design Club's moment to shine. The Design Club puts on a big St. Paddy's Day banquet every year. I got in on it, in spades. Starting Monday, groups of people were gathered to make this event happen. Every time we went through the auditorium during the week, new smells came from the kitchen. Corned beef was cooking on Monday. On Wednesday, after Coffee and Donuts, we got together to peel potatoes and carrots and slice cabbage. Everyone knows carrot splatter can cover your clothes in no time, and it did. I even had carrot splatter on my glasses for two days before I was able to clean it off completely. Early on the 17th, the dinner began. Servers were in place to dole out portions of corned beef, cabbage, potatoes, and carrots. I was at the condiment table with Katherine's husband Roderick and Minnesota-Carol. Roderick was dishing out sauerkraut, Carol had charge of horseradish, and I was the two-fisted mustard dispenser (horseradish or spicy brown). There are only so many ways to offer two different kinds of mustard, but I found them all! It was interesting to see the reactions as people declared their preferences.

The Design Club likes to give away free door prizes. They figure if you've already paid for the tickets, you shouldn't have to pay extra to be in on the door prizes. There were about fifteen bottles of wine and related gifts. I had donated a 9" x 12" acrylic painting of a dragonfly with zentangle details (fine-tipped ink drawings in tiny patterns) on its wings. When the wine-related prizes were gone, Wally pulled out the painting giving it a big buildup. I was a little embarrassed! Paul and Joyce, the forty-one-year residents, were ecstatic to have won the painting. I couldn't have been happier!

After the dinner, the kitchen looked like something out of the parable of loaves and fishes. We had one-gallon containers of leftover food on all the kitchen counters. In fact, there was so much food remaining we ran out of containers. I had a lot of large plastic tubs in the motor home. I ran to get them. On the way back, I happened to look to my left and saw the moon coming up behind the Rincon Mountains. I was so pleased! Just before I entered the auditorium, the moon had cleared the mountains. And there it was ... the Worm Moon!

On the way home after cleanup, I took another look, but the moon was higher in the sky and looked like a normal, albeit bright, moon. The next night, Harry took the dogs out for a brief rest and came back in saying the moon looked pretty. I stepped outside to see it. It was low near the mountains with an orange tint (from the fires in Texas). The palm trees lining Happy Street gave it a romantic foredrop. I called Irv and Kate and told them they had to drop everything and step outside to see it. I walked down Happy Street, knocking on doors. The people who were home were not disappointed. Wayne,

Chapter 11 ...Tucson

the mousetrap neighbor who had recently lost his wife, was one of the people who came out. We had a nice long discussion about life.

END-OF-SEASON PARTIES

We were involved in three end-of-season parties. Betty and Pam organized one of them. Harry and I were invited because I had told the ladies a naughty story about a butterfly while Pam was cutting my hair. They laughed until it hurt. Robert and Betty, Pam and Don, and Harry and I carpooled in Robert's mammoth truck. There were eleven people at the dinner party. When we were seated, seven people snatched the first seats. The four remaining seats were at the far end of the table. Robert and I milled around to one side of the table. As we were sitting down, Robert howled, urgently, "Oh ... no! This ... will ... never ... work! Betty ... can't ... sit ... next to ... Harry."

"Yes, she can," I countered. "He's a big boy." Betty engaged Harry, my man of few words, in conversation throughout the meal. I think she may have made him use up about a month's worth of his words! No one at Happy Hour would have believed it possible!

A second goodbye event was a dinner with Harry's Sunday golf buddies. Irv and Kate, Joe and Kathy (knitting), and Harry and I had a good time as expected.

The third going away party was a potluck with the Happy Hour group. The pièce de résistance was Sue's vegan macaroni and cheese casserole. It tasted just like real macaroni and cheese! Woohoo, those vegans have it figured out!

RINCON SINGERS

The Rincon Singers were performing one last time for Coffee and Donuts. As it happened, it was the same day as the Photo Club's annual show. There were about 267 entries, all displayed in 9" x 12" mats. The rec hall was filled with six-foot standing displays ... all but the corner where the piano resided.

During the practices, Bill, our mild-mannered director, had kept us somewhat on task. Anita, our lead soprano, frequently stopped Bill from proceeding to the next song because we didn't have the timing right. It didn't take more than a quick look at the music to see Anita was right ... Anita was always right! Bill listened ... so did the chorus. And so it went, week after week, at all our practices in the auditorium as we struggled to get better.

When the day of the performance arrived, we had officially abandoned a difficult song we could never seem to get right. As a result, our confidence level was pretty high. We needed a quick tune-up before the performance ... in the rec hall ... even though the Photo Show's contest was in full swing. We gathered around the piano ... jammed together ... bordered on two sides by the tall photo displays. Altos, sopranos, tenors, and basses were mixed together ... no rhyme nor reason. We sang and, oh my goodness, the magic happened! The acoustics in the rec hall were much better than the acoustics in the auditorium. We discovered we sounded good! The excitement we felt lasted as we waited in line ... it lasted as we filed into the auditorium and positioned ourselves in front of the stage ... and it lasted all through the performance. We sang our hearts out without a care in the world ... and to Anita's chagrin, we sang without a care to the timing! But interestingly enough, it really didn't matter! We were the only ones who knew whether or not we hit the right notes with the right timing. The songs we sang were near and dear to the hearts of each person in the audience! As Cindy, a fellow soprano, had said to me repeatedly "All will be good" ... and all was good!

Chapter 12 ... Heading Home

On the Road Again

At Happy Hour, the big topic was determining the best route home. Several of the people were heading to the Northwest. Some were going through Susanville via Las Vegas; others touted the route to Salt Lake City via Las Vegas. We pulled out our map and studied it. We decided to go through Salt Lake City but not via Las Vegas: it was much shorter to get there by driving straight north through Arizona. We had convinced ourselves it would be a better route.

Jeep

Our first stop was for fuel in Casa Grande. In the two blocks between the truck stop and the freeway, I thought Harry had gone wacko! We were on a two-lane road with the truck stop on our left and businesses on our right. I was staring at the phone to get in touch with my navigation duties. Out of nowhere, Harry made a sixty-degree turn to the left followed by a ninety-degree turn to the right ... we were using both the lanes! He finally made a thirty-degree turn back to center ... and to peace. The tow bars for the Jeep had locked up again, causing it to revert to a bucking bronco behind the motor home. Harry had addressed the problem before I even realized we had a problem. It was a little unnerving to sit in the passenger seat behind our gigantic windshield and see the view change so dramatically! In Harry's defense, there was a gap in the oncoming traffic. His little maneuver achieved the desired result, and we were on our way. However, hours later, north of Flagstaff, the Jeep acted up again. I had just given up the driver's seat and was ready for a little nap. All of a sudden, the coach started jerking back and forth. Harry performed the maneuver again. As disconcerting as it was to look through the windshield while the maneuver was in progress, it's even worse when you can't see out any windows! This time the maneuver didn't work ... too bad. Harry pulled off at the next exit, dinked around with the tow bars, and we were back on the road in no time.

SURLY

I went back to bed and got a little rest ... enough to be able to drive but not enough to be cheerful. Just after I took the wheel, the road, which had been getting steadily narrower, became shoulderless. I like to ride the white line marking the right side of the traffic lane and I frequently hit the rumble strip, which can be six inches outside the traffic lane. This road was so narrow there was no rumble strip, and the white line was butted up against a three-inch drop-off! Neither of us felt comfortable with the drop-off. Somewhere before we reached Page, Arizona, Harry had me pull over. I hadn't been driving very long and was still feeling a little surly from my short nap. Being encouraged to switch drivers again didn't help, but we got things sorted out and hit the road once more. In the process of switching drivers, we missed our turn and ended up on an alternate route ... a lesser quality road going farther into the middle of nowhere but still ending up at Page. With Harry sitting behind the wheel, my job was to answer all his questions. And here's what happened:

"How much farther?"

"An hour and 15 minutes."

"What?" he yelled above the din of the road noise.

"I said 'One hour and 15 minutes.'"

"That's what you said ten minutes ago."

"Well, we're supposed to be driving less than the speed limit, so I added ten minutes." (My surliness hadn't melted off.)

After we got our destination concerns resolved, Harry asked if I had the GPS working and would it announce the turns?

Chapter 12 ...Heading Home

"Yes."

"What?" he roared above the din of the road noise, yet again.

"YES-YES-YES!" I shouted, pushing the words out.

Then he asked, "Did you push the Start button?"

"no."

Harry pointed out the humor of the situation, saying "Yes, yes, yes ... no." (It was a line from a BBC comedy, "The Vicar of Dibley.") I was ready for bear, but when I looked at him, I noticed he had a big grin on his face. My surliness disintegrated. After more than thirty-nine years of marriage, a smile from my husband still melted my heart.

We found a comfortable RV park to stay the night. Early the following morning, we connected with Interstate 15 (Las Vegas to Salt Lake City) at St. George and finished our trip home with sunny weather and amazingly smooth freeways. We vowed never to take the direct route again. (A detour through Las Vegas was a longer distance but it would have taken the same amount of time and would have definitely been a more pleasant drive.)

Chapter 13 ... Vancouver

Home Again

We got home Thursday, April 7, emptied most of the motor home in dry weather and settled in to allow the wild and wonderful Pacific Northwest weather entertain us. Within ten days we had multiple rainstorms, several snowstorms (one gracing us with eight inches of wet snow), a few hailstorms and a tiny bit of sunshine. The snowstorm dropped one tree on the driveway and another smack dab into the pond. With nothing to do but wait for the tree guy to come and work his magic, we stayed indoors, pretending it was still winter.

Loss of Credibility

Before we disappeared indoors for an eternity, I decided to put the motor home in the carport so it would be out of the way and plugged in. It's not a difficult thing to do, but it takes a little jockeying. Usually, Harry runs around the coach making sure I'm not getting too close to anything. But this time, Harry wasn't around when I was ready to do it. I backed it up and took a running start from the far left side of the driveway. If I turned right too late, I'd connect the driver's corner with the concrete retaining wall. Who knows who would win ... definitely not the driver. Fortunately, I didn't turn too late. My mistake was thinking I could do it in one move. I might have made it but for the portion of the downspout connecting to the gutter thirteen feet above the ground and five feet above my field of attention. I didn't hear anything, but on checking my mirrors to make sure I was doing a good job, I saw some movement in slow motion. I was not doing a good job! I have to hand it to the gutter people: The nail in the vertical portion of the downspout was absolutely centered. The motor home had disconnected the downspout from the gutter and the downspout arced slowly and gracefully from a height of fourteen feet to a low of one foot. The stick-out portion slowly came to rest below the belly of the coach. Because the coach was slightly angled and the downspout

Chapter 13 ... Vancouver

was arcing slowly, the stick-out portion never hit the coach. The downspout could be fixed. If it hadn't been for a little eight-inch section of gutter that found its way to the top of the coach at the beginning of the fiasco, I wouldn't have had to trouble Harry with the details at all.

Of course, before I was able to fully park the motor home, Harry showed up. I knew I was in for some ribbing. Harry asked me if I could put the slides out without hitting anything. Chagrined, I took full responsibility saying I was totally disgusted with myself. We were a team again. I told him the next time I mention that horrendous mailbox incident, he should chime right in about me ripping the gutter off the barn.

PART SIX

2022–23

Chapter 1 ... Vancouver

The End of an Era

Messiah Lutheran's pastors of twenty-eight years decided to retire and enjoy their grandchildren. The way for me to really feel something is to get involved ... plunge right in! I jumped at the chance to work on the retirement planning committee. The pastors left in a blaze of glory at the end of August, after a phenomenal final worship service followed by a huge party.

Immediately following their departure, our church convened a "Call" committee to find a new pastor(s). We had heard the Call process would likely take at least a year. The bishop in Seattle, two years away from retirement himself, placed two volunteer pastors in our church to shepherd us through the time of the Call process. One was a retired bishop, the other a retired pastor from a nearby city. Who knew so many people would take to retirement at the same time! Baby boomers!

But life goes on and November came up fast. It was time to take to the road again for another winter.

Chapter 2 ... Fixed Itself!

Nothing ever fixes itself ... or does it? We had had the motor home for almost three years. We knew what normal was. Here is a collection of strange incidents occurring during the first few weeks of the trip:

1. As we pulled away from home, we noticed the check engine light was on. We were only a few blocks from our RV maintenance place. I pulled up out front intending to leave the motor running while I darted in for a quick assessment. Before I could get out of the driver's seat, Harry reached in and shut off the diesel engine. He said he wanted to try something. We turned the engine back on about a minute later and the light was cleared. We shrugged and drove a mile down the road when the tow bars started going nuts again. I waited for two lanes of traffic to clear and then performed our wild angled maneuver. It must have been a little disconcerting for the oncoming traffic. The maneuver cured the sway bar problem ... Fixed Itself!
2. Our first night on the road, as we were getting ready to hit the hay, I dry mopped the floor. Corgis are big shedders. I like to dry mop the floor each evening. We have an inboard vacuum system. It's pretty simple: mop the debris to the vacuum port, kick the lever, and with a *shloop*, the port eats the debris. I mopped, kicked the lever, and nothing happened. I kicked it again ... still nothing. The next evening, I tried it again and it worked ... Fixed Itself!
3. There's a button by the front door for retracting the steps. It's pretty simple: Push the button and the steps retract. There's no way to stop it in mid-retraction. On our second day on the road, Harry pushed the button and the steps retracted ... only partially. Push, partial retraction ... push, partial retraction. We were dumbfounded. The next evening, we set up, pushed the button, and the steps fully retracted ... Fixed Itself!
4. When I turned on the water at our first stop, it barely dribbled from the kitchen faucet. I unscrewed the nozzle and checked for

calcium buildup ... nothing. The water pressure was fine; the bathroom faucets worked fine. But the shower spray was also dribbling. Harry checked for calcium buildup and found a ton (or a gram) inside the nozzle. He cleared it out and the shower worked fine for two days. He cleared it again and it worked fine for the rest of the trip. Even though it didn't fix itself, we were pretty happy it was working again.

5. My electric toothbrush started malfunctioning about two weeks before we left to go south. It turned itself off at regular intervals. I had to restart it about four times with each brushing. When we settled in for the first night, I used my electric toothbrush with no issues. It didn't turn off by itself at all ... Fixed Itself!

6. On our third day driving, Harry stopped at a rest area north of Las Vegas. I was going to drive us through Las Vegas. After I started driving, I realized the seat was too far back. I reached down and slid the switch to move the seat forward. It wouldn't move. Harry put a pillow behind my back so I could reach the pedals comfortably, but it was a temporary solution at best. When we stopped for the night south of the Strip, Harry tried to fix the seat. After a little of this and that, he ended up sitting on the floor trying to move the seat with a sudden punch from the soles of his feet ... nothing worked. I set us up for the evening and was startled to see Harry kneeling in front of the commode. There was no sound. I tiptoed back and checked to see if he was okay. He was leaning on the stool trying to check the circuit breakers in the dark closet. I took the dogs to the dog park. When I returned, he had a big smile on his face. He told me he had looked in one of the outside bins and found a fuse extended. He pushed it back in and the seat worked again ... Fixed Itself!

7. No sooner had we left the Las Vegas RV Resort and merged onto a three-lane freeway than the Jeep started bucking again. I slowed to about forty miles per hour and within a mile I was able to pull off to the side of the freeway on an ample shoulder. It was rush hour in Las Vegas on a Monday morning, but we were headed the opposite direction, thank goodness.

Harry suggested I do the wild turning maneuver, but traffic was pouring by steadily. I prayed for a traffic bubble so I could do my maneuver, or for the ability to limp forward to the next exit. My prayers were answered but not the way I asked. I started the motor home and pulled forward toward the exit ... the Jeep was fine ... Fixed Itself!

8. When we arrived at the RV park near Lake Havasu, Harry unhooked the Jeep and noticed the check engine light was lit. We checked to make sure the gas cap was properly seated. Harry started the car a couple more times, but the light was still lit. Then he started it one more time ... the light went out ... Fixed itself!
9. It was more than eighty degrees in the Lake Havasu area. Harry turned on the vent fan in the kitchen. It's normally very quiet, but this time it was clicking like crazy. Harry poked at the screen a couple of times ... peace ... Fixed Itself!
10. We enjoyed the comfort of the fireplace on cold mornings, but it hadn't been working for a month. In keeping with the theme this year, it fixed itself all of a sudden. It was a mystery!
11. After being settled in one spot for five weeks, the ice maker in our motor home's residential refrigerator started to work again.
12. One day, I looked at the coach's electronic display and saw a horrendous thick red line. I decided to let Harry take care of the problem. When he came home from golfing, Harry saw a horrendous thin red line, which seemed even worse: The charge in our all-electric coach appeared to be heading to zero. It was not a good thing! Since two brains are better than one, we commiserated. Suggestions were flying ... albeit slowly. Reboot the coach? Flip the relays on the power hookup? Run the generator? Harry started up the coach and messed around a little, then shut it off. We flipped the relays. All to no avail. We did the next best thing ... we gave up. The next time Harry looked at the readout he realized it had fixed itself! We were really glad to have it working properly!
13. I was getting to be an old hand at flipping relays inside the coach. If the dishwasher made funny noises, it had to be stopped by

flipping the relay. After successfully resolving a couple of dishwater problems, I designated myself "relay queen." Therefore, when we had trouble with the microwave clock not behaving correctly after a park electrical outage, I went back, flipped the relay, and watched it fix itself. I don't know why, but it worked.

Chapter 3 ... Heading South

Getting Ready to Leave

Late October was dedicated to packing. The time had arrived. The day before we left for Tucson, we were expecting a major rainfall in the Vancouver area for the first time in months. When I was having coffee at 7 a.m. with my neighbor Dorothy, she asked when the rain would start. It had originally been forecast for 10 a.m. I checked and saw it had been upgraded to 9 a.m. I jumped up, said my goodbyes, ran home, tended to the dogs, went outside, winterized the tiller, ran the lawn mower until it ran out of gas, winterized it, finished mowing, and put the mower away ... just as it started sprinkling. To finish, I grabbed the blower and blew off the road ... done and done. It took about two hours. Boy, was I happy!

A Disconcerting Event

We left at 9:30 the following morning. I drove the first two hours (with intermittent Jeep bucking). As I was driving by a rest stop, a tow truck pulled onto the freeway in front of us. He was towing a big rig, which was facing backward. (If you glanced up unawares, you'd think the big rig was coming right at you and you were about to die!) It was a little unnerving.

Chapter 3 …Heading South

Real Travelers

We stayed in RV parks instead of rest stops like real travelers. We stopped at Baker City, Oregon, the first night, went through Boise, Idaho, on Saturday to Tremonton (a few miles north of Ogden, Utah, at the base of the Rockies' foothills), and through Salt Lake City on Sunday. It was easy weekend traffic. Usually, we pushed to rack up the miles, frequently driving in the dark. This time, we stopped about three every afternoon and kept a normal schedule. It was pleasant for a change. Costco chili on sticky rice was one of our staples.

Interstate 15 between Las Vegas and Salt Lake City cuts through the mountains in the northwest corner of Arizona. The mountain pass was extremely pretty. It came out of nowhere from either direction. All of a sudden, we were weaving our way through the infamous rocky craigs of the Southwest ... up close and personal. I took a picture to send to my brothers. As I was checking to see if it was any good, I glanced up. There was a more spectacular view. I took another picture. I repeated the process three times before I eventually sent them something, but no picture could compare with the moving reality.

We stopped at a rest area north of Las Vegas to switch drivers. We stayed in Las Vegas RV Resort on Sunday night, making it easy to cut and run to Big Bend RV Resort near Lake Havasu to visit Larry and Wendy for four days. Wendy wanted to invite us for chili dogs but told me she had only one can of chili. I was so excited to reach into my pantry and come up with a fine can of chili from Costco!

In between golf dates, Harry called the manufacturer and checked on the bucking Jeep problems. The mechanic gave Harry some detailed advice about cleaning the hydraulic rods. He followed it to the letter, putting an end to our dramatic bucking Jeep problems. We left on Friday morning for Tucson.

My brothers wanted a picture of something besides cows dotting the hillside. I looked for a cactus or a palm tree, but we weren't far enough south. When I finally found a palm tree, I snapped one shot. Before I could check the picture, the palm tree was long gone. When I looked at the picture, I saw the palm tree conveniently hiding behind a telephone pole. *(Sigh!)*

REFUELING IN CASA GRANDE

We refueled in Casa Grande. It was very crowded. We were third in line. After leashing up the girls, we traipsed across the parking lot to graveled area. It looked okay enough. We walked around and I hassled the girls to "hurry up." Then I noticed Lucy had glommed onto something. It looked like there were a couple of feet hanging

Chapter 3 ... Heading South 217

out of her mouth. I fussed trying to get her to drop it, and after a few chomps, she did. I snagged it with a doggie bag so no other dogs would get it. When I looked at Angie, I was horrified to see she had found one too. I figured there was no way I could get it away from Angie, but she dropped it on command. I was amazed. Dogs ... gotta love 'em.

By Friday evening we were all set up for five months. I was up for the sunrise the next day, but there were no clouds in the sky. It was blue ... blue ... blue ... suddenly bright ... the sun nailed me right in the eyes. I needed to get out my acrylics: One well-positioned painting and I would be home free. "Palm Tree Hiding Behind Pole" would be my first painting.

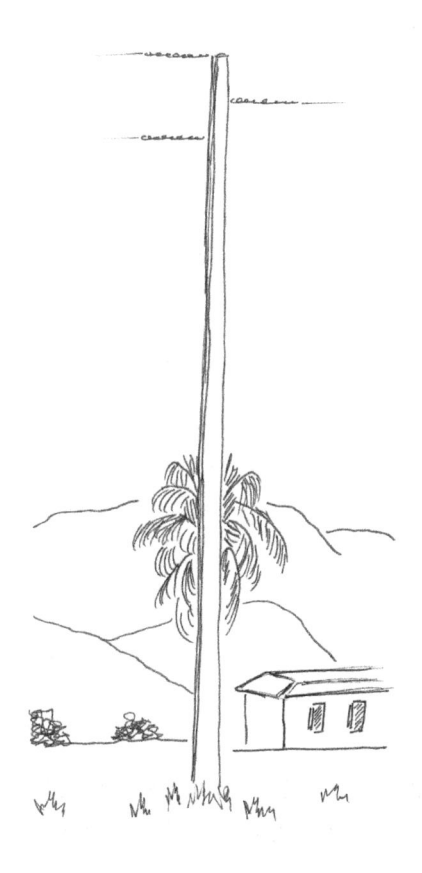

Chapter 4 ... Tucson

Life Is Simple

Life is simple in the desert. At 7:30 a.m. Harry gets dressed for freezing weather to take the girls down the street to their special area. Harry strides along ... 1-2-1-2; the girls walk along next to him taking two steps to his one ... 1-2-3-4-1-2-3-4. I watch their little Corgi butts wiggle all the way down the street. When they come home, the girls run to their crates, turn, and wait hopefully for Harry to remove his jacket. He gives each of them a little treat. Then they jump up to the captain's chairs where they take up their positions watching out the door to see if a big dog walks by. Big dogs get a greeting, little dogs usually don't.

Harry goes off to exercise about noon. Exactly ninety minutes later, the girls bark. They can see Harry chatting with Rich. Granted, they like Harry but when he comes home it's dinnertime. They run to their crates, turn, and look hopefully to their right as Harry enters the coach. He immediately fills their dishes. After their dinner, they retake their post in the captain's chair to watch for other big dogs to come by. Life is simple in the desert.

Jiminy, a shaved Golden Retriever, usually got a greeting. Topaz, the young Boxer mix always up for playing, got a greeting, too.

Evenings were usually pretty quiet unless somebody stopped by to visit. If they came in a golf cart, I had a chance of seeing them from the window by my computer. If they were walking, the girls would sound the alarm until I became aware someone was there. A simple thank you would bring an end to the chaos.

Choir

The choir at TVLC, seven miles north of the park, kept getting better and better. Sandi and Dick from the park began attending. They occasionally brought someone along. Afterward, Sandi always mentioned how wonderful the choir sounded. But the choir never sounded better than on Choir Sunday, the third week of December. It was spectacular. It was bittersweet as we honored a longtime choir member who had passed away during the week but also exciting because we ended with a jazzy version of "Go Tell It on the Mountain." Our choir director had so much energy she almost danced on the pedestal as she directed. Every week, her efforts made the whole choir come alive.

Catch Me If You Can!

On the evening before Thanksgiving, I was peacefully sitting sideways on a cushion on the sofa with my legs propped up. Harry and I were watching an old episode of "Mannix." All the shades were drawn. All of a sudden, out of the corner of my eye, a huge bug about the size of a winged termite, blew past me on the headrest of the sofa. I leapt out of my sitting position with a high-pitched "Aack!" Dancing around the middle of the coach, I brushed myself off, repeatedly.

"What's wrong?" asked Harry.

Trying to feel as nonchalant as I sounded, I replied. "Oh, I thought it was a spider … but it was probably just a flying bug."

After I regained my composure, I looked down at the pillow where I had been sitting and stared at a huge spider staring back at me! It was grayish brown and blended very well with the sofa and pillow in the dim light. It blended too well! It was sitting there quietly, but all eight legs were bent, obviously poised for flight or fight. I didn't want to take any chances. I inverted an empty plastic container trapping it and raced outside, pillow and all. I didn't even stop to try to find the switch for the outside lights. I was stuck with moonlight. Any delay meant an opportunity for my captive to escape. I removed the plastic prison and shook the pillow. Big mistake. It was difficult to determine if my little charge was still clinging to the pillow. In my peripheral vision, I thought I saw something scurrying off to the right. I tried to focus and saw something else scurrying. It was hard to tell what I was seeing. Hopefully, it meant one spider made it to the patio and was heading away from the coach. I couldn't tell for sure. It blended too well with the concrete patio in the dark.

The next morning, having no distractions like "Mannix," I was sitting on the cushion alone with my thoughts. Those thoughts went directly to the possibility of all the little critters who might be living under the hide-a-bed where I was sitting ... and how easy it would be for them to climb up the back of the sofa and visit me whenever they liked. Then I pulled out my trusty phone and googled "spiders of Arizona." A quick scan told me I had met either a very large brown recluse or a common hobo spider. Reading further, I discovered hobo spiders can run up to three feet per second. That's my boy! It wasn't a brown recluse. Cheated death again ... if only in my mind.

With the hobo spider still in mind, I was constantly checking the sofa. But it was time to cook Thanksgiving dinner. Stuffed bell pepper casserole sounded perfect. And it was. Comfort food, to make me appreciate new friends in Arizona and longtime friends (we don't use the O word) in other places of the world, especially those in the Northwest! The encounter with the hobo spider faded to a distant memory.

Save It for a Rainy Day

We had two rainstorms since arriving in Arizona. Back home in Washington, winter rainstorms seemed like they started in November and ended in March. Nevertheless, a typical rainstorm in Arizona started at 9 a.m. and ended at noon. Same day ... what a deal! But the exciting part was what happened before and after. It was fun to see all the clouds gathering. It was especially fun seeing the colorful sunrises.

Before the second rainstorm hit, I happened to be looking out the window at the palm trees lining Happy Street. The rising sun hit the palm fronds, making them glow like gold. With the wind blowing ferociously, it looked like the palm trees were covered with thousands of little gold twinkle lights. Within three minutes, the heavens opened and the rain dumped down. Shortly afterward, Harry got up and our day went on as normal.

Chapter 5 ... Tucson

Bees

I was making lunch at 2 p.m. and heard a popping noise. It seemed to be coming from the kitchen vent above me. I looked up through the screen and saw bees and bee body parts. Turning on the fan immediately eliminated about two-thirds of the bees and body parts. Tapping the screen a couple of times took care of the rest. I finished making lunch and heard a buzzing noise. The bees were back en masse. No amount of fan work could discourage them from coming to the vent area. When I sat down on the sofa to eat lunch, the buzzing seemed to be louder ... there was a new bee gathering around the screened window next to the sofa. We thought it was pretty strange, but they weren't getting in, so we let the bees be. The next afternoon, like clockwork, the bees were back. I don't know why, but it seemed to be a thing. Oddly enough, they came to the kitchen vent only, not the bathrooms vents. They must be kitchen bees. Who knew bees were room-specific?

Nap-Time Sprint

I took the girls out for a business walk. After they were finished, I had them practice taking a nap on the road, while I quickly cleaned up what needed to be cleaned up. Nobody was around to distract them. On the way home, we stopped by a neighbor's house to visit. I had them repeat their little nap trick. There were a few distractions, so they didn't do it very well. I had them do it once more for Sandi's husband, Dick. They did it. When they do their nap trick in the motor home, they immediately get a treat. But after performing twice on our walk with no treat, they were feeling slighted. They knew there was a treat somewhere in the park and they were going to find it. Lucy was like a lead sled dog in the Iditarod race. She knew where the motor home was ... she was on a mission. It was all I could do to hang on as they pulled me down the street. I did manage to stop them before they got to the cross street. Once inside the motor home, they got their treat. It's good to know if they get lost, they'll be able to find their way home ... almost instantly!

Oh, That Harry

Out of the blue, Harry asked, "Are you ready to take a break?"

"I am, with all my heart."

"OK, here," he said handing me a filthy water filter, "clean this out with a mild soap."

I walked to the kitchen sink, picked up my dispenser, and squirted a generous portion of dish soap into the water filter. As I reached to turn on the water, Harry looked at me and smiled sheepishly with eyes twinkling. "Oh, there is one problem. You have no water. And what's more, I can't turn it back on." Oh, that Harry!

Leveler

I came back from an art class to find Harry busy releveling the motor home. First, he let the motor home level itself. Then he opened a nearby door. When the door slowly closed itself, he made an adjustment. Soon it was staying open on its own but a kitchen cabinet was slowly sliding out. He reversed the adjustment a tad until the door stayed open and the cabinet stayed closed. Everything was fine. One would think he was finished ... but no. He went outside and checked the bay underneath the living room slide. The door of the bay wouldn't open ... it was bumping into the bottom of the slide. Back in he went, leveling the coach until he could open the bay door, while the indoor door stayed still and the kitchen cabinet stayed closed. Life in a motor home with an automatic leveling system ... there's always something to do.

Chapter 6 ... Tucson ... The Tall Soprano

Choir

The Choir at TVLC sang for two services on Christmas Eve. It seems whenever I have to sing more than once, I get all excited and can't come down. This minor break from reality is what happened from The Tall Soprano's viewpoint.

Familiar Carols

The Tall Soprano was excited to see all the people filing into the church. She knew the songs were going to be beautiful. The bulletin announced a dozen familiar Christmas carols:

- *Gloria, In Excelsis Deo*
- *O Come, All Ye Faithful*
- *Come, O Come Emmanuel*
- *Away in a Manger*
- *Hark! The Herald Angels Sing*
- *Angels We Have Heard on High*
- *How Shall We Approach This Wonder*
- *What Child Is This?*
- *It Came Upon the Midnight Clear*
- *O Little Town of Bethlehem*
- *Silent Night*
- *Joy to the World*

Call to Worship

The Choir had come early to practice and had run through their special songs. The Director had the Choir in tip-top shape. The first two songs were sung as one. As the pre-service timer counted down to zero, the Director stood up and walked in a stately manner toward her pedestal. She mounted gracefully, looked every member of the Choir in the eye, and with a flourish, motioned them to stand. Her arms poised, she smiled, turned to the Piano, and signaled

Chapter 6 ... Tucson ... The Tall Soprano

the beginning. The Piano, who had long ago proven her worth, pounded the introduction ... **BUM ... bum-bum-bum-bum ... bum ... BUM ... bum-bum-bum-bum ... bum**. It sounded like a full orchestra. The Tall Soprano was overcome. She nearly swooned, missing her cue as the Director brought the Choir to life. Nevertheless, she recovered and came in on the second note: ... **ri-a, een ex-cel-sis De-e-o. GLO-ri-a, een ex-cel-sis De-e-o**. It was exciting ... there was a slight key change upward. The Choir, with the Sopranos perched on top of the melody, was singing in unison: **GLO-ri-a, een ex-cel-sis De-e-o. GLO-ri-a, een ex-cel-sis, een ex-cel-sis**. All that was left was the final De-e-o to resolve the chord. It was to be led, of course, by the Sopranos. Everyone in the church held their breath as the Piano gave a final **Bum ... bum-bum-bum ... bum**. Suddenly, without warning, the Basses, who were sitting right behind the Sopranos, stole the Sopranos' thunder. They came in of their own volition. The Sopranos, especially the Tall Soprano, were visibly upset. The Basses had firmly taken control of the song: **IN EX-CEL-SIS**. They were intent on finishing the coup. The Sopranos were having none of that. They struggled to reclaim the song, repeating their pure crystalline melody: **een ex-cel-sis**. And then the Basses did it again. Booming out the phrase, they tried to finish the carol: **IN EX-CEL-SIS**. To give them the benefit of the doubt, the Sopranos had decided to count to three. They had hit three! They took charge once and for all: **een ex-cel-sis**. The Basses yielded to the Sopranos, but trying to get the last word, they repeated: **ex-cel-sis**. Finally, the Choir yielded to the Director who was determined to put a stop to all the nonsense. The Director charged the Choir to come together in a final prolonged **DE-E-O**.

The Director, still half-traumatized at the outburst from the far-left of her choir loft, regained her composure and turned to the Congregation. With a grand upsweep of her arms, she invited everyone to stand and join in the singing. The Piano continued her Bum ... bum-bum-bum-bum ... bum-ing in the brief interlude. The Organ, a noble man of great stature, brought the organ to bear. Both instruments blended perfectly. Still facing the Congregation, the Director gave a mighty cue. The Congregation and the Choir burst into song together: **O Come All Ye Faithful**. The only people not singing were the Piano and the Organ, who were busy enough as it was, as well as one lone man in the pew near the Altos. The Tall Soprano wondered why he wasn't singing but was soon lost in the fervor of the carol.

The Sopranos sang like their lives depended on it. At the same time, easily able to multitask, they ruminated, throughout the entire first verse, on the outburst from the Basses. Much like the Borg Collective from the Star Trek series, the Sopranos were of one mind. They didn't just think alike ... they shared the same thoughts. By the end of the first verse, they had come to a conclusion: *We are Soprano! No one ... no one ... upstages Soprano!* With a key change at the start of the second verse the insurrection began: The Sopranos came in on the first note with the rest of the Choir, but with the second note they blew through the barrier skittering up the treble staff in a semi-controlled manner. It was actually enchanting: **Sing choirs of angels, sing in exultation, sing all ye cit-**. In the middle of the next word, they came back to the normal melody: **i-zens of.** But it was too much. They had experienced independence and didn't want to give it up. Back up to the top of the treble staff they flew: **heaven above**. The second time they flew they refused to come back. In fact, they started taking liberties. The high E, used repeatedly in the verse, was left in the dust as the Sopranos scurried up to an F-Sharp, bending the note downward to a D Sharp: **Glory to God, All Glory in the High-**. Nonplussed at the sound of the D Sharp, they settled back on the E: **est.** They enjoyed the E. They enjoyed it so much they held it while the rest of the Choir tried to make sense of the refrain: **O Come**. They were having a wonderful time. The Director cued the second part of the refrain as the Sopranos continued their insurrection: **O Come**. When the third part of the refrain came, they were flitting all up and down the treble staff: **O Come Let Us Adore Him Christ, The**. They were pleased with themselves. *We are Soprano*, they thought as one. And

Chapter 6 ...Tucson ...The Tall Soprano

as if to impress their conviction on the Choir and the Congregation, they filled their lungs and soared to a high A holding it in fortissimo for two measures: **LORD!** *Forgive and forget*, they thought, as they sat down in front of the Basses.

THE OFFERTORY

The Choir sacrificed an Alto and a Soprano to instruments. When everyone was ready, the Director signaled the instruments. The Flute set the stage, coming in with somber meditative strains. The Violin echoed, blending each note with the next, rising and sparkling like twinkling stars on a moonless night. The Congregation sat mesmerized. The Director brought the Altos and the Sopranos in on the contemplative stanza. She brought the Tenors and the Basses in to join them on the next line. Instruments and Choir alternated as the softly pulsing anthem resonated throughout the church. The last line came: **Bring your empty lives with longing, then return full-hearted**. The Director swayed with the music, silently singing the words with the Choir until at last they ended with ... **home**. Every mouth formed a perfect O shape for a full three seconds. Bringing her thumb and middle finger together, the Director gave the signal to complete the last word with a reverent **-mmm**, until at last she released her fingers, like a bird lightly taking flight, and the sound faded into eternity. The Congregation and the Choir listened silently as the Piano, then the Flute, and lastly the Violin joined together in the last measure purposefully completing a musical sigh ... bringing peace to the Church ... and renewed hope for peace on Earth.

COMMUNION

During Communion, the Altos led the way to the communion station at the front of the church, followed by the Tenors, the Sopranos, and the Basses. When the Altos returned to their chairs, the Organ cued the next song: "What Child Is This?" The Sopranos, still communing, had yet to return. The Altos, filled with confidence, sang the accompaniment as they had learned it ... without the melody. It was destined to be a fiasco! As the Sopranos returned, they heard the Altos ... as if for the first time. The Tall Soprano, and consequently all the Sopranos, thought it to be extraordinary. The one lone man in the pew in front of the Altos swayed in his pew, his eyes closed, devouring every rich note. It was a melody so unfamiliar and yet so astonishingly lovely. The Sopranos, visibly moved, had a thought surprising even them ... *We are Choir.* They joined the singing with a different purpose: It became a song of praise, "Haste ... Haste," singing their high notes on the one hand, listening for the Altos on the other, "Joy ... Joy."

Recessional

The recessional was the traditional "Joy to the World." The Choir stood. The Congregation stood. The Sopranos, still reeling from their surprising thought, were dumbfounded to see the Director, who had taken up lodging with the Altos, throw a darting look to her right. What is she looking at? they thought, still in unison. The singing began: **Joy to the world, the Lord is come**. There it was again ... another look ... was it a signal? ... A third look ... Was the Director promoting anarchy? Because all eyes were on the Director, no one noticed the Organ, who had been held back by the Director for so long he simply couldn't stand it anymore. His left foot went down halfway as the booming voice of the organ began the second verse: **Joy to the earth, the Savior reigns**. The Congregation was noticeably distraught. They could not hear themselves sing. And so, they doubled their efforts. Words and music not only filled the church but spilled out into the neighborhood. The Director continued throwing darting glances to her right. It appeared the Director was openly signaling the Basses to incite a riot. The Organ, who could see the Director clearly, decided he was not to be outdone. He put the pedal all the way down to the floor at the start of the third verse, inspiring a key change. The Tall Soprano, ever a fan of key changes, had a clear view of the foot pedals. She had been watching the Director with her left eye and the Organ with her right. She inhaled as much air as she could and belted out the third verse:

Chapter 6 ... Tucson ... The Tall Soprano

He rules the world with truth and grace! Everyone followed suit. Each was fighting to be heard. The Congregation could not help themselves, but, being good Lutherans, they all stood stoically in place ... except for the lone Baptist in the third row. The Sopranos, especially the Tall Soprano, the Basses, the Tenors, the Altos, the Organ, the Piano, the Director, and the Congregation completed the song, realizing ... in unison ... *We are one!*

It was a ... very ... Merry ... Christmas!

Chapter 7 ... Tucson

Golf

Harry's men's golfing group abandoned him on New Year's Day. He turned to me. I joined him at Fred Enke, the neighborhood course known for eating golf balls. We had an enjoyable game, but I gave up three balls and Harry did about the same. My most notable loss was a new neon red ball. I whacked it on the back nine. It sailed directly to the ridge and went over. I was elated. On the other side of the ridge was a little trough of sand, dirt, and small rocks ... a drainage trough, which directs everything to the bottom of the hill into a rocky area. Nothing gets lost there ... except my beautiful new ball. I could not find it and was instantly disgusted. Golf ... why bother?!

Ruthe's Birthday

A trio of residents called The Desert Boys frequently entertained at the park: Wally, on the tambourine, was the lead singer; Don and Dennis, on bass guitars, were the backup singers. Their playing was enhanced with Wally's soundtrack machine. They played for Coffee and Donuts monthly and for special events ... including Ruthe's 101st birthday. Sweet Ruthe has so much energy. She takes it slowly but never stops. Her daughter brought decorations, cake, and ice cream. Everybody sang and whooped it up. We had a grand old time. The Desert Boys started playing immediately. Wally announced they were going to entertain for thirty minutes, take a break, and then come back to entertain for another hour. For those on the clean-up committee, it was shaping up to be a long afternoon. Ruthe was there for the whole party ... more than two hours! During the second half of the program, I saw something unusual for an over-55 park. There were dozens of young people out on the dance floor busting their moves. They were all about eighteen or nineteen. It was amazing. The people in the park had seen the ravages of time from age and gravity: jowls and other things south of the jaw line had long since drooped, gaits had slowed, shoulders had hunched ... but when The Desert Boys started playing songs from the 60s, a third of the people stood up. One walker was left by a table as the people moved out onto the dance floor. After three steps, the dancers lost ten years. Three more steps ... another ten years. By the time they started jiving, they had regressed to being eighteen and nineteen years old. They were doing the two-step, a modified twist, and assorted dances from the 60s. It was simply astounding. And who doesn't love songs of the 60s!

Happy Birthday, Ruthe!

Chapter 7 ... Tucson 233

50ᵀᴴ Anniversary

Two couples celebrated their 50th anniversary. A few weeks earlier, when The Dessert Boys were playing for Coffee and Donuts, they invited the couples up to dance while they played a favorite: "I Can't Help Falling in Love with You." It was a treat to see the two couples in each other's arms ... laughing and enjoying each other. Fifty years ... it's a good thing.

Hectic

The park filled up on January 1st. Major activities occurred from January through March. If you got involved, you had to hang on for dear life. I got involved. I looked at my calendar and was stunned to see it was totally full four days a week. And then I did the obvious ... I filled in Monday.

Huh?

With a full schedule, I did my other chores whenever I got a chance. I told Harry I was going to do some errands, including grocery shopping. I asked him the usual question:

"I'm going to the store; do you want anything?"

"Yeah." There was a long pause.

"Can you be more specific?"

"No."

(Sigh!)

Full Calendar

Agility: The Dog Club was in full swing, but Lucy and I had decided to take a break from participating in agility. I still went to the club meetings. (I was well trained at BPA: attend meetings!)

Chapter 7 ... Tucson

Ceramics: Slab rolling in ceramics was a big thing. We rolled out a slab like a pie crust and made pockets, trivets, and vases. I made an 8" x 10" pudgy wood pigeon to hang on the palm tree in front of our RV site.

Dinner and a show: A comedian came from two hours away in the mountains. There was snow in them thar' hills. He braved the elements just to do a gig for our park. With lots of little quips, he had us laughing, continuously. He invited us to write questions on 3" x 5" cards during the intermission. He promised the person with the best question would get dinner and a show. Everyone tried to come up with a question for him. I joined in, but no, I'm not going to tell you what I asked. Suffice it to say I was a little embarrassed when he announced my name along with the question. Oops. I guess nobody else put their name on their card. (BPA taught me to fill out forms, too!) After he addressed all the questions, he picked the winner. I won! He asked me the name of my favorite restaurant. I was speechless. He invited me up to the front while he was digging around in his satchel. I thought he might have coupons for a multitude of restaurants inside. But, with a flourish, he fished out a box of macaroni and cheese. Everyone roared! Next, he brought out an old movie on DVD. Harry and I enjoyed our "dinner and a show" at the first available opportunity.

Painting: In January, McKenna led us in painting a coyote in silhouette in front of a large harvest moon. I thought it was perhaps one of the most challenging and potentially intimidating paintings we had attempted, but everybody jumped in with both feet. We had coyotes of every size and shape, one of which looked like a javelina.

In February, we attempted a simple lighthouse with a clear blue sky, glassy sea, grassy land, and a few birds. It wasn't terribly challenging so I added a battleship ... heading straight for the lighthouse ... complete with guns a-blazin'. My brother said he thinks I've been spending too much time watching conspiracy theories on TV.

The final painting, in March, was a stylized blazing sun with a cactus ... a rainbow of colors.

Slapstick: There were tickets available for a dinner theater downtown. Harry had never been into slapstick, but I always loved it. I went with a group of people on the shuttle. The play was hysterical ... it was a little light on plot and script but well executed. The ad-libbing had us in stitches! If Harry had been there, he would have walked out before the intermission.

Therapeutic painting: A resident named De led a therapeutic painting class. She invited us to think of a time in our lives when we were very emotionally invested. And then she invited us to paint the emotion using whatever colors and whatever shape felt right. The third step was to look at a list she provided and find a positive hopeful emotion next to the one we had already painted. We were to paint the hopeful emotion as well. The paintings themselves were most unusual. Many were bold and graphic. A few people opted to share what they did and why. As they shared you could see how the picture expressed their emotions. A few others stayed after the class and shared their stories in a more intimate setting. It was a powerfully cathartic session.

Rincon Singers: The Rincon Singers met on Tuesdays. We planned to sing a few songs for the 50th anniversary celebration in February and then do a seven-song medley for Coffee and Donuts the following month. After a few practices we started to sound like something ... something good.

Book sales: I had a book signing table at the Craft Fair every Tuesday after singing practice. When foot traffic was light, I did paintings of birds and assorted animals to amuse myself and the other vendors.

Zentangle: A zentangle class (purposeful doodling) was held every Wednesday afternoon. One ceramics lady said she was going to do a zentangle drawing on a trivet. She got several of the ceramics people excited about doing the same.

Church: I initiated a Zoom call every Thursday afternoon and connected with my church buddies back home for an hour of prayer. COVID was responsible for all of us becoming tech savvy.

Choir: On Thursday nights, I had choir practice at TVLC about six miles north of the park.

Bible study: On Friday mornings, my TVLC friend Peggy picked me up for Bible study while Harry was out golfing. The girls, who usually get treats for going to their crates, would run to their beds whenever I put my jacket on.

Spanish class: Spanish class was held on Friday afternoons. The first session was easy enough, but it got complicated pretty fast. Several of us decided to have a couple of study halls on Monday and Wednesday. We found we were spending up to six hours studying each week! We started to understand it ... and then everyone departed for the summer.

BOOK SIGNING

I checked in with my Tucson pastor and asked if I could have a book signing since all the proceeds were going to support World Hunger. He said, "Sure." It was wildly successful. I was there on Saturday night and Sunday morning. One lady came up to me brightly on Sunday morning. I didn't recognize her at all. She said she was already to the "part about the log." I was so surprised. She was well into the book, but I didn't remember signing one for her. She told me she was the wife of the organist. An avid reader, she had jumped right in when her husband brought the book home the night before. We hung out after the service and laughed for ten minutes.

KATHY?

Kate and Irv sold their park model on Happy Street and moved to one across from the clubhouse. They invited quite a number of people to come to an open house. Harry and I were among the first to arrive. After several more people showed up, the women looked at each other. We scratched our heads: The first six women to appear were … Kathy!

Horse Races

Right in the middle of the January chaos it was time for Horse Races. Sallie and Robert joined forces and bought a mare. Sallie dressed her in a miniature red dress with ruffles and a black fringe. It must have been used by a very little girl for a recital. Everybody at Happy Hour was excited to see how perfect the dress was. Sallie named the mare Lolita. The next day, Sallie showed up with a long black wig. It was perfect for Lolita's outfit!

Lolita's head had to be modified slightly to hold the wig on properly. Sallie dragged her husband Don to a craft store where they found a grapefruit-sized Styrofoam ball for Lolita's wig. Don grabbed two more apple-sized Styrofoam balls … and you know what they were for! By the time little Lolita was all dressed up, she had cleavage! Her fringe, which came down to a "V" in the front, was swinging freely. Since Sallie would be the one to introduce the mare onstage, Don insisted she tip Lolita forward slightly when introducing her on the day of the races.

When the big day came, Sallie got up to introduce Lolita. She did it by reciting the words to the song, "Lola." There's something about the way Sallie moves her eyebrows when she talks. The whole room was cracking up. At the end of the night, Lolita fared way better than Queenie had the previous year: She won best-dressed and two races. I was betting on her when she won! I doubled my money. I could afford to take Harry out for coffee … one cup for each of us. Woohoo … I was a winner!

Chapter 7 ... Tucson 239

Surgical Caps

One of the Canadian residents invited volunteers to make surgical caps for kids. She had precut material and elastic. When we gathered in the sewing room, there were two ladies on each task: ironing, serging, sewing, stringing elastic, and finishing. One was running back and forth making sure everyone had what they needed to work efficiently and checking the finished product. It was an amazing team effort. Once we got our stride, we turned out about ten surgical caps every fifteen minutes. We made enough for forty children and ten adults in two hours and had a great time doing it.

Entertainment

William Florian had been the lead singer of the New Christy Minstrels back in the day. He came to the park in 2022 to do a concert of Neil Diamond songs. He did such a great job he was snagged to do a concert of John Denver songs. He brought Raphael, a Tucson bass player, with him again. The crowd loved them. As he did in his Neil Diamond concert, he explained how and why John Denver wrote the songs. Near the end of the performance, he threw in some New Christy Minstrel songs. He was about to finish with more John Denver when someone from the crowd asked for "Sweet Caroline." Without missing a beat, he and Raphael dove right into it. The audience came alive with the "Bah-Bah-Bahs" and the "So good, So good, So goods." Just for good measure, he threw in "Kentucky Woman." Too bad Betty was away on a cruise.

Theater Club

Theater practice started near the end of January. The theater group puts on an annual talent show, except for during the pandemic. I volunteered to do some readings between skits to fill the down time while the sets were being rearranged.

Chapter 7 ... Tucson

Dog Agility

It takes a little effort to keep the agility ring looking spic and span, but there were plenty of people in the club, so we had our pick of volunteer duties. I filled sandbags with Marcia and Jane. We jumped in Marcia's truck, drove four minutes to the sandpile a mile away, loaded four sandbags in seven minutes, and drove the four minutes back to the park. The sandbags were good for another few years. I also volunteered on the painting crew. We needed a taper (me), a painter (Duane), and a sand sprinkler (Jeff). How hard could it be? One hour later all the equipment was sparkling with new regulation blue and yellow colors. Paint dries fast in Tucson! The sand on the wet paint would provide effective traction for dogs as they run up and over the Bridge, A-Frame, and Teeter Totter. Many hands ...!

Flu

Right in the middle of the busy season, I came down with a bad cold. I took some COVID tests and was pleased to find out it was only a cold or the flu: sore throat, congestion ... nothing worse ... but it took me out of commission. Peggy from Bible study said her daughter had adult whooping cough. I know enough not to mess with whooping cough, so I tried to figure out how to negotiate the health care system in Arizona. I made a quick call to my provider and found out all I had to do was go to Urgent Care. I got checked out and was told to tough it out. I took a break from Spanish class, ceramics, singing, the craft fair, and zentangle. I sucked on cough drops and hunkered down. I was sorely disappointed to miss the Variety Show. However, I found out later none of the performers got to see it live. The whole cast, including me, got DVDs. I got to see it after all ... and it was wonderful!

Cousins, Cousins, Cousins

My three dear cousins, Cathy, Phyllis, and Beau, were all in Tucson for their family reunion. They had one free window of time. Cousin

Judy and I had the same free window. She and I raced over to the northwest corner of Tucson to have lunch with them at Grumpy's Grill. Even though we've got snowy tops, as soon as the words started flowing, we were all in high school once again. We laughed and caught up for a couple of hours.

Cousins: Kathy, Judy, Beau, Cathy, Phyllis

Chapter 8 ... Tucson ... Dog Exhibition

The sixth annual Dog Exhibition was held on the first warm day following our cold wet winter. I had recovered from my illness and was glad for the distraction. Participants and observers were grateful to break out the short-sleeved shirts and shorts. Lawn chairs abounded. Special parking behind the lawn chairs was designated for face-in golf-cart parking. Every seat had a great view. As usual there were four categories. The little battery-operated megaphone was brought out of storage. AKC-Carol, in her glittery pink baseball cap, had tutored owners and dogs diligently for weeks. The teams had been practicing since the beginning of January ... but, as always, there was never a guarantee anything would go as planned.

Rally

Rally can be performed with touching and treats. The owner is also allowed to use voice and body language.

Dawn – Labradoodle – Jessie. Dawn and Jessie (eleven years old) made it look easy as they went from station to station performing left turns, right turns, about faces, and any manner of maneuvers required by the course.

Duane – Golden Retriever – Tucker. Tucker's innate grace and ambling manner made him a joy to watch.

Minnesota-Carol – All-American Dog – Topaz. Carol researched Topaz's lineage and discovered about two dozen breeds of dog in his background. He has the body and grace of a Boxer, the head shape of a German Shepherd, and the nimbleness of a fawn. Topaz had been a wild dog the year before, but Carol's constant work with him ... walking, training, and patient handling ... had paid off. He looked like he was having fun demonstrating his accomplishments. His performance was a thing of beauty. (Carol kept a smelly treat in her hand holding it at nose level.) Topaz readily did everything she asked of him, and as a side bonus he pranced around the ring like a horse preforming dressage!

TRICKS

Iowa Carol – Golden Retriever – Tucker. Tucker was going to show us how well his nose worked by finding a treat under one of three cups. Carol brought him into the ring, but he's such a large dog it was nothing for him to lean in and check the cups before Carol realized what was happening. He easily upset the correct cup and found the treat. The crowd roared. Since spontaneity was not on the trick list, Carol had someone hold Tucker's leash while she reset the trick. When she released Tucker, he took off like a missile, nose first, targeting the box on which the cups were positioned. Sniff, sniff, sniff … nailed it again. The crowd roared again.

As she had done the previous year, Carol told Tucker to sit on a box the size of an apple crate. In slow motion, he put his front paws on the box, thought about what to do next, and with a little jump, he was sitting pretty on top of the box. When he got off, she flipped it and told him to get in the box. It was a bit more of a problem for this seventy-five-pound beast. Carol reiterated the command. He jumped a little (although it was more like walking) and his front legs were in … the crowd cheered "Yea." He ambled again and his back legs were in, but his front legs were out. (He was twice as long as the box.) Cheer! Carol stuck with him … he moved … front legs in, back legs out … and again … front legs out, back legs in. Every move resulted in a cheer (we were easily amused). On the next try, it clicked for him … front legs in, back legs in … The crowd gave a mighty yell! Carol commanded, "Sit!" The box was barely able to contain his bulk, but after giving it two thoughts, Tucker slowly sat in the box, folding his tail as needed. The crowd went wild! His next trick was "Catch the Ball." He's a retriever … enough said.

Dawn – Labradoodle – Teddy. Dawn took her Labradoodle puppy into the ring, positioned him on a mat, and announced he was going to do Push-Ups. With the exaggerated movements of a seasoned trainer, she stuck a treat in front of Teddy's nose, shoved her hand to the ground saying "Down!" He went down. Dawn straightened, lifting her loaded grip into the air, hollering, "Up!" Teddy returned to a sitting position. A few more iterations ... Down, Up, Down ... and Teddy's trick was immortalized, leaving Dawn exhausted. The crowd cheered. (I wondered if the day's cheering might have had something to do with everyone being pent up for two months.) Teddy, not a small dog, gave us a demonstration of standing on the wobble board, catching a ball, and running up and across the Bridge.

Laura – Terrier/Beagle – Rosco. Laura told Rosco to hit a four-inch buzzer. He did and got a treat immediately. She repeated the command with the same result. Pretty soon, Rosco took charge and did it without getting a command ... it's all about food! The buzzer was a lot more tolerable than Tucker's Boy-yoy-yoing from the year before. Rosco also demonstrated the wobble board and rolled over on command.

CANINE GOOD CITIZEN

Trish, Judy, Minnesota-Carol, and Tamara demonstrated their dogs' willingness to walk in a circle at varying speeds and then two by two, they met in the center to show how well-behaved dogs were expected to act while the owners had a little visit. Nothing untoward happened!

DOG AGILITY

Agility is to be performed without touching or treats. The owner is allowed to use only voice and body language.

Trish – Australian Shepherd – Kobe. As a beginning team, Patricia had Kobe negotiate three Jumps, the Bridge, and the Table. He had the hair coloring and shape of a Bernese Mountain Dog, which is arguably the prettiest breed on the planet. It was a pleasure to watch him run through his routine. He obviously wanted to perform for the crowd.

Tamara – Havanese – Theodore. Theodore worked pretty well for Tamara until he got to the A-Frame, which peaks at more than five feet. Instead of up and over, he ran around the A-Frame on the first and second try, got a boost from Tamara on the third try but never made it past the three-foot mark. AKC-Carol, who has two Havanese of her own, came to help. From my vantage point, it looked like Carol was trying to shoot a basket from the half-court line: She bent forward at the waist, lowered little Theodore between her knees, and hefted him in the direction of the A-Frame. It was all the help he needed. He continued up and over and walked smartly down the opposite side. Everyone ... everyone cheered!

Iowa-Carol – Golden Retriever – Tucker. Tucker had to go through the Tunnel. He balked slightly at the entrance. The audience got excited at the possibility of a dog going off script but calmed down when Tucker came around and did exactly as commanded. He went through the Tunnel, to the Table, across the Bridge, up and over the A-Frame, and through the Hoop. The audience had to wait for another dog to supply comic relief since Carol had spent hours rehearsing the routine with Tucker. But comic relief was destined to come soon.

Kevin – Labradoodle – Justice. Kevin got his exercise running Justice around the ring. He started with Stay at the Jump and then they were off: Jump ... Jump ... Hoop. Justice was on her best behavior until she got to the Hoop. There was something very interesting near the Hoop, and Justice was all about exploring. As it happened, there was a dog on the other side of the privacy fence. We didn't know it, but Justice did. After a couple of false starts, she finished the course with Kevin.

Tom – Shih Tzu – Gizmo. There was one remaining team. Carol introduced Tom and Gizmo stating we were about to see a competition-ready team. When you hear those words, you know it's the kiss of death! Tom walked into the ring with a "Come on, Gizmo," got to the center, and realized he was dogless. Off-lead demonstrations ... what's not to love! The first Jump was a hard one. Gizmo sat there, snuffled his nose, and trotted around it. The second Jump was a piece of cake and soon Gizmo was running through the Tunnel on command. Things were progressing nicely for the team ... until Gizmo's "reverse" switch kicked in. He turned around and went back through the Tunnel the way he had just come. Then, his "forward" switch kicked in as he turned again and ambled through the Tunnel in the right direction a second time. He came out, but before he hit the Table for his full five seconds, he took a couple of detours to the fence next to the Tunnel. Finally, the audience had their comic relief. Tom just shrugged. I looked back at the Tunnel and saw Carol blocking one of the ends ... just in case. But soon Gizmo got bored with the fence and sauntered to the Table. Tom told him to go across the Bridge, up and over the A-Frame, through the Hoop, and through the Weave. Although he was in no big hurry, he did everything Tom asked of him. For his last challenge, Tom told him to take the Teeter Totter, which he did with the ho-hum attitude of one who has long since mastered the maneuver: He trotted slightly past the midpoint, waited for his body weight to lower the other side, and walked off pretty as a picture. As he meandered out of the ring with Tom, the Sixth Annual Dog Exhibition came to a happy close.

Chapter 9 ... Tucson

It Never Dawned on Me I Might Be Wrong

You would think since Arizona does not participate in Daylight Savings Time there would be no time issues to deal with. But ... you would be wrong. (Part of my problem was getting a new phone in February and not checking to see how the time change worked.)

I had no shortage of opportunities to tell time. I had a phone and a tablet in the living room, a battery-operated clock with large numbers on the shelf above the fireplace, and a clock on the microwave. Harry had only one opportunity to tell time: his phone in the bedroom was set up to display a large digital clock.

I got up around 6 a.m. and meandered into the living room as usual. I opened the blinds and checked for clouds in case we were to have another beautiful sunrise. With no clouds changing color, I had no way to judge the passage of time. I had already missed dawn. At 6:30 a.m., I sat down to pray and checked my tablet for news or whatever. When I looked up later, the clock above the fireplace read 7:30. Harry was due to get up at any minute. I continued to look at the clock above the fireplace. Harry was sleeping in. It was Sunday: I had to leave for church and didn't want to be late. I needed to leave at least by 8:45 a.m. to take him to the golf course so I could be at church by 9:15 a.m. Harry was oversleeping, and I was getting pretty anxious. At 8:30 a.m. I couldn't stand it any longer. I started clattering around in the kitchen. I figured he hadn't set his clock. Pretty soon he came out and got ready to take the dogs for a walk. "You slept a long time," I said, noncommittally. He growled something back at me about the time change, but I still had no clue. After he left with the dogs, I started looking at every clock. There were different times everywhere. It never dawned on me I might be wrong. It took all of five minutes of concentrated thought to realize I was indeed wrong and another five minutes to reset all the clocks. Good Grief! When are we going to get rid of the time changes?

Quarantine

My illness quarantine was over. I returned all my activities to my schedule.

During singing practice, I stood next to Katherine, another soprano. We were going to sing for Coffee and Donuts the next day. One of the songs was Roy Orbison's "Crying." While we were all singing the lamenting words at the end, with Kleenex and hankies dangling, Katherine honked realistically into her Kleenex. It got a good laugh during practice and again during the performance.

Bright and early Thursday, I showed up to peel potatoes and carrots for the huge St. Patrick's Day dinner, only to find out Katherine and her husband Roderick had tested positive for COVID. I self-quarantined for three more days and focused on outdoor things and painting while waiting for three consecutive negative tests. I was so pleased to learn I didn't get COVID, but I was sorry I had to miss the St. Patrick's Day dinner. Then I heard someone who had been peeling potatoes and carrots had tested positive the next day. Quarantine ... it's a good thing!

A Glimpse of the Past

Lots of visitors show up at the park throughout the season. Usually, they can be found walking around the Loop with their hosts. But when Robert and Betty have visitors, they are often nieces, some in their early twenties. They're easy to spot ... young professionals sipping their specialty coffee drinks purchased outside the park while flitting from place to place in Betty's fancy golf cart, wearing a Rincon RV Park smile. Like Ava and Annie embarking on a career of promise and a life of excitement ... we were those girls, once.

THE CHILDREN'S SERMON

On Sunday, at TVLC, Pastor Stephen gathered all the children around and told them they were going to play Telephone. They all appeared to know what that meant ... but they didn't. He whispered to the first child. It seemed to take a long time. The little boy was stoic and didn't respond at all. I wondered if it was part of the game. Pastor Stephen gave up and went on to the second child. The second attempt got all jumbled up, too. The third little boy caught it and whispered it to a little girl, but it got stuck again. It was pretty funny. Pretty soon, everything clicked and the kids were "telephoning" each other. And then, when they started giggling, it all went to pot. Finally, Pastor Stephen couldn't stand it any longer. He intervened and asked what the last one had heard ... it was something about an orange at end of life. He announced he had originally said, "My March Madness bracket fell apart." The kids weren't even close! Somehow, he managed to get the lack of communication to factor into the day's sermon and quickly ended with a prayer. I love children's sermons. They're so unpredictable.

Chapter 9 ... Tucson

A BIG POT OF STEW

I was pretty smart in high school. I got all the right answers. But then I graduated, and it was all downhill from there. For example, I made a great big pot of stew. When I finished putting the stew away, I needed to soak the pot before washing it. The water pressure was pretty lousy. Instead of putting the pot in the sink and listening to the water dribble into it for the next five minutes, I thought how smart it would be to put the pot on the counter, swivel the faucet around, and let it fill, silently. Sadly, I couldn't seem to hold a thought for very long. While waiting for the pot to fill, I got distracted and sat down to watch TV with Harry. Fortunately, I got up to do something after only one hour. I was horrified to discover a big flood on the kitchen counter. The recessed induction stovetop was a pool ... when I walked, I could see a little wave action. The water on the counter seemed to be puddling in the back left corner. Rather than bother Harry with those details, I grabbed a big towel and started sopping up water. I was pleased to find the counter sloped slightly toward the back; I was also pleased to find it was pretty well sealed. When I finished, I thought it might be wise to check outside to see if there were any wet spots below the slide. I took a little bitty flashlight and went outside to check. I didn't see any glistening gravel. Things were looking good. Back inside, I pulled out the bottom two drawers and felt way in the back to see if any of the carpeting underneath the kitchen area was wet. The initial test was dry. I put a paper towel on the end of a stick and stuck it as far back as I could. It came back dry. Boy was I happy! All was well in my world again.

OCTOPUS PAINTING

While I was at the craft fair, I painted a pretty good-looking Gila monster. It was the last craft fair of the season. One of my new friends, Dick, came by on his mobility scooter, saw the Gila monster, and declared (in his slow-talking manner) he had never seen a painting or print of an octopus. He was into whales and octopi. Although he had lots of prints of whales, he none of an octopus. It sounded like a challenge to me. I whipped out my phone and googled image of octopus. Up popped a picture.

"Is this an octopus?" I asked.

"Oh, yes ... it's a Great Pacific Octopus," he drawled.

"Do you like the colors?"

"Oh, yes," he said meditatively.

"Do you like the background?"

"Oh, yes," he said leisurely.

I had all the information I needed. A week later, I had finished the most amazing painting I had ever done. We both loved it. I hated to give it up. (See image on back cover.)

More Octopus Work

I stopped by to visit Dick a number of times during the last month of our stay. I had already given him the painting. Even though I had a picture stored on my phone, I missed the painting. I went to the ceramics room, rolled out a slab of clay, traced the octopus, and started playing with glazes. I layered all sorts of colors on the clay like I did with the painting. With each session, the project got more detailed, and the colors got sharper. After each session, I snapped a picture of the progress and ran across the street to show Dick on my way back to the coach. He was getting excited, too. The final firing was on a Friday morning, the day before we were to return to Vancouver. It was a pretty tight timeframe, but it got done. I picked up the octopus at 6 p.m. It was still warm. It was stunning. It wasn't the same as the painting, but it was special in its own right. I went across the street to show Dick. When I appeared at his doorstep, he knew exactly why I was visiting. "Just a minute," he said in his calm voice. He edged himself up straight in his chair, his eyes sparkling in anticipation. He examined it carefully and agreed it was a winner. As an added bonus, the frame he ordered had come in. I got to see the painting in its new dark brown frame. It was stunning. It was a satisfying end to the mad-dash efforts of the previous few weeks. (See image on back cover.)

Chapter 10 ... Heading Home

Please Fix Yourself

There's always something crazy about traveling. We started experiencing the craziness immediately. When we left the park the radio system, which included the rear camera, wouldn't work. I couldn't see the Jeep behind the motor home, nor could I see enhanced views of the left and right of the coach when signaling. Those views were essential for switching lanes safely. Harry sat on the floor in front of the console, fiddled with the system, and finally got it to work.

The low voltage light was flashing on the dashboard and the check engine light was lit below it. We'd seen that scenario before. It was a quick fix. We shut off the engine and started it again ... the problem was resolved. We were headed home.

Fixed Itself ... Not!

On the first day of our journey, we stopped and refueled. We were experienced at running through our refueling process: Harry jumped out, poked the nozzle into the coach, dealt with the fuel, and ran off to take care of the windshield. I jumped out, grabbed the leashes from the little drawer under the steps, and took care of the girls.

When Harry finished with the windows, he checked the hose. There was no activity. The pump registered 102 gallons ... $500. He went in, paid the bill, but for some reason they were unable to give him a receipt. He came back out and checked the fuel gauge. It still showed a quarter full. He tapped it a couple of times to no avail. By that time, I had returned and had put the heavy retractable leads in the shallow drawer beneath the steps. I saw him tapping the gauge. "What in the world is wrong now," we both wondered out loud. After spitting and fuming a few minutes, Harry went back in to talk with the cashier. When he returned, he poked the start

Chapter 10 ... Heading Home

button and filled the tank "again." This time, when he finished, they returned his first $500 and charged him for the fuel that was actually pumped. Evidently, it's important to push the start button.

On the second day of our journey, we were experiencing 83° weather. We stopped for refueling. We went through our efficient procedure again. This time there were no problems with the refueling or the dogs. Everything was going smoothly. Harry started the generator so we could have air conditioning on the road. I put those heavy retractable leads back into the shallow dog drawer, jumped into the passenger seat, and we were on our way. But as we slowly pulled out of the refueling bay there was a horrible crunching metal noise. We felt something jarring the coach. Harry stopped immediately and backed up a tad. We were horrified and perplexed. We both jumped up and started out of the coach when Harry said, "Well, what the heck is the awning down for?" We were both shocked. Somehow, the awning had extended itself during our stop. As we were driving off, it had fought with a concrete pillar and lost. As best we knew, there was only one way it could have been extended ... with the button in the cabinet above the driver's seat. Neither one of us had gone near the cabinet. I wondered if starting the generator could have had anything to do with it. It seemed unlikely, but it's an all-electric coach, so who knows. We both shrugged. It was a mystery we were pretty sure we weren't going to solve. Harry pushed the button hoping it would retract and it did. It retracted to within six inches of the coach. It was a very welcome sight. Good enough to go.

After a trip of everything fixing itself, we were ending with something actually breaking and doing some real damage. Nevertheless, it appeared the only damage was to the awning arm and the cover ... not to the body of the coach!

We stopped at two more RV parks on the way home. Harry talked to other RV owners to see if they'd ever had a problem with their awnings mysteriously extending. They offered no help ... it wasn't a common problem. It was destined to remain a mystery.

Dryers Don't Fix Themselves

About three weeks before we returned home, our poor little house sitter, Alyssa, was in the middle of doing the laundry when the dryer died. I got on the phone and arranged for a new dryer. We were going to be home on Tuesday, May 2, about noonish. The dryer, a new machine, demoed as a floor model, was going to be delivered on Friday, May 5. I wondered if anything could go wrong with the plan. I knew the answer: Oh, so many things! And so I thought it prudent to do a load of laundry when we hooked up on our last night ... the night of my seventy-fifth birthday. (Never travel on your birthday!)

Doing the laundry was a little bit noisy. We closed the doors to keep the noise down. As a result, I frequently forgot to deal with it ... which bugs Harry. Doing laundry on my birthday at an RV park was probably doomed for failure. Neither one of us was very thrilled about the idea of tending the laundry, but I wanted a basketful of clean underwear, just in case! No sooner did I get the laundry started early in the evening than I got a phone call from the dryer people: They were going to be able to deliver it the next day and asked if I was going to be there. "Oh yes," I chirped, "I sure will be."

"Will you be able to pay by cash or check?"

"Oh sure, no problem." I hung up the phone. I was so happy! Actually, I was not happy ... I had started the laundry unnecessarily. But what was done was done.

I don't know how I happened to realize it, but I suddenly discovered I was a day off. We were still a day away from home. There was no way I could be home at 10 a.m. the next day to accept the dryer and make payment. I called Alyssa to see if she would be available. She assured me she would, but she didn't have her checkbook. After a little fancy talking, the appliance store agreed to deliver the dryer while I agreed to stop by and pay them later in the day.

Chapter 10 ... Heading Home

We continued our evening in the motor home, finishing up the laundry and putting all our clean underwear in a special easily identifiable container, even though it was no longer an issue. The next morning, we were on the last leg of our journey home. It looked like we'd get home early in the afternoon. The dryer would be there. I knew unloading the motor home and doing laundry would be easy.

I received a call from the appliance store at 9 a.m. while Harry was driving. They said they discovered a large dent on the back side of the dryer when they were getting ready to load it. They were going to give me a large discount to go along with the large dent if I still wanted the demo model. Harry had other ideas. He barked a flat "No!" (There was no telling what happened to the insides of the dryer, with the outside dented so badly.) There was no other dryer of the same quality in the store. They said they would have to order a new one and it would take ten days to get it shipped. I was immediately happy I had done the laundry and started to wonder if we were going to have enough underwear to last another ten days. At any rate, at least I knew what we did have was in an easily identifiable container.

Chapter 11 ... Vancouver

Arrival

We got home at the expected time. Harry unhooked the Jeep at the bottom of the hill. I drove the motor home up the hill, parked, and stood up to look out at the front yard. I expected to see pop weeds (bitter cress) everywhere. The front yard had been full of it the previous year and it had all gone to seed. I was shocked to see a couple of different kinds of weeds, including a strange kind of ajuga. I stood there staring at it. I couldn't move. I thought perhaps overseeding might be the way to get rid of weeds; there would be so many fighting for the same soil they'd choke themselves out. Then I saw my little Cocoa Bean and went out to greet him. The weeds could be dealt with another day.

The Rest of the Story

The coach was almost empty. The last thing I tackled was the dog drawer under the front step. And there, in the shallow little drawer stuffed to the limit with dog paraphernalia, was a remote control. I picked it up and wondered what a remote was doing in the dog drawer. But it wasn't a normal remote ... it was the remote for the awning! Immediately, I went into the house and told Harry the mysterious extension of the awning was obviously my fault. I must have put the dog leads in the drawer on top of the remote, pushing the button by accident. Harry agreed I was to blame. It took me another two days to wonder why in the world Harry kept the remote for the awning in the dog drawer. Oh yes, I was definitely to blame ... or was I?

Thank Goodness It Didn't Happen in Tucson

Ten days after we got home, I was driving home on the freeway when suddenly it felt and sounded like I had driven over two steel I-beams ... Thunk, thunk. Slight pressure on the gas pedal resulted in a Vrrrrr sound. The Jeep was sounding like it was in neutral. I

Chapter 11 ... Vancouver

limped off the freeway at thirty-five miles per hour. I was glad for a downslope and found a safe place to park. I was also glad I had my cell phone with me. I got busy making phone calls: my mechanic for advice, the Jeep dealer for an appointment, my insurance agent, the tow service, and Harry (who came and picked up my golf clubs and my faithful little companion, Cocoa Bean). Within two hours, I was driving home with a rental car. The transfer case had gone out. Harry and I were reeling at the thought of what might have happened if it had blown up in Tucson. We were also reeling at the thought of paying thousands of dollars to get the problem fixed ... but Harry kept thinking and finally remembered something ... something really good! When the service coordinator called me a few days later with the bad news ... our bill would be more than five thousand dollars ... I meekly asked him after a bit of a pause, "And how much is covered by the extended warranty?" There was a pause as he absorbed the question. We were fortunate this mishap occurred a month before the expiration of our five-year extended warranty. We were totally covered!

Bolstered by this good news, Harry contacted our insurance agent and found out our awning problem was almost completely covered by our motor home insurance. We were lucking out right and left!

CELEBRATION OF LIFE

After we got home, I went to a celebration of life for Gary, the grandfather of five of the little girls who came to my tea parties in the late 1990s (see *Life at Two Ponds*). They are all gorgeous women in their twenties and thirties becoming accomplished in their fields, marrying, and having children of their own. They told me they have cucumber sandwiches like we had at the tea parties whenever they celebrate special life events. How fun is that!

ADDENDUM

It took me a full day to find the supposedly easily identifiable container with my clean underwear and another full day to find my stepping-out clothes. I had to be at church by 2 p.m. and was running low on clean clothes. I spent the morning putting things away until I finally found my long warm pants. I was back in business.

PART SEVEN

2023–24

Chapter 1 ... Downsizing

We had to downsize by one dog before this trip. We discovered the Corgis were highly competitive and we had been living under increasing amounts of dog tension for eight years. Harry told me one of the girls would have to go and I would have to decide which one. I couldn't make that kind of decision, so I buried my head in the sand and hoped the whole issue would go away. Harry decided for me: My dog Angie would have to find a new home.

Reluctantly, I got busy with an online search. Out of the blue, a woman named Carole popped up. She lived a mere thirty minutes from me. Her Corgi, Milo, had died a few months earlier. We communicated via multiple email messages. With all the questions she asked, I knew she would love and care for my special Angie. But, on the morning of the meeting, she called to say she had changed her mind. I asked her why. She said she had had to ask too many questions. Go figure. Nevertheless, it was too good a match to abandon. After a few more conversations and a visit, Angie went to live in her wonderful new home. Carole, an artist and massage therapist, absolutely dotes on Angie ... and Angie dotes back. I couldn't have asked for a better placement.

Chapter 2 ... Moab

Easy Trip South

We were getting smarter by the year. We left Vancouver on a Saturday to avoid traffic in Portland, Boise, and Salt Lake City. It worked. We turned left at Provo and went to Moab. The red rocky cliffs and boulders were a welcome change. In fact, there were some big red boulders in the campground. Harry looked at one of those boulders and suggested I swing wide when it came time to leave. I looked at the boulder and knew I wouldn't hit it with an ordinary turn. Nevertheless, I decided to swing wide anyway, because who wants to have a scratch on a motor home. (And, of course, I'd be driving this time, unlike during that horrendous mailbox incident that resulted in a three-foot scratch on our first motor home, six years earlier.)

Moab ... The High Point

On our first day, we went golfing. I was tickled to find Virginia Creeper running rampant on the golf course: climbing on fences, climbing up into trees, spreading in and around bushes. It was everywhere. It was perfect timing: Virginia creeper turns bright red in the fall. Even better, the golf course, itself, was very forgiving. We had a nice time.

Harry and I thought it would be fun to do some kind of a tour in Moab, but he didn't want to do any work. The front office suggested a rock-crawling tour. There were two types. One would put each of us in the driver's seat of a one-seater ATV, the other would put "Luke" in the driver's seat of an eleven-seater Hummer. We opted for Luke and the Hummer. Another couple joined us. Luke came to pick us up and off we went. The tour propaganda assured us it would be the high point of our vacation. Well, we weren't on vacation; we were retired. Perhaps it would be the high point of our retirement. I had my camera out the whole time. When things got a little hairy and scary, I simply looked through the lens and pretended I was watching it on TV. Occasionally, I'd hit the wrong button on the camera: Selfie mode assured me I was having a good time. It was definitely a high point!

At one point, we went down a sixty-degree eight-foot hillside. When we stopped, I took a picture of me standing next to the hillside called "The Wall" and another picture of the Hummer. I sent those pictures to some people back home. In almost every case, I got a comment back saying "OMG! Are you nuts?"

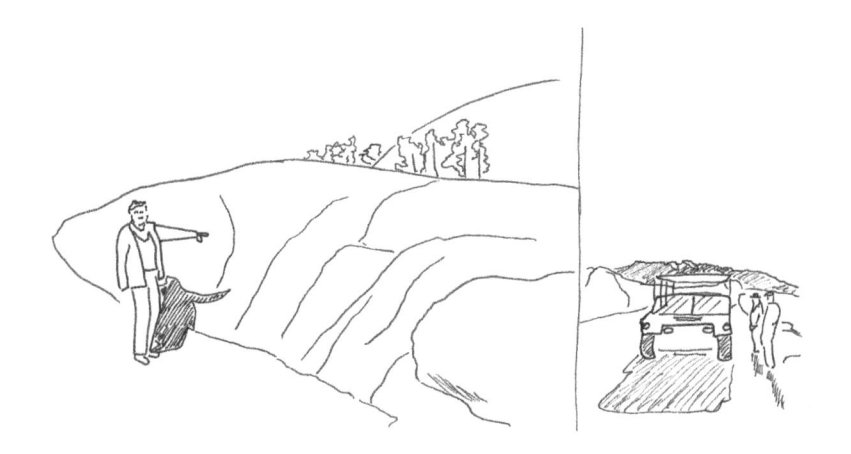

Lasagna Taste Test

We asked Luke about his favorite place to eat. He suggested Pasta Jay's. When our waiter came to take our order, he said we were welcome to wait a long time for whatever we wanted ... or we could order lasagna, which was already made. It was an easy choice. We enjoyed it so much we decided to go out for lasagna once a month at different restaurants.

Stop!

The following morning, we got up and started moving out at 7:30 a.m. I slowly swung wide to the right as planned, creeping forward to make sure I was nowhere near the big boulder at the left. In fact, I was watching three big boulders. I was nowhere near any of them. I could see Harry in my side-view mirrors from time to time. All of a sudden, he flailed his arms and yelled loud enough for me to hear in the closed coach, "STOP!" It's not something you want to hear at 7:30 in the morning in a quiet campground. I stopped. I looked in the mirrors but couldn't see why Harry had sent up the alarm. In fact, he had to tell me there were not three boulders to watch out for ... but four. He said I had moved a boulder. I was grateful to hear the boulder was movable. He got in the coach and, without further incident, we drove to Williams, Arizona, west of Flagstaff to visit Irv and Kate in their new home.

Chapter 3 ... Williams, Arizona

Bell Bottoms

After setting up at the Grand Canyon Railway RV Park in Williams, Harry invited me out to peruse the damage. I looked at the back bin door on the passenger side and saw a crease about three inches from the bottom. It was bad. The whole length of the bin looked like it was wearing bell bottoms. I could live with a crease on a bin door. But as I continued to examine the side of the coach, I saw another crease, and another, and another, and another ... every bin door was creased. Almost the full length of the coach. No longer will I besmirch Harry because of "that horrendous mailbox incident." This was worse ... way worse. I was exceedingly humbled.

Irv and Kate

Irv and Kate had moved from Columbus, Indiana, to Williams, to avoid the long trips back and forth while snowbirding. During the day, the boys went golfing, while Kate and I checked out the house and the town before meeting them for lunch at noon. In the evenings, we went to restaurants and enjoyed each other's company. It was a nice way to ease into the winter.

Chapter 4 ... Tucson

Winter Activities

Going south through Phoenix on a Saturday morning was an easy trip. We were all set up in our park in Tucson for the winter by early afternoon. Harry immediately started golfing with his men's group. I joined the ceramics and lapidary clubs. By the middle of the month, I had completed a commissioned painting of two Belgian Malinois dogs. We were back in business in Tucson!

Back in the Saddle, Again

The activities started in full swing. I rejoined the choir at TVLC: Music Sunday, the big event with challenging music, was coming up fast. I rejoined the Rincon Singers. Our Christmas presentation was scheduled for Coffee and Donuts on Dec 13th. I started working on what I thought would be a simple glass fusion project. It immediately morphed into a big project, but I quickly learned a lot. Several people commissioned paintings of their pets. And, I was working my heart out in the ceramics room. Things were going great. Lots of activities, lots of plans.

Sad News

After we were ensconced in Tucson, I heard from Alyssa back home: The coyotes had done what coyotes do. My little Cocoa Bean had met his demise. There were lots of advantages to living above a gully ... coyote population wasn't one of them.

Lasagna ... DOA

In keeping with the concept of going out for lasagna once a month, we went to Nate's with Irv and Kate. The meal was called Monster Lasagna, but it was not as flavorful as Pasta Jay's in Moab. We came home with lots of leftovers and a little extra: Three days after our excursion, Harry came down with COVID ... and after three more days, I followed suit. Irv and Kate had lucked out. They each had a cold. Harry and I had never been sick together at the same time in our forty-one years of marriage, but this time we suffered through it together ... in the motor home. Harry took the chair; I took the sofa. There were enough blankets to keep us toasty warm. Laundry day occurred in the middle of our infirmity. I got up to check the status, walked slowly through the coach, made it as far as the bed, and toppled to my left with a groan. I was exhausted from walking twenty-five feet! (Later, I laughed as I told my friends I had done a lot of groaning ... to get my fair share!) Robert and Betty dropped into stealth mode and left some cans of chicken noodle soup on our steps one night. Besides tasting good, it was pretty nice to be missed! After five days of isolation, moaning, and groaning, we both masked up and peeked outside. After seven days, we felt better and the masks came off. We were still sleeping a lot but it was nice to be back among the living. After my isolation period, I decided I wouldn't go into any large gatherings of "old" people ... which pretty much killed anything but going for groceries. Music Sunday came and went: I enjoyed the singing from a pew. As for continuing the Lasagna Taste Test ... Dead on Arrival!

Dog Club

AKC-Carol didn't return to the park. She decided to pursue another college degree. The Dog Club was playing catchup all season. We limped through our meetings but did manage to engage with people who wanted to learn how to do agility. The Dog Exhibition was put off for a year.

Open Mic Night

Something new was added. De, the therapeutic painting instructor, started Open Mic Night. Anyone who wanted to share with the group could do so. I shared a reading from my new book each month. Once, when De needed a filler between acts, she invited me up to give a demonstration. With nothing but imagination and movement, I taught people how to drive a golf ball. A couple of

Chapter 4 ... Tucson

guys came up to me a day or so later and said they were going to try my method.

Andrew, the dentist-turned-magician, was the last act two months in a row. He was amazing! He had us believing he was clairvoyant. Even when things seemed to go awry and the audience started feeling smug, he salvaged the act, leaving us with our jaws wide open. Harry chose not to attend. When I got home, poor Harry had to listen to my excited blow-by-blow recitation of Andrew's magic act.

Chapter 5 ... Tucson

Robert and Betty's Christmas Party

Robert and Betty, who have a home in the middle of Happy Street (one of the longer streets in the park), had an intimate Christmas gathering ... for dozens of their closest friends!

Betty drove her hot pink golf cart, accessorized with its twelve-inch jet black eyelashes, around the park for days inviting people and not remembering who she had invited. (Everyone identified with the lack of remembering.) She and Robert spent two weeks preparing for the festivities, cleaning the house, decorating to the nines, buying special mugs at the dollar store for hot buttered rums, and making a variety of cookies, fudges, and bourbon balls. At the last minute, they prepared slow cookers full of meatballs, wienies, and broccoli cheddar dip. They set out shrimp platters, vegetable trays, and a punch bowl full of crimson punch. They never do anything halfway!

On the morning of the party, the street was almost blocked with party paraphernalia: twenty chairs as well as multiple stools and benches. From my vantage point at the end of the street, with the sun reflecting off the asphalt, it looked like the furniture had melted on their driveway and had drifted toward the low spot in the center of the street.

Harry and I left our motor home at exactly 1:59 p.m., walking hand in hand up Happy Street to the party. It was a gloriously sunny December afternoon. Except for the bedroom where Ozzie was confined, nothing was off limits, but the food and drinks were located conveniently on the driveway. The chairs and stools were full. People were milling around chatting. I actually started to understand what Jimmy the Scot, a neighbor from across the street, was saying, despite his thick highlands (or lowlands) accent. Perhaps it was the hot buttered rum drinks. Whatever ... it was a lovely party!

The next day, Robert and Betty invited the Happy Hour group to their house ... for leftovers and to-go plates. By Boxing Day, and not a moment sooner, Robert and Betty had recovered!

Lucy, Fetch

Some dogs live to run after an object, snag it, and bring it back only to have the process repeated ... incessantly. We had been hoping for such a dog. We wondered if maybe Lucy was the one.

According to the park rules, you could walk your dog on a six-foot lead in certain areas of the park but never off lead. You could let your dog(s) run loose in any of the three enclosed areas but nowhere else. However, there was a fenced concrete "alley" (a walkway) leading to a locked gate. It was a drainage route formerly doubling as a park exit, but the gate had been permanently locked a few months earlier. The alley was at least 100 yards long and secure enough to let Lucy off lead.

Harry told me he took Lucy to the alley and threw the ball for her. She ran, fetched, and brought it back to him. I could picture the whole thing in my mind: Harry doing an overhand throw, the ball bouncing all the way to the gate, Lucy running full tilt for 100 yards, snagging the ball, and returning. In my mind, it was a thing of beauty.

One day, Harry asked me if I'd like to go with him. I jumped at the chance. I was excited to see Lucy at her finest. When we got to the alley, Harry took out the ball ... a treat ball with a special hole in which to stuff treats. Lucy liked it. At the time, it held no treats. Harry revved up to throw the ball. Unlike what I had imagined, he gave a slight underhand toss of about fifteen yards. It bounced a few times before Lucy caught up with it. It was a little disappointing. I was expecting the second try to be an overhand throw, but he gave another easy lob. Lucy ran her little heart out, her little black rump going up and down like someone bobbing for apples in fast motion. She snagged the ball and ran it back to Harry, dropping it en route and booting it with her front paw. At least Harry was able to get the ball without too much trouble. When he threw it a third time, she sauntered up to it and sniffed it a little. With a dismissive sneer, she was finished. No amount of cajoling helped. Evidently, Lucy was too smart to do mindless repetitive actions to make us happy. Too bad for us. When I asked about her stamina, Harry told me she usually burned out after two throws.

The next day he took her out again. When he came back, I asked him how it went. I was hoping he got three runs out of her but no such luck. Since we had been using the ball as a treat delivery system inside the motor home, she kept looking around while running ... to see if any treats had bounced out of the ball. Another failed experiment. *(Sigh!)*

ANGIE ... SHE'S A PIP!

For years we've had stories of both Lucy and Angie. Even though Angie was no longer with us word of her escapades did get around. Carole sent me pictures of Angie frequently. In all the pictures, Angie was having the time of her life ... ears perked up and smiling. On Christmas Eve day, Carole sent me a cute picture of Angie wearing a Christmas tree hat made from shiny green garland, but her ears were pinned back and she was looking askance at the camera. I texted back: Now there's the Angie I know and love so well ... ears pinned back with a guilty sideways look. That comment started a whole slew of texting with Carole who was getting ready to load up gifts and head to her daughter's place for a couple of days of family celebration:

Kathy: Will poor little Angie girl have to wear her hat?

Carole: I have a story on Angie.

Kathy: Uh-oh!

Carole: Yep, this is why her ears were down.

Kathy: Oh, she's been naughty.

Chapter 5 ... Tucson

Carole: First off ... you have mentioned she has a sensitive stomach. I beg to differ and I'm thankful she didn't end up at the vet.

Kathy: First off ... she's a pig ... p-i-g!

Carole: This is kind of a long story, starting with: I normally bake about eight kinds of cookies for Christmas. My family loves most all of them, I think. This year, I was cutting back so I asked what were their favorites. They said Florentines. Yippee-Skippy, they're fun to make! I started making them but screwed up the batches by making a double recipe. I ended up going to the store twice to get more stuff. At the same time, I was making my favorite crabcakes. A couple of my best friends love getting them from me, so I thought, why not do it at Christmas? That was percolating in the kitchen, as well. But that's just the backstory.

Kathy: Oh, I'm getting very nervous. How bad can it be, I'm wondering.

Carole: I left home for a couple of hours and came back to this:

- She had eaten all of the Florentines ... about twenty-five that had not yet been covered with chocolate.
- She ate four crabcakes.
- She ate half of the filling for another cookie I was designing.
- She ate all of the treats I keep in a plastic container. Actually, she just chewed open the plastic container you gave me and ate everything inside. She didn't eat the plastic ... that was a plus.
- She figured out how to open the bread box and consumed or chewed up a whole bag of English muffins.
- She ate about a quarter of a cup of chocolate chips, and
- She ate a couple of bags of dried fruit.

Of course, the mess was all through the house (it's a small house). God only knows how she came out of it unscathed. It severely cut back on the number of Florentines available for my family who are waiting patiently for a double recipe. They now get only two each. I still had enough of the filling to design some new cookies, which have been a hit with my neighbors ... but Angie has been in such hot water.

How did she do it you might ask: She climbed up on a chair, and then jumped up on my piano keyboard, and then jumped from the piano keyboard to the bar side of the kitchen counter, and began her sweep of the area, consuming everything in her path. She even ate birdseed, because the bird was sitting there in her cage with some birdseed out front. When she tried that, she knocked it all over hell and back! Yep, you were right, she'll eat anything, absolutely anything she can get her paws on!

Kathy: Lololololol!!!!!!! Evidently you weren't paying attention when I sent you this picture, way back when. (Picture of Angie in the motor home standing on the sofa resting her chin on the counter while eying a freshly made casserole two feet from her nose. She was hoping I would turn away and leave the room!)

Carole: Mea culpa. I have now rearranged the house so she cannot acrobatically get to the kitchen counter. And I have sent out a fire warning to my family for Christmas: Hide all items that could possibly be considered edible in your bedrooms as soon as you open them!

Kathy: Very good idea ... very, very good idea! Don't you just love her!

Carole: Yeah, but she is now innocently sniffing a dish towel. As if I need more drama!

Chapter 5 ... Tucson

Kathy: She was always so much more fun than Lucy!

Carole: Ummmmmm, fortunately I don't carry a grudge. But I'm now questioning your idea of fun!

Kathy: Well, I think you hit the nail on the head. You have to think of everything in advance ... everything! I just kind of got used to it. Here in the motor home, we have the treats on the shelf above the fireplace. We leave a whole bunch of treats on top of the container so we don't have to open the container each time. Not so when we had Angie with us! Don't you just love her innocent demeanor?

Carole: Oh yes! I soon realized that getting mad at her and glaring at her for a half an hour wasn't really gonna get me much. I just chalk it up to Christmas high jinx. My friends love hearing my stories anyway, so this is another good one for them.

I'm still cutting around the bites she made in the English muffins so I can have one. [emoji of bewildered face]

Wow. I have told friends it would have been interesting to watch Angie during her holocaustic efforts on my kitchen counter. I bet my parakeet was yelling at her the whole time, especially when Angie was messing with her bird food.

Kathy: She is such a tub. Did she throw up ... or worse?

Carole: Oh sure, three big urps. Tough on the oriental rugs, but that's life.

Kathy: What a pip!

Carole: Yep, I'm just glad I avoided a big vet bill.

Addendum: Later in the day, Carole's granddaughters took Angie for a walk up the hill to deliver gifts to friends. Angie slipped out of her collar. She was in a strange location with people she hadn't known long. It was a recipe for disaster, but before anyone could panic, Angie ran back down the hill and stopped in front of Carole's daughter's front door, emulating a pointer. She knows who butters her bread!

CHRISTMAS EVE

On Christmas Eve, the choir sang for two services at TVLC. We had two special choir songs and, of course, there were Christmas carols for the congregation's participation. When the congregation is singing, we don't have a choir director. We follow the organist.

I noticed Lars, the organist, would give a little jolt with his body when he wanted emphasis from the congregation. It was fun to follow his lead. His jolts got a little more dramatic with each verse, until during the last verse, it seemed like he was body-slamming the organ. And every time he increased the volume, body-slammed the organ, and decreased the tempo, the congregation responded enthusiastically!

The best carol by far was "Joy to the World." By the time he hit the third and final verse, he had started using the foot pedals. The sound was blasting off the walls. "HE RULES THE WORLD with truth and grace!" He played it and we sang it like it was a life-threatening imperative!

Chapter 6 ... Tucson

Angie ... At It Again

Two weeks after Angie's holocaust, I got another text from Carole.

Carole: Today I was compelled to leave Angie at home while I worked with a client. I thought I had dog-proofed the kitchen perfectly. When I returned home, she had chewed open that bag of hollyhock seeds.

Aside: I had given her a big plastic sack of hollyhock pods still on the stem. Each pod had dozens of seeds. There were dozens of pods!

Kathy: Where did you keep it?

Carole: I have an antique grocery scale that hangs from my ceiling. They were in the scale. Angie managed a straight-jump to the keyboard piano, then to counter. I googled hollyhock seeds and found they were not toxic to dogs, and she kindly left me two. My fear is that hollyhocks, the magenta variety, will be sprouting out of her bum on one of these trips outdoors!

Lucy, Fetch ... Please

Harry continued to take Lucy to the alley to practice their fetching. Some days he came back encouraged because she was up to four tosses before deciding it wasn't worth the effort. Other days, he came back convinced she'd never be a fetcher.

Another Day at the Races

The annual day at the races arrived. Sallie, Robert, and I had purchased a horse. We dressed her up to look like Robert in bib overalls but with pigtails because she was, after all, a filly. We named her Roberta. She also had a malfunctioning wardrobe.

When the time came to introduce our horse, Sallie took the microphone and signaled me with clicking noises from the top of her mouth, simulating a horse's clopping. I sashayed Roberta to the front of the stage. Sallie read the poem "Roberta the Racehorse."

Roberta the Racehorse

Kathy had a racehorse
A chestnut through and through, *(tilt)*
But every time she raced the horse
The chestnut threw a shoe. *(release)*

This clever mare keeps tools in tow
To fix her errant boot.
Two nails and a hammer and
The shoe boo-boo is moot. *(show)*

This little mare is perky
And feeling sort of frisky.
She gets her speed and courage from
Kentucky's finest whiskey! *(pull)*

Our horse is named Roberta
She ambles down the track.
And when she isn't racing
She gambles some out back! *(pull)*

Roberta is a genteel mare
She'll call you ma'am or sir.
And so dear friends, if you are smart,
you'd ... better ... bet ... on her!

Tilt the horse forward to show two styrofoam balls forming cleavage under v-neck blouse.

Release fishing line, shoe drops 12 inches, dangling.

Show toy nails in front pocket and toy hammer hanging from overall loop.

Pull sharply on fishing line: left front hoof pops up with a mini-bottle of fireball whiskey dangling from hoof.

Pull sharply on fishing line: right front hoof pops up with numerous bills waving in the breeze.

We didn't win best-decorated horse because the people who owned Number 4 were pretty well liquored-up before the audio voting started. The hooting for the vote was greatly aided by the liquor. Sadly, the person who was supplying the liquor was one of the owners of our horse! We shot ourselves in the foot!

Once again, we had six races. I bet on three different horses for each race ... and often forgot which horses I had put money on! However, during the fifth race, as I was cheering for Number 4, on whom I had bet $2, Don leaned in and told me we would make more money from an Owners Pool win than I could possibly make on a single bet. I immediately saw the wisdom of his comment and started rooting for Roberta. She won! I'm pretty sure it had nothing to do with my rooting. I ended the night rich enough to buy dinner for two. I was coming up in the world!

CERAMICS

In January, I started teaching ceramics classes. The Ceramics Club was raising money to buy a pottery wheel. The money from the classes went to the wheel fund.

The first class was gnome ornaments. A few days before the class, two ladies agreed to be my guinea pigs. I rolled out some clay and had them cut out their ornaments and smooth them. It took about an hour. The glazing, which was the fun part, also took quite a long time. They stuck with me for four hours. I learned a lot in a short amount of time. I immediately precut twenty-eight gnomes and set them aside to dry.

On the day of the class, I held up a tool and told the students I would demonstrate how to punch a hole in the top of the hat. I punched a hole in some dry clay: it immediately crumbled! Uh-oh, I was in trouble. Thank goodness the class saw it crumble. We switched to water and a sharp needle, which produced slightly better results. However, some of the gnome hat tips popped off anyway. I was starting to sweat. I was on the verge of refunding everyone's money. Some of the ladies decided they didn't want to have an ornament.

Chapter 6 ... Tucson

Instead, they planned to put their gnomes outside in a flowerpot. I was relieved. For the broken tops, a little water, a little reshaping, and a little patience resulted in a satisfactory hat. We were back on track. Out came the glazes and soon the hats, noses, and beards started to take shape. The rest of the class was enjoyable. I loved the creative designs the ladies used for their hats. We set the gnomes aside to be fired on the weekend. Afterward, they came back to check their glazing before the final firing.

My next class was a six-inch hummingbird ... with the hole already punched! The word was getting around. Fifteen people signed up. I had to split it into two classes. Unfortunately, two beaks popped off as the hummingbirds were being put into the kiln. A quick repair fixed the problem. Other projects included a partridge, an overweight dragonfly with a stubby body (to avoid any breakage), and a desert scene candleholder.

THEATER

Our Theater group was doing another variety show. I signed up to sing a song by Dennis Day from back in 1951. Joe, of Kathy and Joe, recruited me for his skit. We started rehearsals at the end of January: two two-hour rehearsals per week. It was an intensive effort. The dress rehearsal was scheduled for March 1st and the show for March 2nd.

PAINTING

The subject of McKenna's monthly painting class was an adobe house. I had a Christmas card from Marg showing a sepia painting of a nighttime procession in front of Taos Pueblo, circa 1934. It was a little challenging for a ninety-minute class, but I got right to copying the painting with a little more color. Afterward, Betsy, a classmate, said she recognized it. I had thought I was painting some adobe buildings. I hadn't realized it was a real place!

Several more people asked me for paintings of their dogs. Sometimes I put the unfinished paintings in the window so the people who walk by every day get an opportunity to see the paintings develop step by step. Some finished paintings stayed in the window for the season to distract passersby from looking straight into the motor home! *Oooh!*

GLASS FUSION

I continued to work with glass fusion. I had only one real failure. I tried to do a head of Angie, my rehomed corgi. I was surprised when I took it out of the kiln: A wide three-inch triangle had broken off one of the sides. I threw more glass at it and refired it. The patch held, but a tall three-inch triangle broke off in the same location. After three attempts in the kiln, adding glass each time, the piece was getting pretty heavy. When it shattered the third time breaking in two places, I decided to glue it. One part held; the other part didn't. It was time to give up. I used a hammer to reduce the glass to shards and started again. The new piece looked like a Swiss cheese version of Angie ... holes throughout but recognizable. I decided to stop fussing ... I was happy.

Chapter 7 ... Tucson

Theater

Within a week of the first meeting, ninety percent of the show was scoped out. By the following week, the skits were becoming polished and the order was determined. After five weeks of practice, we had a dress rehearsal, followed by the big event. The tickets sold out! My solo was "The Corn Keeps a'Growin'," recorded by Dennis Day in 1951.

I was going for a farm-girl look. I had on a short-sleeved, red polka dot, high-neck dress with a full petticoat. Black socks with black dress boots gave the impression of cowboy boots when on stage. Stage makeup included dark brown eyebrows, cheek blush, red lipstick, and freckles. I used the yarn pigtails from Roberta's day at the races ... a wide-brimmed sun hat covered a multitude of sins. I skipped my glasses. A big white elastic belt around my midsection made it easy to clip on the electronics for the headset, which was worn underneath the pigtails.

When I got up on the stage, I wanted to give the people just a little time to get used to my persona before I started in on the song. I greeted them with "Haa," to which they replied, "Hi!" I didn't realize they were going to be so interactive. I launched into my preamble in my best farm-girl accent: "This here's a song that mah pappy used to play for me when I was a little girl back in Port-land, Or-e-gone. They's three verses: The first verse is about biz-ness ... and it has a ba-ad ending. The second verse is about love ... and it has a ba-ad ending. The third verse is about two men and licker ... and you know it's gonna have a ba-ad ending. The fo-urth verse ... well, it's jest swee-t." To finish the introduction, I expanded my accordioning cardboard cornstalk to its full eight feet, announcing, "This here's mah co-rn-stalk."

Chapter 7 ... Tucson

After announcing the title once more, I started the song, hoping I wouldn't forget any of the verses. I was grateful to Lyn, the director, for requiring us to attend all the practices. There were no unwanted hesitations and no forgotten lines. When I got to the end of the third line of each verse, I slowed down to get ready for the fourth line. After blasting the fourth line of each verse, I gave a high-pitched hoot and sang the refrain.

After a purposeful bow, I retraced my steps and quietly maneuvered backstage until I got to the women's side where my microphone was turned off and removed. Completed ... what a hoot!

The Corn Keeps a'Growin' recorded by Dennis Day in 1951.

Oh, the corn keeps a'growin', the corn keeps a'growin',
The corn keeps a'growin' all the time the time.
Even snow stops a'snowin', and the crow stops a'crowin',
But the corn keeps a'growin' all the time.

Now Alfie owned a farmland, and Ralphie owned a calf,
And Alfie raised alfalfie, while Ralphie raised his calf.
They said let's us be partners, but couldn't stand the ... gaaaaffe ...
When ... Ralphie's calf ate Alf's alfalfie, Alf ate Ralphie's calf!

OH! The corn keeps a'growin', the corn keeps a'growin',
the corn keeps a'growin' all the time.

Now Anna had a sweetheart and Abe McCabe was it.
He hankered so for ice cream, she couldn't make him quit.
Came Gabe a perfect stranger and Abe was in a ... fiiiit ...
When ... Abe McCabe saw Ann with Gabe, then Abe and Anna split!

(continued)

*OH! The corn keeps a'growin', the corn keeps a'growin',
the corn keeps a'growin' all the time.*

Old Mulligan loved Brandy and Milligan loved gin.
The flavor one would favor the other was agin'.
When someone switched their glasses, they drank each other's ...
breeeew ... Now ... Milligan's a sober man and Mulligan's a stew!

*OH! The corn keeps a'growin', the corn keeps a'growin',
the corn keeps a'growin' all the time.*

Now Millie's sister Molly loved rich young Willie Shaw,
But Millie was the filly that Molly's Willie saw.
And so young darling Molly just married Willie's ... paaaa ...
And ... after Millie married Willie, Molly was her ma!

*Oh, the corn keeps a'growin', the corn keeps a'growin',
The corn keeps a'growin' all the time the time.
Even snow stops a'snowin', and the crow stops a'crowin',
But the corn keeps a'growin' all the time.*

Ceramics

It was a super month for free-form ceramics classes. We made flat hummingbirds and dragonflies and graduated to 3D candle-holders (a curved adobe house with cacti, on a round base). I gave some basic instructions and sat back to watch everyone's creativity sparkle.

Monochromatic Painting

I had one class billed as monochromatic painting, but I wouldn't tell anyone what it was about. Ten brave souls showed up. Each person got a different subject (Tom Selleck, Marilyn Monroe, Lucille Ball, javelina, rattlesnake, bowl of cacti, birds, and more). I gave them four washed-out black-and-white copies of their subject. Then, I told the class there would be one answer to any question they asked me, and one answer to any question I asked them. My answer would be "Who cares!" and their answer would be "OK!"

We immediately plunged into our project with smiles. Each person had three brushes (large, medium, and small) and a bottle of acrylic paint. They took the large brush as instructed, poured some paint into a small container, and painted the darks on their first sheet. They watered down the strong color and painted the mediums. They watered it down again to paint the lights, leaving the white highlights alone. They had only ten minutes to do it. After the ten minutes, I told them to take a fresh copy of the same subject and repeat the process with the medium brush for ten minutes. Then they took a third copy repeating the process with the small brush. With each new instruction, they responded "OK!" When anyone asked me a question, the whole class shouted, "Who Cares!" Who knew teaching could be so easy!

When they were finished with the first three pictures, I had them use their paint and their small brush to paint the darks on their final picture, then they traded paints with another person and painted the mediums. They traded again and painted their lights with a third color. It wasn't really monochromatic painting at that point, but it was interesting. Each person took someone else's four paintings to the far end of the room so we could see how they looked from a distance. Since everyone had a different subject, no one felt compelled to compare their work that of the others. We were able to focus on the differences between the brushes and the colors. It was all very interesting and positive.

PAINTING

The demand for paintings caught me by surprise. In addition to the two Belgian Malinois (Rue and Piper), I was pleased to paint whatever people wanted, including:

- A Shih Tzu (Carly),
- A raccoon on a ceramic slab,
- Another Shih Tzu (Gizmo), the agility star,
- A lovable little mix (Wookee),
- "Divine Mercy" from a holy card for Carly's mom,
- A pair of Cairn terriers (Annee and Lilly),
- Debbie's husband (Richard) with their sheltie (Bella),
- A black shepherd named Goose (painted in blues and reds) as a wedding gift for a friend of the daughter of a friend of Laura in the Dog Club,
- A beagle with a funky ear sticking out sideways (Boo Boo),
- Two doodles (Bear and Wags),
- Another painting of Bear and Wags,
- A potcake dog (Hazel), and ...
- Four paintings of my dear friend and muse Helene, who had passed away during the month.

Theater Cast and Crew

Chapter 8 ... Tucson

Valentine's Day ... Finishing Each Other's Sentences

Harry and I don't seem to go for fanfare. We just love each other ... pure and simple. We have our own ways. Here are two of them:

About midday we met in the middle of the coach. I threw my arms around his neck, smiled, kissed him, and said, "Happy-y-y-y ..."

All I got was Tim-the-Toolman Taylor's grunt: "Hu-uh?"

It was not what I expected. Changing my eyes from normal to sparkly, I said with a bigger smile, "Hap-py-y-y-y ..."

Pretty soon he gave me, "Valentine's ... "

To which I responded, "Day!"

Finishing each other's sentences ... how hard can it be?

Valentine's Day ... Three Little Words

It was the end of the day. I put my arms around his neck. He put his hands gently on my waist. We kissed a Valentine's Day kiss and then Harry said to me those three little words every woman dreams of hearing. Actually, he said five words and it ended with three words a woman would never dream of hearing ... "Are you putting on weight?" (It stung a little because it rang of truth. During our holiday COVID escapade, I dropped my guard and started eating crackers. By January, I was in full cracker mode ... and growing.)

The next day, as I was walking down the street, Irv drove by. He asked if I wanted a ride to the ceramics room. I accepted and told him about Harry's three little words. It took him by surprise for a moment, but he recovered quickly, saying, "Oh, that silver-tongued fox!" When I was visiting with the ladies in the ceramics room, I told them about the three little words. As expected, they were all disgusted and mildly horrified. From the feedback I collected,

Harry was the only husband who would dare say such a thing! Later in the evening, I told Harry all the ladies in the ceramics room and Irv were mad at him. I was giving him an easy lob. I expected him to take the hint and show a tiny bit of contrition ... but no! He countered with "There's a scale in the weight room." Oh good grief! I couldn't seem to win.

The following Thursday, I was at choir practice at TVLC. We shared joys and concerns at the end of practice for prayers. I raised my hand and said in a voice loud enough for all the hearing-impaired people to catch, "Please pray for my husband ... who thinks I'm putting on weight!" (Take that, Harry!)

Easter Rest

You know how busy the Easter season can be if one is connected with liturgy. I was connected ... through choir. In addition to our normal one song per week, we had been practicing for the installation of a new pastor and for Holy Week services.

The song for Maundy Thursday, about Jesus in Gethsemane, started with, "The wind in the olive trees." It had some eerie slides in it: first the piano would slide up four notes, then the whole choir would slide up the same notes. There were at least six slides in the song, making it sound exactly like wind in the olive trees. At one point, we took a deep dive, sliding from F down to middle C with a vengeance. It was very effective. I was starting to think it might be my favorite song.

We were each given a booklet of eight new songs for Good Friday.

We had only two new songs for Easter Sunday. But the processional for Easter about did me in. The one thing most of the songs in the last seven years have had in common was the music catering to the sopranos. The sopranos dance up to and beyond the limits of the treble staff. We can always hear the melody so we always know where to go. Our part is the top note of the music. It's easy to be a soprano: read the top notes, watch the piano's melody, come in on cue. When the sopranos cut loose, all the people in the congregation "Ooh" and "Aah." It's just easy! Not so on Easter Sunday!

Our choir director chose "Joy in the Morning" for the processional. No one seemed alarmed. I'm pretty sure the choir director said all but three people knew the song. Laura and I, two of the three sopranos in the first row, were two of the three singers who didn't know the song. I had never even heard of it before. It started simple enough, but then the words started coming fast and furious as the pace picked up to double time. The music stopped catering to the sopranos. After the pianist had a turn, she let in the tenors and the altos until, after three false starts, it was finally the sopranos' turn to show up, disheveled. Trying to keep up with the rest of the sopranos, I felt like I was being dragged by a horse like a sack of potatoes over exceedingly rocky ground ... bumping up and down ... getting hang time! Thank goodness we had other songs to practice. If we had worked on that song one more time during rehearsal, I would have thrown my sheaf of papers into the air and melted into the carpet.

Fortunately, the choir director had emailed the audio to us so we could listen and practice on our own. By Maundy Thursday, I was starting to get it. I continued practicing until I felt like I was getting a sense of the song ... like I was driving a buckboard over bumpy ground rather than being dragged behind a horse. It was not an easy song. In order to anticipate when to come in, the sopranos had to watch the music, wait for the tenors and basses to sing their phrases, wait for the altos to sing their phrase and lastly ... lastly! ... the sopranos could come in. Why would anyone write a song having the sopranos come in last? To make matters worse, this happened in more than one place, and it seemed to be different each time. The sopranos were definitely not being catered to!

The day before Easter, I thought, *I think I know this, so I'm going to sing it like I know it.* Everything was great. I had pencil marks all through the piece: arrows reminding me to drop down in a tough spot, words to indicate what was coming at the page turn or the beginning of the next line, circles around the triplets so I could hear them three times before the sopranos were to come in. It was work! Personally, I didn't think sopranos should have to work so hard to learn a song. It was a challenge for me because I wasn't used to paying attention to what everyone else was doing all the time. But at the very end, it was wonderful. As we sailed up toward the high G, the words were repetitive ... Joy, joy, joy, joy ... *Joy!* There was a quarter note rest before the fifth and final "Joy." The whole choir took a deep breath and belted out the final "Joy."

The quarter note rest made sense to me. I nailed it at every practice. Occasionally, someone jumped the gun and sang out of turn, causing the choir director to make a point of cautioning us about the rest. But it wasn't a big deal to me, because I watched for it, I could see it clearly, and like I said, it made sense. I didn't even need to mark it in pencil. A quarter note rest is a pretty big blot of ink on a page.

So there we were on Easter Sunday, having one final practice before the first service. During our warm-up, thirty minutes before the service started, my Bible study partner Peggy and her husband Jim came in. The choir was in the middle of stretches. As I lifted my hands with everyone else, I pointed to my wedding ring and pointed to the back of the church. Peggy frowned slightly and looked over her right shoulder. She looked back at me and frowned again. I repeated my gesture (by that time, the choir was already lowering their hands), pointing more insistently to the back of the church. She turned all the way around and saw a man sitting alone in the back row. After a final gesture to my wedding ring, I had succeeded in getting her to realize it was my husband way back there. She and Jim jumped up and went back to introduce themselves to Harry. They chatted for quite a while. I was secretly glad I had been instructing him in the fine art of chatting during the last forty-one years. I refocused my attention to the warm-ups and then to the songs. All my markups really helped. I still felt in control of the processional. When we came to the quarter note rest, I waited, as did the other choir members. Then with a blast of her hands, the choir director hit the air in front of her, prompting us to nail the high G ... *"Joy"* ... which we did! It was a phenomenal ending! We sat down and enjoyed the prelude as people meandered in for the early Easter service.

After the prelude, the choir director motioned for us to rise. She cued the piano and brass. They began with panache. The pastors processed up the aisle as the choir started singing. All of the marks made sense. When I got confused, I simply stopped singing until I could figure out where we were. But at the very end ... I forgot about the rest. There I was, all by my lonesome. I was in the middle of hitting the high G ... solo. It was not meant to be a solo! I pulled the plug as fast as I could, but what was done was done. In retrospect, it might not have sounded so bad, in fact, it might not have been noticeable but for my right hand. Since I was holding the music with my left arm and hand, my right hand was free to do its own thing. It shot up to my mouth ... snapping to attention like a rookie saluting a five-star general ... my rigid palm quivered in place as my fingers effectively covered my open mouth. I was doubly horrified. When I went to the restroom afterward, I stood in front of the mirror and repeated the gesture hoping it was perhaps hidden by my music folder. It wasn't! But, even worse, I saw my eyebrows go way up as my eyes bulged.

I went outside afterward and began talking to Jim, lamenting about what had happened. I never did ask him if he heard it. I assumed he had seen and heard everything. It was probably not a valid assumption, since he's hard of hearing. I was telling him about my big mistake and followed it with something about my hand covering my mouth. "That," he exclaimed, "was your big mistake!"

"Joy in the Morning"
The Choir / Band
Jennifer Watson Director

Chapter 9 ... Tucson

Art Times Three

I'd gotten excited about doing one theme in acrylics, pottery, and fused glass. McKenna's monthly painting class was supposed to be mountains at sunset. I found a picture of Seven Falls at Sabino Canyon and used it as my subject for the class. Since there wasn't enough time to paint as I usually do, I used broad brushstrokes in oranges, yellows, and reds to paint the layers of hills, not paying too much attention to how I mixed the colors and not even trying to achieve shades of brown. I had planned to go back and repaint the hills with browns. There simply wasn't enough time and I was left with brightly colored hills. And, magically, I loved them. I left the hills and spent the rest of my time working on making the water shimmer and highlighting the mountains. I was happy with the results. (See image on back cover.)

I repeated the Sabino Canyon subject in relief as a ceramics project. It was very successful. (See image on back cover.)When I tried to do the same subject in fused glass, the glass shattered. The upper left corner of the glass project jumped away from the rest of the glass during the firing and landed an inch away, melting down the side of the clay support and becoming friendly with the bottom of the kiln. It was a little disappointing, but two out of three worked for me.

Caring Neighbors

A new group started up in the park. It was all about neighbors helping neighbors. I got in on the ground floor. Quite a number of people expressed an interest in being volunteer helpers. It was very touching. Those who were in the park year-round were doing a little bit during the summer to get a feel for what to expect. We were all gearing up to hit the ground running when October arrived.

Good Dog Scavenger Hunt

The Dog Club sponsored a Good Dog Scavenger Hunt. One didn't have to be in the club to participate. All one had to do was get someone to witness their dog obeying an easy command correctly. The witness had to sign a form attesting to the dog's good behavior. The eleven commands were as easy as Sit, Stay, Down, Come, Walk Calmly on a Loose Lead, etc. Once the form was complete, the owner brought it to space 387, whereupon I took out my calligraphy pen and signed their Good Dog Certificate. Several people completed their Scavenger Hunt before I realized I should probably do it, too. Lucy helped. She got her certificate and had me put it in the window next to the paintings.

Rincon Singers

The Rincon Singers included seven altos, six sopranos, and a couple of tenors and bases. We dressed up in western garb to go along with the park's theme for the season, singing western songs at Coffee and Donuts in late February. Several people wanted me to wear a sombrero, so I donned Roberta's pigtails yet again and went along with the fun. It still amazes me when people have trouble recognizing me in disguise.

Morkie?

Our friends, John and Arlene, said they were planning to get a Morkie (Maltese/Yorkie mix) in the fall. Since John and Harry have a history of getting the same breed at the same time ... Airedale, Westie, Bouvier ... we started thinking about our next breed. We'd been talking about a Greyhound, Mastiff, Bichon Frise, or Maltese. It was my pick and I was leaning toward a small companion dog. Morkie sounded like something I might want to research. I tucked it away in the back of my mind.

Chapter 9 ... Tucson

Let's Go Swimming

For a few days, Harry had been making noises about going to the pool. In fact, he said, "I either want to go to the pool or take a nap." We looked at the weather forecast: Take a nap won. Thursday was picked as the perfect day to go to the pool. Thursday came and went. All thoughts of going to the pool were wiped from my memory.

On Saturday, at two in the afternoon, I was deep in thought, writing an important letter. Harry announced he was going to go swimming at 3 o'clock and asked if I wanted to go. Pool stuff is not something I enjoy, but marriage is. I said, "OK," and immediately refocused on polishing the letter. No thoughts of pool were dancing in my head.

At 3 p.m. on the nose, Harry got up and started moving around, changing his clothes. Suddenly I realized we were going swimming. Life is simple, if you're a man: Harry changed his clothes, went to the front door, and put on his hat, saying, "Are you coming?"

"Oh ... oh yes," I responded, distractedly. I jumped up, ran the ten feet to the bedroom, whipped off my clothes and plowed through the bottom drawer where I had last seen my bathing suit ... Not there! "Oh shoot!" I mumbled softly. I went around the side of the bed, opened the overhead bin, and started pulling things out sideways at an awkward angle. I knew there were bathing suits up there. I grabbed the first one I could find. It was well used, which is a euphemism for "threadbare and won't hold in the bulges." Too bad for me. I ran ten feet to the bathroom, whipped open the closet door, pulled on my bathing suit coverup, ran back into the living room, spun around, and asked Harry if he could see through my suit. I was pleased to get a negative and even more pleased he made no additional comments about any body parts normally kept under wraps. I pulled down the dress quickly as I turned to face him. My goal was to protect him from seeing the ravages of time most visible from the rear (aka, the rear). Well, maybe I really meant the ravages of crackers eaten in January. The coverup seemed to fit, but it felt kind of funny. I pulled it off, turned it around, and pulled it back on. It fit a lot better when it was on correctly. We had a ten-second discussion about which was front and which was back. As I slipped on my shoes, grabbing my hat and sunglasses, Harry turned and took one step down and reached for the door handle. But as he took a second step down and opened the door, I mumbled something about needing a towel. I slipped off my shoes, ran the full length of the coach to the bathroom, grabbed a towel, hurried back to the front of the coach, slipped on my shoes and exited the coach … one step behind Harry … smiling. After locking the door, we calmly walked together to the pool. (He was calm, I was faking it.)

When we got to the pool, Harry went through the gate while I took a quick detour for a speedy restroom break. I knew I didn't have much time. I looked in the mirror as I walked by, shook my head, and sighed. Once in the stall, I set down the towel, whipped off my hat, pulled off the dress, all the while wondering where I was going to put everything so nothing would fall into some place unacceptable … [nature's call] … I pulled the necessities back on, grabbed the rest of my paraphernalia, and walked to the door. I shook my head again as I looked in the mirror, stopped at the door before going out, gave a deep sigh, cursed myself for eating all those crackers in January, straightened up, sucked in my stomach, tried to convince myself I was the complete package … and walked out.

Harry was standing by the chairs. I had expected to see him in the pool. Maybe I had been faster than I thought. Harry was putting on his shirt … probably to keep from getting sunburned. "Are you going in?" I asked.

"I've been in."

I thought he was kidding. It was strange because Harry rarely kids around. Nevertheless, I kept thinking we were going in the pool. When he reached for his hat, I asked, "Are you really finished?"

"Yes," he said, "but you can go in."

Chapter 9 ... Tucson

"I'm not going in!" I said with a little too much emotion. Whereupon we picked up our things and left the pool area. On the way out, he said he had done one lap but found it too noisy and crowded.

And so we went home ... he, looking all sorts of calm, and I, laughing on the inside! Life with Harry ... always the unexpected.

Chapter 10 ... Williams ... Festivities

Our date of departure was timed to drive through Phoenix at about 10:30 on a Sunday morning. We left our 80° weather in Tucson and drove north to Williams to visit Kate and Irv again. The timing was perfect; we sailed north through Phoenix in moderately heavy traffic, without even slowing down. (I shuddered as I thought of Highway 60 to Wickenburg.)

We set up at Grand Canyon Railway RV Park again, rested a little bit, and walked the few blocks to their home. Kate asked if we wanted to sit down. Harry and Irv took the recliners, I took the place that was most likely not Kate's spot. I noticed there was a big bouquet of flowers. *How lovely*, I thought. Kate settled right in front of me, which forced me to look at the flowers. Suddenly, I realized there was a Happy Birthday balloon floating above them. I squealed in delight and thanked her profusely. Evidently, I had bellyached a lot about traveling on my birthday because of the previous year's dryer episode. "Evidently" nothing ... I know I had. And next to the flowers was a tiny little book of sweet, meaningful quotations. I felt extremely special. We both had a laugh about how blind I was.

Williams is a tiny town of about 3,500 people. But it is known as being the Gateway to the Grand Canyon. Consequently, a lot of people stop there. We all headed off to one of the most popular restaurants in Williams, which happened to be right across the street from the RV park. After dinner, Kate invited us back for some strawberry cake, but we couldn't eat a bite ... we were stuffed. It was disappointing because it was Kate's signature dessert, and she had worked hard on it. Irv was even more disappointed because he wanted to sink his teeth into the cake, but Kate put her foot down. She wouldn't let him cut the cake until we were all there.

The next day while Irv and Harry went golfing, Kate and I sat around laughing for four hours. By mid-morning, Kate and I got a little hungry and cut into the cake. I was afraid to imagine how displeased Irv would be about missing the cake-cutting. Later we had a bite of lunch and heard from the guys, who were on their way home. When they got home, Kate cut large pieces of cake for everyone. I could tell Irv was pleased. Each one of us was even happier when Kate cut the remaining cake right down the middle and sent us home with half.

Once we got back to the motor home, I put the flowers and the balloon on the shelf above the fireplace so they wouldn't compete with Harry's view of the TV, a move doomed to failure. He repositioned the flowers next to my table and put the balloon in the little bathroom! Oh, that Harry!

During the course of the next few days, we changed elevations multiple times as we drove through the mountains. Every time I looked into the little bathroom, I saw the poor balloon becoming more and more emaciated. It was not pleased about all the mountain passes we had to traverse.

Chapter 11 ... The Little Dog

On Tuesday, we got up early, had breakfast, and took off for St. George, Utah, via Las Vegas. We went by the little valley of mini-mountains, again. It was as cute as could be. I discovered it was called Willow Beach. The first time I saw it I was driving and couldn't look closely. This time, rather than snap a picture, I opted to look to my heart's content. I thought perhaps on another trip I'd snap a picture so I could do a painting.

In order to get from Nevada to Utah, we had to cut through the northwest corner of Arizona on highway 15. It's one of my favorite scenic routes. I took fifty-nine pictures as we were going through its Virgin River canyon. The rocks towered steeply on both sides of the highway. They were very interesting to look at ... lots of layers, colors, and textures ... the kind of mesmerizing rocks that can make a person wonder about so many things.

When we got to St. George, we were looking for Temple View RV Park. The GPS was telling Harry where to go ... nicely. After turning right, we saw a temple perfectly framed in our view. We had arrived at the park. Two other big rigs arrived at the same time. The man in front of me was telling the registration people he had the cutest little dog, a Shih Tzu/Bichon mix. I thought it would be nice to see the little dog. After I registered, I went outside and saw the man driving by in his motor home. We proceeded to our spot ... as luck would have it, we pulled in right next to the man with the little dog. Being a creature of habit, I promptly started my setup duties forgetting all about the little dog ... until Harry took Lucy outside after dark. I heard a little dog barking. I quickly put on my shoes and dashed out of the motor home. There was a man walking down the street with a little dog, but since it was dark, I couldn't really see what it looked like. When Harry came in. I asked him if he had seen our neighbors' little dog. He had. I was disappointed I didn't get to see it.

Chapter 11 ... The Little Dog

As we were going through the tear-down motions the next morning after breakfast, I saw our neighbor pull away and again I realized I had missed an opportunity. Then I saw a blonde lady out front talking with Harry. It was our neighbor! I wondered if I should ask to see the little dog. I decided not to broach the subject because they were already on their way. Off they went. Shortly thereafter, off we went, too. When we got to the front exit, there they were ... and then they were gone. We got out on the street and drove down to the intersection, and there they were, and then they turned while we had to stop for the light. I sighed. Casually, Harry mentioned he had told him about the spacious RV park where we stayed north of Salt Lake City in Tremonton. I realized perhaps I might get to see the little dog after all. We poked along at sixty mph in an eighty-mph zone and had no problems getting through Salt Lake City at two o'clock in the afternoon. An hour later, we were in Tremonton. On the highway, we passed a big motor home towing a gray Jeep. "Is that our neighbor with the little dog?" I asked Harry, expectantly.

"No," he said, "they had a white Jeep." I gave another sigh. When we got to the park, there were several large motor homes, I was disappointed to see none of them had a white Jeep.

The next morning, the temperature was below freezing. I didn't want to do anything involving going outside in the cold. Harry walked Lucy. After we had breakfast, he told me the motor home with the white Jeep and the little dog had come in late in the day, but they had already left. I was ready to kick myself for missing yet another opportunity.

Utah is such a beautiful state. We enjoyed cresting the hills and getting a bird's eye view of the gorgeous mountains, hills, and valleys before us. The balloon in the little bathroom was not as pleased as we were.

Southern Idaho is a lot flatter than Utah. Interstate 84, the main drag, is a major trucking route. When we went through Twins Falls, we decided to take a break and pulled into a rest stop. It was huge.

We both remarked how unusual it was. After a quick rest, I took Lucy out for a little walk. As I turned to come back to the motor home, I almost missed the huge motor home towing a white Jeep parked right next to ours! I looked at Harry and asked, "Is that our neighbor with the little dog?" Before he could answer, I saw a woman waving through their front windshield ... it was the blonde lady! I went right up to the door and, as she opened it, I saw the little dog, looking as cute as could be. We had a nice visit, which was cut short by drizzly weather. As we turned to go our separate ways, I stopped and introduced myself, finding out they were Carla, Marco, and Kona Bear. I returned to our coach, but right before Harry started the motor, I grabbed my phone and ran out again. I almost ran into Marco as he was coming around the front of our coach. We exchanged phone numbers in the rain and off we went. Who knows if we would ever see each other again! At least we had a way to connect.

Harry said we had to stop at the next rest stop so he could feed Lucy. The rest stop was pretty crowded with lots of trucks. As I slowly maneuvered behind the trucks, there was a little white Jeep sticking out! The little-dog people were there! We went to the far end of the rest stop and parked. I texted: *We're at the same rest stop as you are!* Carla fired back: *I see you!* And then she texted they were going to A-Frame RV Park in Baker City where we had a reservation for the night! I knew I would get to see the little dog again ... and Carla and Marco, of course.

I took some pictures of the little dog when we stopped for the evening. The next morning, bright and early, they left for Gig Harbor, Washington. We were a few minutes behind them. I wondered if I'd ever see them again. As we were leaving, I saw them again, hooking up their Jeep at the entrance to the park. We waved goodbye again. On the way home, Carla and I texted quite a bit. She mentioned

Chapter 11 ... The Little Dog

they would likely go north when they got to the Columbia River. I looked at the map ... it looked like a more direct route for them. When we came to the place where they would turn off, I said a mental goodbye to the three of them.

Quite a bit later, we entered the scenic part of the Columbia River Gorge. I thought it might be nice to text her some pictures of the route not taken. I got right on it, sending a picture of the hills on the Oregon side of the Gorge and one of Mount Hood in all its glory. The picture of the paddle wheeler going down the middle of the river wasn't as striking as I had hoped, so I decided not to text it. A few minutes later, I got a text from Carla: *The paddle wheeler is having a beautiful day on the river.* I took another look at the pictures I had sent but there was no view of the paddle wheeler. They had changed their route and were actually about five minutes behind us! We enjoyed quite a bit more texting until we got home. Then all bets were off. We were deep in the throes of homecoming and two hours later, so were they. I can't help but think I'll see the little dog and the little-dog people again, perhaps with a little dog of my own.

Chapter 12 ... Vancouver

Who Cares

The shock of coming home was not as traumatic as in previous years. I had seen the same sight five years in a row: The grass and weeds were about two feet high in places. With mild resignation, I thought, Who cares ... *I'll get to it in due time*! I put on my Vancouver hat and started life anew.

Petey

No grass ever grows under Harry's feet when there's a dog to be gotten or a car to be boughten. We were a two-dog couple, and we'd been down to one dog for nine months. After being home for a week, he started sending me email messages about Morkies in the area. "In the area" is a misnomer in the internet age. The pups in the first email were from Chicago. The pups in the second email were from Florida and Ohio. The one pup in the third email was from Spanaway, Washington. The breeder and I clicked. Less than three weeks after we arrived home, my yard work was done and Petey ... a five-pound, four-month-old Morki-poo (Maltese/Yorkie/Poodle) ... was scheduled to come to live with us in Vancouver. Life as we knew it was about to change once again ... for the better!

Chapter 12 … Vancouver

Epilogue

DOROTHY

Two weeks after returning from our snowbirding trip, I was coming home from choir practice at Messiah Lutheran at dusk. An ambulance passed me and turned left on Highway 99. I continued straight, saying a silent prayer for the family and friends of the person who would be visited by the ambulance. As I approached my property, dusk had morphed into night, but the neighborhood was lit up by the lights of the ambulance and a firetruck ... at Dorothy's house. I got a sinking feeling in the pit of my stomach. I parked and went across the driveway. One of the four responders passed by. "I'm a neighbor, tell me what I can do," I blurted out. He said it would help if I could lock up the house after they left. Not knowing how long they'd be there, I raced home, grabbed the key tightly in my left hand, and returned as quickly as possible. I parked in my driveway and went to Dorothy's back door ... and waited ... in the dark. Pretty soon, I thought my lurking was a little creepy. I went into the laundry room, an alcove inside the back door. I could hear the guys and Dorothy talking. Since I was still hovering in the dark, it wasn't too long before hovering felt creepy, too. I proceeded into the unlit dining room, still acting much like a shadowy six-foot statue, when a tall fireman walked in through the back door, did a double take, and hollered, "Dorothy, does someone else live here with you?" His question punctured the balloon holding back all my frustrations. Words started pouring out of me, leaving sentences in the dust ... "her neighbor ... friend ... will lock up when you leave," and who knows what else. It got sorted out quickly and I went back to listening.

I got the gist of their conversation: Dorothy, who had just turned ninety, had gotten up to leave the living room when she stumbled over the footstool, fell, and broke her leg. Since she couldn't reach the phone, she crawled across the room and pulled the phone off

Epilogue

the end table. She dialed 911 and they came right away. The four men worked as an efficient team. Their voices and mannerisms were the epitome of kindness: "Dorothy, we're going to have to cut your jeans off. Is that okay? ... If we don't do it, they'll do it at the hospital." I heard a soft, "Yes, that's okay." She and I had had a conversation about ratty jeans within the past week. *Oh, please be the ratty ones, please be the ratty ones*, I muttered in my mind. (They weren't.)

Once they got her situated in the ambulance, I asked if I could see her. They said it would be fine. The ambulance was parked on the slope in the driveway. It was a pretty steep climb to get into the vehicle. I knew I'd have to grab something to clamber in, and it was unlikely to be graceful, but I couldn't see anything to grab ... except the gurney. That wouldn't work! I must have looked like I was about to do something that would produce disastrous results because, out of the blue, one of the guys quickly fiddled with the bumper and a step magically appeared. Once in the ambulance, I greeted Dorothy and was pleased to hear her say, "Oh, Kathy!"

We got right down to business. "I've got your phone charger and your purse."

"Oh, good!"

"And here is your iPad."

"I don't want it."

At that point, it was clear the guys were anxious to leave.

"Do you want to hold on to your charger?"

"No, just put it in my purse."

I stuffed everything in my hands except the iPad straight into her purse. As I struggled to debark gracefully, I had a feeling something was wrong.

"Something's wrong," I muttered as I stood a few feet behind the ambulance patting my chest and my hips. I had four pockets in my pants and two in my jacket. I checked all the pockets for something, but I didn't know what I was looking for. Suddenly, I realized I no longer had her house key. Up went my arms. I started sputtering. Back up into the ambulance I climbed, without touching the gurney. After a little rummaging in her purse, I held up the keys with satisfaction and debarked a second time. I was sure we'd laugh about the gurney incident when she came home.

After her husband Morry died in 2016, I often grabbed my morning coffee, cinched up my bathrobe, and headed up to Dorothy's, where we would talk about everything and nothing for an hour or more, always laughing ... mostly at ourselves. Eventually, it became the way we started every day. Once in a while, I'd show up with way we started every day. Once in awhile, I'd show up with something hidden in my hand. I'd hold out my fist and drop something magical into her palm: berries picked on the way over, a strange leaf, or some other treasure. Other times, especially in the later years, I'd take a video while I was walking to her place and we'd watch it together marveling at a deer walking through her yard or a brand-new family of ducklings skittering across the pond.

Sometimes we'd argue about property lines even though both of us knew it wouldn't make a hoot of difference as to how we were living our lives. I asked her, "If I can prove it with county documents, would you believe me?" I laughed and threw up my hands when she said, "Probably not!"

Once she asked what Rodney's address was. I said it was probably in the 10600s or 10700s. She was having none of that! She declared it must be in the 10900's. I knew I was on solid ground because 109th Street was a couple of blocks north of me and Rodney, my neighbor, lived a little south of me. We went on and on, until I said we should jump in the car and drive to Rodney's to check it. I thought that would kill the conversation, but she surprised me when she said, "Okay." We both straightened our bathrobes and piled in my car (I must have been too lazy to walk that morning). We drove the three blocks to Rodney's house but couldn't see the address sign, so we continued driving three more blocks to 109th Street. I stopped the car and waited for her to look around and discover the street sign, which was partially hidden. She was shocked when she saw the sign. We laughed and went back to her place, grateful that no one was around to see two dotty old ladies driving around in their slippers and nighties.

I loved how she always chastised herself for not visiting her friends and relatives more often ... and there were a lot of friends and relatives ... when in reality, she'd call or visit each of them about twice a month.

She was always washing her windows ... sometimes twice a year. Each time she was ready to start she'd ask me how to get the blinds down. I wasn't much help because I'd have already forgotten. (It was counter to what you'd expect for a planet with gravity.) Years earlier, I had to put a memo in my cell phone to jog my memory. And sure enough, early in 2024, she called me when I was in Tucson and asked how to remove the blinds. Ours was a good friendship.

I got Petey ten days after Dorothy's fall. He went with me to visit her in rehab almost daily until it was clear she was failing. Dorothy was an amazing woman who could handle just about anything ... except the complications of a broken leg at her advanced age. She died peacefully, one month after her fall ... yet another person leaving a hole in a lot of hearts.

Swiss Cheese Hearts

I'm glad to have a bunch of holes in my heart (like those made from Helene, Mom, and Dorothy). It means I truly love my friends and family.

My maternal grandmother died when I was eight. I remember how soft and fuzzy her face was. Her oldest daughter, Auntie Lois, had the same soft fuzzy face. Grandma always planted marigolds in her front yard. Throughout my life, every time I deadheaded marigolds, I raised my hand ceremoniously to my nose to breathe in deeply, remembering Grandma Beaucage.

In Dorothy's last few years, she had more than enough to take care of without having to deadhead her flowers. But she did plant a garden every year: marigolds, beans, tomatoes, zucchini, and cucumbers. When I'd walk up the hill to her place at 7 a.m. in my red bathrobe with coffee mug in hand, I would cruise by the raised beds deadheading marigolds and searching for cucumbers.

I watched as Dorothy slowed down during her last ten years. One of our favorite topics was trying to figure out how to get up off the ground without anyone knowing there was a problem. Every year, we had to put a little extra thought into the process as our bodies continued to rebel. But every year we figured out what would work for us for a time. Never in my wildest dreams did I consider the possibility of her having to crawl across the floor dragging a broken leg. I know if she had survived, we would have found something about the whole situation to get us laughing like crazy.

Dorothy never lost her fascination with new life. Between the two of us, we had four spring-fed ponds. There was plenty of habitat for mallards, wood ducks, and hooded mergansers. Every year, we'd keep an eye on the ponds in hopes of seeing little ones. Whenever we'd see ducklings, we'd count, compare, and recount. Mama ducks would shepherd their charges through the duckweed and algae covering the ponds and through the tall grasses around the banks. How they could maneuver from one pond to another was an endless fascination for Dorothy.

Now … when I raise my hand ceremoniously to my nose and breathe in deeply the smell of marigolds … or when I get stuck on the ground like a beetle lying on its back … or when I count a new batch of ducklings … I'll look into one of the holes in my Swiss cheese heart and find Dorothy's face smiling out at me.

Epilogue

Lest You Are Left Wondering

A full two years after the beginning of Messiah Lutheran's "one-year" call process, the hiatus was over: We had new pastors. The interim pastors had been amazing with their clear messages, senses of humor, and caring mannerisms. They coddled and challenged our grieving congregation into appreciating and even enjoying the journey.

The MIL (malfunction indicator light) icon coming on was the result of a small leak in the coolant, discovered by the service department in the summer of 2024.

The thick red line on the control panel, which made it appear we were in imminent danger of losing all power, was a temporary condition. It occurred when power from the park was interrupted. The coach knew how to fix the problem and provided us with a red line of warning while it fixed itself. We just happened to look at the control panel at the wrong time.

The Jeep kept dying because the wiring in the harness (from the motor home to the tow vehicle) was configured incorrectly. We took it to someone in the know and never had a problem afterward.

The bucking bronco experience was caused by a problem with the hydraulic arms used to tow the Jeep. Harry researched it online, got some magic lubricant, and we were good to go … or so we thought. Harry was fussing with the hydraulic arms one day and discovered the spring on one locking mechanism wasn't as beefy as on the other. Harry tied it down with a fifty-cent bungee cord and we were finally good to go!

When I got home to Vancouver, I pulled out the scale and found Harry had been all sorts of right. I abandoned the crackers and slowly lost ten pounds over the summer.

A Message to You

Thank you, Dear Reader, for going on this six-year journey with me, vicariously! Watch for a book about little Petey coming soon.

About the Author

Kathy Hoffman was born and raised in Portland, Oregon, with her six brothers. She has a BS in Mathematics and enjoyed a 28-year career as an engineer with the Bonneville Power Administration. She later volunteered as a math tutor, and then went on to sell and service insurance policies with husband in his Vancouver, Washington, State Farm Agency until they retired ... but her passion is, and has always been, laughter.